"In SMALL VOICES SILENCED, Author Sherrie Clark's descriptive writing put me into her story with her, taking me with her on her tumultuous journey through the foster-care system. Her joy and pain were so real that I couldn't help but become emotionally engaged. I found myself riveted, turning the pages as fast as I could, and unable to put it down. A well-written, fantastic read!"

FLOY TURNER
Best-Selling Author
Special Agent, Florida Department of Law Enforcement (Ret.)

"I have found few advocates in my twenty-three years of working with the foster care system. This is what makes the Clark family and their moving story so special. SMALL VOICES SILENCED shows how all too often, foster families who open their hearts and homes to damaged foster children become victims to this unfeeling system. It also opens the readers' eyes to what is happening to our children in such a poignant way, that you can't help but be enlightened and appalled about the behind-the-scenes antics of this secret society we call the foster care system."

GEORGI MCALLISTER
Volunteer Coordinator
CUDAS UnHooked
Former Foster Parent

"I was able to read your beautiful, as well as infuriating story SMALL VOICES SILENCED. Good book--touching and heartwarming story. Well told."

ROBERT FULMER
Consumer Protection Representative (Ret.)
for the Attorney General
State of Washington

"SMALL VOICES SILENCED was moving and genuine. The reader is invited into the home and heart of author Sherrie Clark. Each page takes the reader into another phase of navigating through the foster-care system and running into the roadblocks that can prevent caring and committed foster parents from extending themselves in the capacity they long to. Gratefully, the Clarks kept their hearts and home open to God and to the hope that their family could heal from the initial pain of loss and move forward with a blessed outcome!"
DEBORAH FURGASON
M.A., Licensed Professional Counselor
Stevens Point, Wisconsin

"SMALL VOICES SILENCED is a well-written poignant love story, thriller, and mystery all wrapped into one captivating page turner. Although it reads like a novel, you have to remind yourself it's a true story. As a former foster parent, I couldn't help but nod in agreement and cheer as Clark unfolded, exposed, and battled the corruption embedded within the foster care system, the side no one knows about until now."
DEBBIE DYKES
Educator/Teacher
Former Foster Parent

"SMALL VOICES SILENCED is a wonderful read. I had trouble putting it down at night! Anyone thinking about entering the world of foster parenting would benefit greatly from reading this book, as it offers an unfiltered view of the system from a first-time foster parent.
JACKIE STITT
Teacher
Nashville, Tennessee

"I read SMALL VOICES SILENCED: THE SECRET SOCIETY OF SACRIFICED CHILDREN in two days and in between bouts of my busy schedule. The book held my attention with each page as I remembered that author Sherrie Clark had lived the story, sharing her heart with readers. This book is a must-read for every parent as well as an eye opener as it depicts the reality of how our foster children fall through the cracks of justice."

MARSHA GEOGHAGAN
Program Coordinator, WJEB TV-59 (Ret.)
WJEB TV-59
Author

"I finished the book SMALL VOICES SILENCED in one day and loved it. It was moving, and I felt their pain and anguish. This is truly a great story about a loving family who wanted to do more. All new foster parents should read this book. I was so happy for them at the end. I would love to read more from this author. Thanks for sharing a wonderful book and moving story."

ANNARITA ELLIFFE
St. Augustine, Florida

"I read SMALL VOICES SILENCED, and I couldn't put it down. I highly recommend everyone reading this book."

REV. BRENDA DORMANN,
President, Endtime Handmaids/Servants
Jacksonville, Florida

"The story reads like a suspense novel, but it depicts events that are all too real! I thought I'd seen just about everything in memoir; I was surprised to find myself moved to tears. I'll never forget these two little girls."

MARCIA TRAHAN
Editor and Personal Essayist

"I could not put this book down! It grabbed my attention from the very beginning. SMALL VOICES SILENCED reads like a novel, but this is not fiction. It shows the good, the bad, and the very ugly side of the foster care system and took me back to those days when I used to work in the foster care system. Sherrie brings life to each page of this book; she takes you there! It actually played like a movie in my mind. This book tells the story of Sherrie and her husband Darryl's first-hand experience with the foster-care system.

"For Sherrie and Darryl, caring for the fatherless was more than a just an 'Amen' on a Sunday morning; they lived it. Through their story we clearly see the devil's hands, the power of God, and two people who were not willing to give up. I believe that every aspiring foster parent should read this book and that this book should be a mandatory part of every social work curriculum. This book should make it all the way to the President of the United States to provoke changes in this broken system."

ANGEL CASIANO
Author
Podcast Host, Beyond Opinions
Pastor

SMALL VOICES SILENCED

The Secret Society of Sacrificed Children

Sherrie Clark

Storehouse Media Group, LLC
Jacksonville, Florida

SMALL VOICES SILENCED: The Secret Society of Sacrificed Children

Copyright © 2018 by Sherrie Clark

All rights reserved. No part of this book may be used or reproduced by any means, graphic, electronic, or mechanical, including photocopying, recording, taping or by any information storage retrieval system without the written permission of the publisher except in the case of brief quotations embodied in critical articles and reviews.

Storehouse Media Group's books may be ordered through booksellers or by contacting:

Storehouse Media Group, LLC
Hello@StorehouseMediaGroup.com
www.StorehouseMediaGroup.com/Contact

The views expressed in this work are solely those of the author and do not necessarily reflect the views of the publisher, and the publisher hereby disclaims any responsibility for them.

Any people depicted in stock imagery provided by Thinkstock are models, and such images are being used for illustrative purposes only.

Certain stock imagery © Thinkstock.

ISBN: 978-1-943106-33-2 (softcover)
ISBN: 978-1-943106-32-5 (hardcover)
ISBN: 978-1-943106-34-9 (ebook)

Library of Congress Control Number: 2018906185

Printed in the United States of America

Storehouse Media Group rev. 2nd ed. date: 08/15/2018

Dedication

This book is dedicated to three special girls who were the inspiration behind this book:

Janna, I thank God for his faithfulness through you. Graci-An and Molly, wherever you may be, you will always have a part of my heart.

Epigraph

Regarding your title search, I wanted to share two suggestions. The first is *The Lamb Cries*. I had a visual of a baby lamb bleating in a field with no mother to come and protect and care for her. So, she stayed there alone, bleating, and no one came. I think of all these children who are screaming inside but are too little to voice it. They don't even have the words. They are just standing there with tears and afraid. I then think of Jesus—the Lamb of God—and I KNOW He cries about this.

Then the title *Small Voices Silenced* came to me because I feel so strongly that foster parents like yourself and my daughter are the ones who have to become *the voice* of the child. You all are the only voice that is raised on their behalf, purely motivated by love and compassion. You are the voice of the little ones who are silenced until the system often silences you.

—Rev. Margie Ussery

Acknowledgments

My family deserves a big thank you for supporting me while I wrote this book. A special thank you goes to my husband Darryl Clark for his ongoing encouragement and input. Nobody knew this journey better than you. I owe a big debt of gratitude to my children—Devlin, Tristan, Liam, Micah, and Janna. Thank you for being such good sports during those hours when I stayed glued to my laptop, working on improving page after page of this book.

Thanks go out to those who read and critiqued my first draft. It was over twice the size it is now, but it contained only half the story. So, thank you to Lynn Bowen and Grace Clark (both of whom have since gone on to be with Jesus), Pastor Rick Crook, Debbie Dykes, and Yvonne McLin for your patience in reviewing all of those pages of jumbled words and for the valuable feedback you provided.

Thanks to Ally Machete for performing the initial editorial evaluation. Your honesty challenged me to find the best possible way to tell this story.

Thanks to Rev. Margie Ussery for coming up with the title to this book. You were able to capture its essence in three words.

Thanks to all of you who helped me settle on its subtitle: Pastor Angel Casiano, Audrey Kendrick, Dr. Apostle Blanca B. David, Darryl Clark, Deborah Furgason, Debbie Dykes, Fran Futrill, Devlin Kidney, Diane King, Kathy Robinson, and Rhonda Biondi. I chose each of you to help me with this project because of the unique perspectives I knew you would bring. Of course, I'd be remiss if I didn't also thank you for your encouragement and support.

Thank you to Marcia Trahan for going over and beyond the call of duty when performing a professional line edit. You did an outstanding job.

Thanks to David Edmonson of Edmonson Photography in Dallas-Fort Worth, Texas, for taking my picture for this book. I appreciate everything you did to pull it all together and for sharing your wonderful artistic talent.

My biggest thanks go to God for his faithfulness and for never forgetting the promises he has made to his children. Otherwise, this story would have remained a tragedy and not the beautiful testimony it is today.

This section would be sadly incomplete if I didn't point out my appreciation to Jesus Christ, who guided me through every word I wrote and held me with every tear I cried.

DISCLAIMER

This book is designed to provide information on the foster-care system from the perspective of foster parents. It's based on actual events that occurred during our involvement with the dependency system and on documentation we have in our possession. Incidents are relayed according to my written documentation at the time and to my memory. I have made every effort to recreate this story as accurately as possible.

My immediate family and a few friends gave me permission to use their real names. To protect the privacy of the other children and their biological parents, I changed the names of everyone else involved in this story, the names of the agencies, and any identifying information. I also modified some of the circumstances. Furthermore, I purposefully didn't divulge the details of the cases involved, including the reasons why the children were removed from their parents.

The purpose of this book is to enlighten and entertain. The author and the publisher do not provide counseling and legal advice, and they have no knowledge of your specific needs. If you need any legal and counseling advice, please contact a licensed professional counselor or an attorney directly. The author and publisher shall have neither liability nor responsibility to any person or entity with respect to any loss or damage caused, or alleged to have been caused, directly or indirectly, by the information contained in this book.

Contents

Introduction 1

Chapter One: Lost and Found 7
Chapter Two: The Call 13
Chapter Three: Down the Rabbit Hole 35
Chapter Four: Once Was Not Enough 67
Chapter Five: Rules of Engagement 99
Chapter Six: Falling through the Cracks 133
Chapter Seven: Is Anybody Listening? 163
Chapter Eight: Preparing Lambs for Slaughter 199
Chapter Nine: The Shattering of Our World 231
Chapter Ten: Coming Out of the Pit 257
Chapter Eleven: Through a Tiny Baby Girl 285

A Conclusion: The Beauty from My Ashes 315
Afterword: Janna's Impact on the World 317
About the Author: Sherrie Clark 321

INTRODUCTION

Deceit, manipulation, corruption, secrecy, conflict: these are the components of a juicy novel.

But what if all of these and worse belong to a real-life tragedy, a real-life thriller, a real-life horror story?

And what if this tragedy/thriller/horror story involves our children, those as young as newborn infants?

And what if all of this real stuff is happening right here in our own backyard and is being committed by the very ones sworn to protect the children?

Follow me as I take you into a world where the behind-the-scenes antics are stranger than fiction. This is a place where the transgressions inflicted upon the innocent are so appalling that they have literally made strong men weep. This is a place where the small voices of its victims are silenced in preparation for what is soon to come. This is a place where a secret society is alive and well and sacrifices its children on a daily basis to personal agendas, a financial bottom line, and apathy.

Ladies and gentlemen, welcome to the world of foster care.

Small Voices Silenced: The Secret Society of Sacrificed Children is a true story that provides insight into this unique world. What we personally witnessed and heard during our tenure as foster parents were things that most people would be horrified to learn.

We had fallen down a rabbit hole and into a foreign land where children were the only commodity, justifying the existence of many of its inhabitants. These denizens chanted their mantra "in the best interest of a child" while at the same time indulging their need for power. Once obtained, its misuse became a life force of its own. Children weren't just falling through the cracks; they were being crammed.

Within these pages, you'll come along with me on a roller-coaster ride, reaching peaks of exhilaration and then plummeting into the valleys of devastation. You'll see complete strangers making decisions that impact children for a lifetime and do so without crucial information.

You'll cruise along with us and feel the sway of the car as the train makes a dramatic turn, causing us to go down a destructive track. You'll hear us trying to warn those who are controlling the train to stop.

You'll see our efforts ignored, our voices silenced, and you'll witness the crashing of the train. You'll feel our frustration, knowing that there were those who could have prevented this wreckage but instead waved the train to its final destination.

But what you don't know and what you won't see is that this happens *all* the time.

How Did We Get Here?

My husband Darryl and I never wanted to become foster parents. We didn't think we could handle becoming attached to a child and then having to give her back. Our reason for getting involved in the foster-care system was to fulfill a desire that we had shared for many years: adopting a child.

So, when it came time to turn our dream into a reality, I called the adoption toll-free number, full of naivety and excitement. We then began the process by attending the required foster/adoptive parent training as "adoptive-only" parents.

During one of the classes, a caseworker overheard the instructor trying to convince us to consider fostering. She opined her unsolicited advice, explaining that adoptable children "don't come out of the chute that way." In the state of Florida, if you have a foster child in your home for six months, then you're given first choice to adopt that child should he or she become available.

This gave us a new perspective and had us asking, "Should we, or shouldn't we?" What were the odds that our foster child would become available for adoption?

After many discussions, Darryl and I decided to take a chance with our hearts. We changed our status to "foster-to-adopt" parents. As a result, our lives were changed forever.

Why This Book?

Darryl and I had unwittingly placed ourselves in the unenviable position of seeing, hearing, and tasting the injustices that the system exacted upon innocent lives. Once we became involved, we knew we couldn't walk away. We knew that if we quit, the system would replace us with another foster family until this family was also either horrified or used beyond recognition.

We didn't want to be part of the problem but part of the solution. We, therefore, made the conscious decision to pull ourselves up by our bootstraps and stay, even if we were forced to stand on wobbly legs from the near-lethal wounds. The children caught in this system's web needed our help—someone's help—for their voices had been long lost amidst the power struggles.

Our righteous anger at what this system was doing to these children became its own powerful force, propelling us to throw fear and intimidation to the wind, stand up to the bully, and say, "Enough. No more. There has to be a better way."

I realized that we were a mere cog in this mammoth, rusted wheel of dysfunction. I could only do what I knew how to do: write. I could sound the alarm, telling others about the travesties experienced by these children. Unless people are made aware of the problem, they don't know it needs to be fixed.

And that was my initial mission—to be the voice of the voiceless by exposing the corruption that lies behind the façade.

The Testimony

But then I realized I hadn't written the ending, and so my focus became twofold. If I was going to reveal the bad side, then I must reveal the good. I needed to instill, or re-instill trust that mankind was capable of doing what was good, what was true, what was right. I needed to be fair and show the heroes who turned the tables, their emergence reinforcing our naïve ideology of a system looking out for the best interests of our children.

So, I deleted some of the bad and condensed the rest because in all fairness, my first attempt had only contained half of the story. I had been remiss in not sharing the joy despite the tragedy. I had omitted the part that encourages us all to not give up, even during those times when the pain becomes unspeakable. I had been negligent by leaving out a very important lesson: when we come to the point of realizing we're powerless, that's when God demonstrates his faithfulness.

And I finished the story. I included the blessings we experienced within the same system that had once almost destroyed me. But if not for the heap of ashes where my heart had once resided, I would never have experienced true beauty.

As a result, this journey had come to a close. For within these pages, you'll read about more than the wrongdoings of the foster-care system. I'll share with you a beautiful love story and a testimony of promises fulfilled.

You'll learn to never give up, even in the darkest of storms. For where there is hope, there is faith. And where there is faith, there are miracles, some of which can come in the smallest of packages.

Chapter One

Lost and Found

The cries are what first catch my attention, their release from muted lungs telling me their source is a young baby.

They continue and continue.

I hear no other sound, no cooing by another to calm the infant. I feel drawn to find it, to see the cause behind this relentless wailing.

I leave my cart by the eggs and start my search.

Each aisle, outlined by tan metal shelves full of grocery products, is void of life. The only movement I see is a dust ball scurrying along the gray linoleum floor. Where did everyone go?

Then I come to aisle nine where I see a lone, metal grocery cart parked in its middle. The cries are definitely coming from it.

There's still no one else in sight. Walking over to it, the cries become louder. It's empty except for a pink blanket covering what looks like a large mound in its wire basket.

I look around again, and still I can't see anyone. Is this a joke? What's really under the blanket? Is there a camera waiting to capture my surprised expression when I uncover something totally unexpected?

The cries become ear-piercing, so I jerk the blanket away. Lo and behold, strapped in a dark-blue infant car seat carrier is the most beautiful baby with blond hair and blue eyes. She's wearing a pink dress and pink booties.

Why is she here? Why is she alone? Where is her mother?

I take the liberty of picking her up in hopes of calming down her screams. She succumbs to my rocking her back and forth in my arms. Her eyes close, and her breathing becomes steady and even.

I walk around the store with her, looking for her mother, uncle, big brother, or whoever brought her here. Perhaps someone walked away from this baby to fetch a forgotten product and is still searching for it, but I don't see anyone.

The only other person in the store is the young checkout clerk with purple and black hair and an eyebrow ring. She's sitting in a chair by a cash register, blowing bubbles with her gum while reading a magazine with a motorcycle on its cover. I ask her if she knows whose baby this is.

Without taking her eyes off the magazine, she gives me an abrupt, "No," and then blows another bubble.

I look around, trying to decide what to do next. I look outside and notice that it's dark, but I have no idea what time it is. I have no watch. I don't see any clocks around.

"Can I use your phone to call the police?" I ask the clerk.

"Don't have one," she says, eyes still fixed on the pages before her. She blows another bubble.

"Okay. I'm taking the baby with me to get help."

The clerk offers no response. I go and get the infant car seat and leave the store with the baby.

I find my car. I buckle her in the backseat, and we start the drive home. It's so, so dark outside; it must be later than I thought. I need to get home. I figure I'll just take the baby to my house and call the police from there.

I find myself driving down an unfamiliar two-lane highway that looks more like a paved pathway through dense woods, yet I sense that I'm on the right road. It's so dark, without even one star in the sky. The shroud of thick fog forces me to keep my headlights on low beams.

If not for my slow driving, I might not have noticed the little girl standing alone on the side of the road. Even with the reduced visibility, I can tell that no one else is around. I see no cars parked, no cars behind me, none in front of me, and no oncoming traffic; I see only a thick mass of trees. I can't drive by and leave her there any more than I could have left the baby in that grocery store all by herself.

I pull over and get out. She appears to be around four or five years old, and she looks scared.

"Where's your mommy?"

She gives no answer. I try asking again. She just stands there without speaking a word.

I have to get home; I have to call the police for the baby, but I can't leave this little girl here alone.

"Are you okay coming with me?" I ask her. "I can take you to my house, and we'll see if we can find out where your mommy and daddy are."

She follows me to my car and climbs inside without prodding.

This has been a very strange day.

The exact details of what happens next are a big blur. For some reason, both girls end up staying with me for a longer period of time than planned.

Despite the differences in appearance—the baby's fair-colored hair and skin in contrast to the older child's olive skin and dark hair—the two girls are both very loving and affectionate. We have fun doing girly things like playing dress-up, wearing jewelry, and painting each other's nails. Even though the baby is too young to walk or even stand, she joins in the festivities with her smiles and squeals. I hold her while the three of us silly dance, and we all laugh.

They're everything I ever wanted in a daughter. I find myself loving them with utter abandonment and without hesitation. I'm so very happy. My world's complete.

Then from nowhere in particular, a voice speaks, gentle yet strong, resonating like surround sound throughout the room: "But they're not yours."

I see no one, yet I'm not startled, nor am I surprised. Intuitively, I know who spoke. "Yes, Lord." I become defensive. "But I love them so much."

The voice responds ever so softly, in the same tone an adult uses to reason with a child. "But they belong to someone else. These girls have parents who love them, who've been searching for them and want them back."

Deep inside, I know He's right, but I sure don't want to hear this. I can say nothing.

The voice continues, "I won't tell you what to do, but you know what you have to do."

I do. I walk over to the phone and finally make that call to the police to report finding these two little girls.

Before long, the two families come and get them. It's over; they're gone forever.

The realization causes me to collapse on the floor, roll myself in a fetal position, and cry and groan like a seriously wounded animal. Oh, I don't think I can bear the pain of the loss.

Then the Lord speaks again. His voice is like velvet, each word applying a soothing balm on my newly open wounds and caressing my very being from the inside. His love is undeniable, and I can feel its warmth even through my grief.

"I'm proud of you. You did the right thing, even though I know that was the hardest thing you've ever done. I know you love those little girls like they were your own. Because you were obedient in doing what was right in spite of the sacrifice, I'm going to bless you doubly."

Then I wake up.

I sit up in bed and look out into the dark. Touching my face with my fingertips, I feel my cheeks still wet from the tears.

That was some dream. Even though it felt so real, I'm relieved to learn that it was only a dream.

For if I ever had to suffer through that kind of intense loss and pain in my waking hours, I truly believe I would not survive.

Chapter Two

The Call

"Mrs. Clark? This is Nancy at Placement. We have a two-day-old baby girl that we need to place. Will you take her into your home?"

I was silent as I tried to remember who or what Placement was.

I held my cell phone to my ear. Then it hit me. Placement was the division that placed foster children in foster homes.

My face became flushed with excitement. Was this really *the call*?

For the past several months, we had dreamed of getting a call like this many times over while sprinting through each and every hoop that was required to become licensed foster parents. Then, after learning thirteen days ago that we had finally been approved by the state, my husband Darryl and I jumped every time the phone rang. With thirty-two children entering our local foster-care system every week, we were sure we would have been called long before now.

Logic overcame skepticism when the idea hit me that this call could be *the call*. It made sense that it would eventually come.

As I sat in the dimly lit restaurant, the pounding of my heart was joined by a temporary paralysis that engulfed my entire body. I could only stare straight ahead at the shellacked blue-and-gray swordfish hanging on the dark-brown wood-paneled walls. Then I realized I hadn't said anything to this person on the phone named Nancy, not even so much as a grunt.

After coming to terms with the reality that this was *the* call, I then became conscious of the fact that she wanted us to take a *brand-new baby girl*. I had given birth only to boys—four to be exact. Paralysis turned into a tingling sensation, like fingers palpating their way from the top of my head to the tips of my toes.

I looked across the table at my oldest son Devlin. Today was his birthday, and he had asked me to take him to this small seafood restaurant for a birthday lunch. The food tasted delicious in spite of the establishment's outdated interior design. The multicolored indoor-outdoor carpet had seen better days, and the red vinyl-covered booth bench had been worn down to the point of feeling comfortable.

Devlin held his menu opened in front of his face, engrossed in reading about the appetizing dishes and their descriptions. He was oblivious to me, my phone call, and the possibility that life as we now knew it might very well change forever.

The first words formed by my lips were, "Wow! Well, that came out of nowhere. Do they actually come that small?" I didn't know foster children went into the system at such a young age.

Nancy chuckled. "Yes, ma'am, they sure do, and all the time."

Different thoughts hit me all at once. I knew I needed to give Nancy an answer, and the mother in me wanted to tell her yes. But I needed to talk with my husband Darryl to see if he was okay with having such a young baby at this time of our lives. We had never discussed the possibility that our foster child would be a newborn; it had never crossed our minds.

I was afraid to ask Nancy to let me call her back. What if she found a family who would agree to take this baby and agree to take her NOW?

A deep breath of air filled my lungs before I forced myself to say, "I need to speak with my husband first."

I couldn't believe I had managed to articulate those words. What if he said no? Finally, that long-awaited phone call had occurred, but would it be for naught?

"Yes ma'am, Mrs. Clark. I've already spoken with your husband. That's how I got your cell phone number. He told me to call you."

Oh my! I reasoned to myself, albeit on an illogical level, that if Darryl had her call me, he would be in agreement with my answer, right? Wasn't that a demonstration of his trust in my judgment? Who could say no to taking in a brand-new baby girl? My excitement and anxiousness increased with each millisecond.

I didn't want to ask the next question but knew I had no other choice. Darryl deserved a vote in this huge decision. We had discussed adopting a child for the past five years. Researching options had led us to decide to adopt through the foster-care system because so many foster children needed a permanent home. We had just expected that foster child to be somewhat older.

"What did my husband say?" I asked, barely able to get the words out of my dry mouth. I took a quick sip of water while my ankles tightened their grip around each other under the table. I wasn't quite sure I wanted to hear the answer.

"He said it was up to you."

I couldn't believe I remained in my seat and didn't move. "Then ... he won't mind if I say yes, will he?"

"No, ma'am, Mrs. Clark. I don't think he will," Nancy said with another chuckle.

"Then yes! Yes!" I blurted out with unsuppressed joy.

I now had everyone's attention in the restaurant. Their initial looks of shock and annoyance were replaced by smiles. They must have assumed I had accepted a marriage proposal over my cell phone.

My son's attention jerked from the menu and onto me. Eyebrows raised, he mouthed the words, "What's going on?"

With a huge grin on my face, I held up my right index finger to signal that I'd explain in a moment. He accepted the delay but not without squirming.

"Thank you, Mrs. Clark. I need to tell you that the baby is still at the hospital. I don't know if you'll have to pick her up there or if she'll be brought to your home. You'll have to discuss that with the Child Protective Investigator from the Department of Children and Families. I'll have him call you right away. Is this a good number where he can reach you?"

"Yes. Yes, it is. Please have him call me on this number," I almost begged.

After hanging up with Nancy, I kept the phone to my ear and allowed myself to daydream. I loved my four sons, but images of holding a tiny infant wrapped in a pink blanket put a smile on my face, one bigger than the grin I wore after my first kiss. I saw a baby girl full of innocence.

Devlin leaned forward. "What just happened?"

"Devlin, we're getting a two-day-old baby girl!"

He smiled from ear to ear. "Wow! Really? Are you serious, Mom? This is the best birthday gift I ever got."

I had considered that as well. What a wonderful gift to be given on your birthday—a brand-new life. This was one birthday I knew he'd always remember. I knew I would remember this day.

"When?" he asked.

I shrugged. "I don't know. I've gotta wait for the Department of Children and Families investigator to call me. I've never done this before. I don't know the process." His questions were the same questions I had.

"Why do they have investigators?"

I did know the answer to that question. My eyes met Devlin's eyes. "They investigate reports of abuse or neglect of children. Sometimes they have to take the child out of the home and place her in foster care. This is where we as a foster family come in. I guess here, someone from the hospital must have called the Department of Children and Families, or DCF, regarding this baby." I leaned my upper body toward Devlin. "I need to call home before the investigator calls me."

Sure, that my husband would be just as ecstatic, I dialed our home number. Darryl answered the phone after the fifth ring.

"Hi, honey," I said. I felt as if I were about to tell him I had a positive pregnancy test. "I just got a call from Placement. You've already spoken to her, right?"

Waiting to hear his excitement, I was amazed at how composed he sounded.

"Yeah, about that phone call. We need to talk about it. This is a newborn baby. We never talked about that possibility."

It was like he had thrown a bucket of cold water on me, jolting me out of a beautiful dream. I now had to consider that it may have been just that—a beautiful dream.

Swallowing became difficult. "Nancy from Placement said she already told you about it. Didn't you tell her that it was up to me?"

"Yeah, I know. She called at a bad time, and I couldn't really talk with her. The dog got loose at the same time Micah fell and scraped his elbow. I guess telling her to call you was a knee-jerk reaction. I just needed to get off the phone at that time."

I envisioned the drama occurring at home and his trying so hard to multitask through both incidents simultaneously. Had my presumption led me to conspire with Nancy in an effort to justify my own desires?

I didn't know what to say.

The disapproval in his voice couldn't be overlooked. "Sherrie, you did tell her we'd get back to her, didn't you? Did you at least tell her you'd call her after we discussed it?"

I felt like a little child who had been scolded. My face became hot as the heat from some internal furnace rushed to it, and a knot formed in the pit of my stomach. I didn't want to answer his question, yet he had a right to know.

"I am so sorry. I felt you had left the decision up to me, so I told her we'd take her. I don't know if it's too late to change our minds. DCF's going to call me any minute." The grip on my phone tightened.

There was a silence ... a long silence, or was time merely teasing me by ticking by ever so slowly? What would I tell Nancy? We had waited so long for this call, and turning away this baby would be difficult.

Finally, he spoke six simple words: "Okay. When do we get her?" He was such a good man.

Feeling like air had suddenly been restored to me, I took in a big gulp of it. I thanked my husband. I told him I still didn't know any of the details, but I'd call him when I did.

As soon as we finished our call, my cell phone rang. The caller introduced himself as Mr. Berg, the DCF investigator. We decided to meet at the hospital first thing in the morning to pick up the baby.

I tried to hide my sigh of relief for the delay. As eager as I was, we didn't have anything for a baby: no crib, no diapers, and not even a car seat to bring her home.

Hanging up, I looked over at Devlin with a smile. "Devlin, how would you like to do some shopping on your birthday? You can help me pick out some stuff we're going to need for a brand-new baby girl."

He grinned. "Let's do it."

My excitement prevented me from eating my food. Devlin, on the other hand, didn't seem distracted in the least from eating a good meal.

Watching him enjoy his birthday lunch, I reflected on what seemed like another life when over a decade ago, I was in a hospital bringing a beautiful baby boy into the world. Here, that beautiful baby sat across from me, growing up before my very eyes. He was my firstborn, and without a doubt, his arrival had changed my life forever.

Now I faced another dramatic change. This time, however, the definition of a whole family would be altered. We were bringing in a new baby, and a girl to boot. This baby would be our first foster child and possibly our first adopted child.

I was glad that Devlin had taken such an interest in providing a home for a child who didn't have one. He and I had spent hours on the computer together, looking at the pictures of children available for adoption and discussing their profiles.

I smiled as I studied Devlin's handsome face framed by thick brown hair. He got his hazel eyes from his father, although he could have gotten his full eyebrows from either of us. The generous dark eyelashes, though, he got from me, but his hair color was from his father.

My mind then switched to the baby, and I couldn't help but wonder what she looked like. Did she have fair or dark skin? Did she have blonde, brown, red, black, or no hair? What color would her eyes turn out to be? Did she look anything like us? Whatever her physical features, I realized it didn't matter.

After Devlin finished eating, we stepped outside the restaurant to walk to our car. I involuntarily squinted as the June sun pounced on my bare eyes. I didn't mind because at last, we were off on our mission.

We visited a couple of stores and bought everything I could think of for a newborn baby. By the time we were finished with our shopping spree, I was amazed that everything was able to fit in our car.

On the way home from the store, my mind raced as I tried to think of what we needed to do between now and first thing in the morning. With each of my pregnancies, a certain process had evolved. After discovering early on that I was pregnant, we'd take our time over the next seven months or so to prepare ourselves, our home, our children, and the dog for the pending arrival. As time moved closer to the birth, we became impatient to bring that new life into the world and home to our family.

Surprisingly, I discovered that whether giving birth or taking home a baby already birthed, we experienced the same levels of anticipation and joy. As for the preparation time—well, that was another issue because whereas most parents have several months to prepare for a baby, we had only a few hours.

Expectations

That evening, I fixed Devlin a special birthday dinner so that the whole family could celebrate with him. Of course, the topic of having a new baby in our home monopolized our dinnertime conversation.

Darryl and I listened as the kids chattered about their self-assigned roles with a baby "sister." I had been concerned about Micah's reaction to having a new baby since he had held that position in the family for the past several years. He seemed fine, even excited about the idea, but something told me he didn't quite grasp what to expect.

Liam, our second-to-the-youngest, said that he agreed with everyone about being happy with the news. As the family jokester, he entertained us with animated accounts of each of his brothers taking care of a baby.

Like Micah, I don't think Liam understood how our lives would be changed. In retrospect, I don't think I could truly appreciate the degree of how the dynamics within our family would be altered. I couldn't anticipate how our daily routine and overall lifestyle would never be the same as the result of that fateful phone call on that beautiful June day.

Tristan, our second-to-the-oldest, had a giant smile, his big green eyes getting even bigger as he analyzed the comments from each person. Toward the end of dinner, he asked, "Are we all going to pick her up together?"

Darryl and I glanced at each other. Although the older three had a different biological father, Darryl had been in their lives for the past seven years.

He said, "Your mom and I don't think the hospital is quite ready to take all four of you on at the same time. So, I'm staying here with you guys while she goes and gets the baby."

Tristan looked at me. "Can I go with you, Mom?"

Quietly, I breathed a sigh of relief. I was feeling uncomfortable with the idea of making that forty-five-minute drive home alone with a newborn. "Sure, Tristan, I would appreciate your help."

For the rest of that evening, we enjoyed a jovial atmosphere within our home. I unpacked the items bought earlier and organized them. My excitement acted like a stimulant, and my body felt like it could run a marathon.

I made myself go to bed sometime after midnight. Falling into a deep sleep proved to be impossible.

I just couldn't get out of my mind that within a few hours, we'd have a brand-new baby girl.

Small Beginnings

Tristan and I left at eight o'clock that morning to pick her up.

During the drive, he slept in the backseat. The quiet allowed me to daydream about the baby. Since we didn't know anything about her, my imagination had no boundaries.

When we arrived at the hospital, we met the DCF investigator in front of the labor and delivery ward. Mr. Berg fit the mental image I had of him when we spoke the previous day. He was probably well into his fifties, of average height, and a little thick around the waist. He wore his gray hair in a crew cut, and he carried a thick, worn black briefcase in his left hand.

After the ward's steel doors opened, an older nurse wearing blue hospital scrubs greeted us. We all followed her down a hallway that seemed infinite, passing soft pastel rooms. Each room held a hospital bed and bassinet.

We were then led through the last doorway on the right and into a small room with walls covered in a light-yellow paint. The pale hue made the tight area appear more spacious.

This multifunctional room acted as a supply closet, furniture storage unit, and maybe a designated area for bonding in nontraditional situations. Several shelved rolling carts filled with a multitude of baby products lined the walls. Two different corners of the room each held steel chairs, their back and seat portions covered with blue vinyl cushions. In the middle of the room sat one white wooden rocking chair.

Mr. Berg walked over to a rolling stainless-steel bed tray and pulled it in front of one of the chairs. He sat and pulled some papers out of his briefcase, stacking them in three piles on top of the tray. There appeared to be a lot of papers, and I suspected they all had to do with our taking the baby.

Seeing those papers brought home the reality of the situation, and the butterflies in my stomach increased their fluttering. *Any moment now ... any moment now* became the chant within my head.

I looked over at Tristan and noticed that he was fidgeting more than usual. Although he had undergone two other new arrivals over the past few years, he possessed a more mature and serious demeanor this time around. Of course, he hadn't been allowed in the delivery room when I gave birth to Liam and Micah, so being just moments away from meeting this new baby girl marked a new experience for him.

He remained quiet and stayed by my side. His big green eyes seemed to study everything and everyone around him.

After a few minutes of waiting, another nurse came into the room and introduced herself as Karen. She smiled warmly when she informed us that we had come just in time for the baby's feeding.

"I'll go and get the baby so the foster mom can feed her," she announced.

Fortunately, I was sitting in the room's only rocking chair, which seemed appropriate for the feeding of a newborn. Tristan pulled his chair next to me.

I then realized that I had been so caught up in the excitement, I had forgotten to ask about the baby's name.

"Mr. Berg, can you please tell me if the baby has a name?"

"Now that you mention it," he said, "I don't really know myself. Let me see." He took a red folder from one of his piles and opened it. He flipped through its papers.

"Hmmm." His eyes scanned one of the pages. "Yep. Yep, she does have a name. Says here it's Graci-An. Hmmm. That's a cute name." He smiled as he closed the red folder and returned it to its designated place in its designated stack.

That must have been *the* red folder our class instructor had talked about during foster-parent training. She explained that a red folder must accompany every foster child because it contained the child's records, including medical information and sometimes the reason for removal from the home. It also held other valuable information and documents, such as various foster-care forms, instructions, resources and their phone numbers, and anything else that had to do with that particular child.

So, our first foster child's name was Graci-An. Tristan and I looked at each other. I could tell that his fidgeting had increased even more.

I tried to pass the time by focusing on the items on the tray in front of me—the disposable diapers small enough to fit a doll, the individually wrapped nipples, and the small bottles of formula. It had been awhile since I had a reason to use any of these products, yet it didn't seem that long ago. I smiled as I sat there enjoying my memories of being in labor and delivery wards similar to this one when I gave birth to each of my sons.

I then looked at my second-oldest child. Tristan's physical attributes were different than those of his older brother Devlin, from his blond hair to his fair skin to his perfect rosebud mouth.

I remembered my surprise at Tristan's features when they put him in my arms for the first time. I had been so accustomed to Devlin's appearance that I just assumed his younger brother would look similar. Whereas Devlin was probably more of a combination between his father and me, Tristan resembled my side of the family.

Tristan and I had always been close. As a baby, he responded to the mere sound of my voice. Somehow, his knowing I was in the room with him seemed to soothe his cries and discomfort, and he calmed down immediately. Not much had changed since that time. Now even years later, my voice still calmed him.

Nurse Karen interrupted my nostalgic musings by pushing a clear bassinet into our little room. Inside, a small bundle was wrapped up like a pink burrito.

The nurse handed her to me. I'll never forget that small face looking up into my eyes as if asking, "Who are you?"

Tristan moved closer to us. "She's beautiful, Mom. Look how cute and tiny." He smiled as he took his index finger to slowly and gently caress her face.

I held her in my arms and remembered how much I enjoyed that feeling. She weighed only six pounds and had the biggest blue eyes and a tiny, turned-up nose above a little pink mouth. She looked so beautiful but so fragile.

The nurse slipped a small bottle into my hand. I placed it into Graci-An's mouth. Without any nudging, she began sucking.

As I fed her, the investigator sat at his "desk" and asked me a stream of questions, using my answers to complete his paperwork. I kept my eyes on Graci-An, taking in every feature. I couldn't help but think about her mother who had just given birth to her two days earlier. How did she feel about having her baby taken from her? I couldn't imagine it.

Verbalizing my thoughts, I said, "This poor mother. To have your baby taken away from you has got to be traumatic."

Mr. Berg quickly retorted, "Don't feel bad for this mom. She knew what she was doing. She chose to make decisions to the detriment of her child. This baby would be in a bad situation if she stayed with the mom."

He was so adamant, his response so vigorous. What had this mother done to warrant such drastic action on behalf of the state? I couldn't help being curious, but I didn't dare ask. I was under the impression that we weren't supposed to know this information. We were so naïve that we didn't know any better.

After about thirty minutes, the nurse came back into the room with discharge papers. She stood next to me and explained them, pointing out that I needed to take the baby to the pediatrician within the next forty-eight hours for a checkup.

Numerous things bombarded my mind at the same time. Here we were, starting all over again—middle-of-the-night feedings, immunization shots every few months, changing diapers. I looked back into that tiny face and knew I didn't mind. Having this baby in our lives for however long would be worth any inconvenience.

After the nurse left the room again, Mr. Berg walked over to me with a stack of papers to sign. When I finished, he took off his reading glasses. "How long have you been a foster parent?"

"This is our first foster child," I said, returning his eye contact.

Mr. Berg walked back to his briefcase and started packing away his papers and files. He then shrugged. "You never know how things work out. I just gave a foster baby to a family last week, and I think they're going to adopt him."

He stopped packing and looked back at me. "But you do know it doesn't always work that way, don't you? We have to look for family members to take this baby. I may call you at three o'clock today to pick her up. I may call you in three days or three weeks. You know that's a possibility, don't you? You know how this works, right?"

I knew all too well, which was the reason Darryl and I had initially wanted to adopt a child outright rather than serve as foster parents first. But during our training, a caseworker explained that our chances of adopting would increase if we fostered children.

The drive home turned out to be uneventful, which was good. Graci-An sat in her new car seat and slept. Tristan sat in the backseat next to her. Neither he nor I said much. I think we both got lost in our own thoughts.

Pulling into our driveway, we were greeted by my husband and three other eager boys waiting to get a glimpse of Graci-An. Darryl showed no emotion as he opened the door to our car and removed the car seat carrier from its secured base. He slowly and carefully carried her into our home as if she would explode into a thousand pieces if he jiggled her too much.

Once inside, he placed the carrier on a large chest next to the front door. I unbuckled Graci-An and took her out to hold her. Darryl stepped back, the muscles in his face relaxing.

He said, "She's just so small."

"Yes, she is. But don't you worry. I'll get her growing so that she'll be bigger. Before long, you won't be so nervous holding her."

I then carried Graci-An to our room where we had set up her new bassinet. A trail of boys walked down the hallway behind me, each one talking faster and louder than the next. I felt like a mother duck with her ducklings all in tow, although my sons were not as calm or quiet as baby ducks.

After I placed her in the bassinet, the boys gathered around like proud parents and then fought to be closest to her head.

I laughed and said, "Baby girl, enjoy this while you can. You may not understand what's happening now, but mark my words. One day you'll love having so many guys fight over you."

I looked over at Darryl, who had joined us. He was still a handsome man after all these years. I've always been proud of having him by my side, whether in public or in the privacy of our home. He was at least a head taller than me, and he had always maintained his weight at a healthy proportion. Although I loved his thick black hair, I've got to say that his kind eyes and happy-go-lucky attitude were what first caught my attention many years ago.

He walked over to me and put his arm around my shoulder. I glanced up at him. Was he happy that we had Graci-An now that she was no longer a faceless newborn but an adorable baby? Hopefully his big smile and the sparkle in his eyes conveyed the answer to my question.

I looked back at the boys as they fawned over the baby. I then looked at Graci-An sleeping despite the noise surrounding her and wondered if she would only be with us for a little while. I didn't know, but I hoped she'd stay with us. Until then, I consciously and subconsciously put up a wall over my heart in case we lost her. Admittedly, the wall was a thin one.

Out of the corner of my eye, I saw Darryl's gaze move down to me. He bent his head to reach my mouth and gave me a kiss.

"She's going to do just fine in this family, sweetheart," he said. "I'm glad we have her."

New Alliances

"Seems like the state can't find a suitable family member to take her."

Mr. Berg's report came a short two days after we brought Graci-An home. He paused for a few moments before continuing. "Supposedly, a relative came forward and wanted her. Even went to court wearing shorts and flip-flops, but she failed the home study. Looks like you're going to have her for a long time." I could almost hear a smile on his face over the phone.

His words "a long time" reverberated in my mind. I pondered them for a while, thankful that someone wouldn't be knocking on our door for "a long time" and taking Graci-An away. This presented the first piece of hope I had since getting *the call* on Devlin's birthday.

I knew I already loved her. That thin wall I had placed over my heart—the one installed to prevent heartbreak should she be removed—started teetering. I didn't think it would take much more to make it come crashing down.

I glanced over at her; she was sleeping. I wanted to do a jig but decided to call Darryl instead to share the good news. Something inside prevented me from telling the children. I needed to remain cautiously guarded. It was too soon to read too much into where this would go. I just couldn't get the boys' hopes up now ... not yet.

Darryl seemed distracted when I told him. I didn't know if he was busy or just didn't want to get his hopes up as well. Hearing some enthusiasm, some squeals of delight erupting out of him would have been great. I'm a girl, and that's what we girls sometimes need.

So, I decided to call other girls—two other foster parents to be exact. In spite of not knowing either of them for very long, we had formed an immediate camaraderie.

I had met Loren Dixon when we were both at the pediatrician's office, me with one of my sons, and she with one of her foster children. I learned that she had been a foster parent for over two years, and I valued her experience with the system.

I met Faith Mead toward the beginning of our foster-parent training, and she had received her foster-care license about the same time we had. Not only were we both rookies, but our lives outside of the foster-care system seemed to parallel each other. We belonged to the same church denomination; we had sons who were the same age; and we happened to know some of the same people.

Plus, I knew that no one would quite understand the excitement like another foster parent. Neither Loren nor Faith disappointed me. Maybe they didn't exactly squeal, but close enough.

Both of my new friends wanted to know all of the details. I sensed they enjoyed listening to them almost as much as I enjoyed giving them.

The Reprieve

Graci-An adapted wonderfully to our family.

This isn't to say that our lives didn't change. We did find ourselves taking on a new routine, I more so than the others. That was only natural and unavoidable.

For instance, frequent pediatrician visits became part of my schedule as she began her series of immunizations. We had also taken on middle-of-the-night feedings and diaper changes.

I guess for the past few years, Darryl and I had gotten spoiled sleeping through the night for the most part. When my sons were infants, none of them slept through the night. Pulling your body out of bed at the most agonizing times to feed a crying baby results in sleep deprivation, no matter what your age. Nevertheless, this time we were older and not quite sure if our bodies could bounce back like they did when Micah was an infant.

With five children, our lives were full, but only temporarily. Graci-An was eleven days old when Devlin, Tristan, and Liam left to spend the summer with their father. Micah didn't go since he had a different dad.

Our family, therefore, shrunk from seven to four, and our house became much quieter. Even though we could appreciate the peacefulness that's expected with three fewer children, my oldest sons' absences created a tremendous void in our lives.

Every summer after his brothers left, Micah would enjoy our undivided attention during the first few days. But as he got older, he missed his brothers more and more. Keeping him busy helped, so we enrolled him in a summer-camp program. Instead of days filled with moping around the house and asking every other hour when his brothers were coming back, we hoped his being with other children would take away that sting of loneliness.

But in the evenings, he hung around Graci-An and me. If he wasn't entertaining us with his uncanny ability to act out stories he had heard at camp, he was hugging and kissing the baby. His propensity to show affection affirmed his blond-haired, blue-eyed, angelic appearance and contradicted his all-boy, rough-and-tumble character.

While Micah was away during the day, I took advantage of the extra time I had with Graci-An. I carried her most of the time when she was awake, and when she slept, I either worked or took a break, grabbing a book to read next to her. Frequently, I found myself looking up from the pages to watch her peaceful body stretch and sigh.

I knew I was getting more attached to her every day despite that wall over my heart. But I couldn't help myself. I could tell that Micah and Darryl were getting more attached to her as well.

We enjoyed the simplicity of life ... for a little while. If not for our assigned foster-care support specialist Sandra Curtis calling to schedule her mandated monthly home visit, I might have thought the state had forgotten about Graci-An.

I wasn't very familiar with the support specialist's role, so Loren filled me in on what to expect. Sandra needed to make sure that as licensed foster parents, we remained in compliance with the state's requirements. Her job also included encouraging foster parents and answering their questions.

Loren said, "Just brace yourself for all of the interruptions and disruptions that are soon coming your way."

Although I listened to Loren's words of wisdom, they didn't quite sink in. My lack of experience prevented me from seeing beyond what I had already experienced and what was before me. It was like telling someone with a perfect driving record what to expect when they get into a car accident. You can't foresee yourself in that predicament because you're a careful driver.

But while being a careful driver does prevent a lot of accidents, those who put all of their trust solely into their own driving abilities aren't taking into account the actions of other drivers. There are some accidents you can't avoid.

So, for a while, with no one else calling and until Sandra Curtis came to visit, we pushed Loren's advice aside and relaxed.

It was a matter of out of sight, out of mind.

Chapter Three

Down the Rabbit Hole

The fall was quick and painless.

It started with Julia Harvey, Graci-An's newly assigned caseworker. She called us after Graci-An had been with us for over three weeks.

She wanted to schedule her first home visit, and she didn't give us much warning. She needed to see us, our house, and Graci-An Friday morning, which happened to be the next day.

We didn't know what to expect from a caseworker's visit. The only way I knew how to prepare was to clean my house, scrubbing it from top to bottom.

Darryl rescheduled a couple of morning appointments for the afternoon so that he could be with us. We were blessed that his sales job gave him the freedom to work at home.

The next morning, he took Micah to camp while I fed Graci-An breakfast. I then went through her assortment of adorable outfits and finally decided upon a pink sundress with a matching bonnet. Dressing her was so much fun, reminding me of playing with dolls as a little girl.

After Darryl came home, he and I waited in our dining room for Julia's arrival. Graci-An was awake in my arms, but for how long was anyone's guess.

The clock inched toward the nine o'clock position. I glanced around one last time to make sure nothing had jumped out of place, especially since the caseworker would be going through our whole house.

We didn't have a formal foyer. As soon as you walked through the front door, you found yourself in the midst of a large, open great room with yellow walls and a tan-and-white tiled floor. The left side of this room held the living room; straight ahead was a doorway leading into a bedroom; and the right side was our dining room.

When the doorbell rang, Darryl opened the door. A tall, middle-aged woman with short brown hair and a brown leather portfolio stood on our small front porch. She wore black slacks, a pink button-down shirt, and black loafers. Her olive-colored skin and dark-brown eyes made me think that she was perhaps of Hispanic descent. She appeared almost bored, like she had done this a thousand times before, and here she was again.

She introduced herself using a matter-of-fact tone. Darryl invited her inside and motioned toward our dining room table. "Please have a seat, Ms. Harvey."

Before Julia sat down, she walked over to me with a huge smile on her face. I wasn't her point of interest, though, because her eyes focused on Graci-An. Julia cooed and talked to her.

So much for her initial bored and matter-of-fact demeanor, I thought.

After a few minutes, she pulled herself away from Graci-An and reverted back to her unemotional disposition. "Before we get started, do you mind showing me your home? I especially need to see where the baby sleeps."

I gave Graci-An to Darryl, my eyes meeting his for a moment. His smile encouraged me.

Turning around to Julia, I said, "Sure. You've probably figured out that this is our dining room." Moving my hand to the only closed door in the vicinity, I said, "This is our youngest sons' bedroom."

She opened their door and stood, scrutinizing the tan-colored room. A wide window stretching from one side of the room to the other lined the back wall. The floor had the same tile as the great room did.

Julia walked back out. Turning to our right, she followed me through our living room, which was occupied by two blue couches and a brown coffee table. We then entered a narrow tan hallway.

Immediately to the right was Devlin and Tristan's bedroom. She stopped to examine it, stepping onto their parquet floor. The walls were green, and on the right side were bunk beds, the top being a twin bed and the bottom a full-size bed.

We walked into the next bedroom. The light-yellow walls and white tile floor gave this corner room a larger and more open appearance. A wooden crib with an animal mobile dangling overhead stood against the left wall. The back wall had a white love seat that could pull out into a twin bed.

I said, "This is Graci-An's bedroom. She isn't sleeping in here yet because we still have her in a bassinet in our bedroom."

Julia looked around and nodded. I started down another hallway, which was at a ninety-degree angle from the previous hallway. The first room on the right was a large blue bathroom, and straight ahead was a doorway leading to our bedroom.

When Julia entered our room, her eyes scanned it from the white crown molding that separated the white ceiling from the brown walls, down to the beige Berber carpet that covered the floor. Our headboard stood against the back wall, and to the left were Graci-An's bassinet and yellow shelves filled with baby products—diapers, formula, wipes, blankets, and clothes.

Watching her face, I waited until I sensed she had seen everything she needed to see. When she looked at me, I turned to go back to where we had started. Walking through the dining room, I took her through a doorway and into the cozy white-and-brown kitchen.

The next room over was the den with orange walls and a brown-tiled floor. The left wall consisted of two large windows, one on each side of the glass door that led to the green concrete patio and a large, fenced backyard.

When the tour ended, Julia and I walked back into the dining room. We both sat down at the table, and she gathered her papers from her zippered notebook. Placing a green form in front of her, she rummaged through what appeared to be a large, black canvas purse before bringing out a blue pen that must have been hiding in its depths.

She explained, "I have to complete this green form during every home visit that's done. These are just routine questions, like, 'Does the child appear clean?'"

"By the way," she continued, "the bio mother called me. She wants to see the baby. A supervised visitation schedule will probably start next week."

Visits? Our simple world was about to end.

Darryl sat at the table with Graci-An still in his arms. "How often are the visits?"

She continued writing. "They'll be every other week, and each one lasts ninety minutes. I'll call you and let you know the details when they're confirmed."

I refrained from squirming. "Where will the visits take place?"

She looked up, her eyes slowly moving between Darryl and me. "That's part of the details I need to confirm. Don't worry. You'll be notified with the time, days, and location." Her brown eyes held my gaze before returning to her green form.

Darryl frowned, pushing his eyebrows together. "Julia, can you tell us why Graci-An got taken away from her mother?"

Julia kept her eyes fixed on the form in front of her and shook her head. "It's all confidential information, Mr. Clark. I can't tell you anything, but it's pretty bad."

Darryl's eyes opened wide. "Should we be concerned, then?"

Julia continued writing without looking up. "No. These visits are supervised. A monitor is with the parent and child every moment. She'll be fine."

She handed the green form to us. "There's a hearing scheduled in two weeks. You don't have to go to any of them. They're not mandatory."

Darryl and I glanced at each other. I said, "Oh no, we want to attend as many as we can. What's this hearing about, and where's it being held?"

Her eyes were focused on the task of packing away her papers, but her voice was directed at us. "It's kind of a status hearing for all parties. It's the first one since the shelter hearing when they first removed the baby and took her into the system. It'll be held in the dependency court in the downtown courthouse. I'll call you with the time."

After she left, Darryl and I gave each other a hug with Graci-An sandwiched between us. But I had a sense of uneasiness, something I hadn't felt since becoming involved in the foster-care system.

Darryl walked away to make some phone calls. I chose not to say anything to him about my feelings and tried to shrug them off, but to no avail.

I couldn't think of any reason why I felt this way except for the upcoming visits. I knew they were part of having a foster child, and I agreed with this aspect and understood the reason; biological parents needed to see their children and vice versa.

But that ominous feeling continued to gnaw at me. I knew it went beyond Julia telling us that this case was "pretty bad."

The Visitation

On Tuesday, we received notification as promised.

In two days, Graci-An would visit with her bio-mom. The event would take place at Julia's agency. Evidently, her offices housed one of the many visitation centers in town. We were grateful that this one was located about five minutes from our home.

Still, I couldn't shake off that foreboding. Of course, we had yet to learn the reason for Graci-An's removal. No one had told us anything. We presumed that to be the status quo.

While I dressed Graci-An Thursday morning for the visit, I pondered my apprehension. Perhaps it was concern over Graci-An being returned to someone who, according to Mr. Berg, chose to make decisions to the detriment of her child. But surely the state wouldn't do that. Surely it wouldn't place an infant back with a parent whose actions had threatened her baby to the point that the state needed to step in to protect her.

We arrived early at the visitation center and saw two women and one man sitting in the waiting room. I didn't know if one of the women was Graci-An's mother since I had no idea what she looked like.

All three stretched their necks to see the baby in the infant car seat that Darryl carried in his hand. We walked to the only desk, and the receptionist instructed us to sign in.

I turned around to find an empty seat. Out of the corner of my eye, I mentally noted the physical details of the three individuals sharing this room with us.

The man appeared to be young and had a shaved head. He wore denim shorts and a white T-shirt that showed off his various tattoos.

One of the women had a sad but attractive face. She had fair skin. The bangs of her short, thick blonde hair covered the top rims of her ocean-blue eyes. She stood, and her height appeared to reach close to six feet. Her flowered jumper fell loosely over her slim frame.

The other woman came over to get a closer glimpse of Graci-An and began talking to us. Her bubbly personality intensified her chatty demeanor. She introduced the tall woman as Gretchen Gray, Graci-An's mother. "And I'm Candy, and this is my boyfriend, Jonathan."

Before we could respond, a woman in an impeccably tailored navy-blue suit walked into the waiting area and over to us. She stood straight, shoulders back.

"Hi. I'm Lilly Turner, Julia Harvey's supervisor. You can leave the baby with me, and I'll take it from here."

I looked over to the receptionist, and she gave a slight nod in confirmation.

Darryl handed the car seat carrier to Lilly. She turned toward the group, and we left.

For the next ninety minutes, Darryl and I spoke very little. I don't think either of us wanted to say anything negative, even though that's how I felt. Darryl's furrowed brow and the expression in his eyes made me think he might feel the same way.

When we returned to pick up the baby, the same three young people were in the waiting room, but we didn't see Lilly Turner. The car carrier containing a sleeping Graci-An sat on the floor next to Gretchen.

I was relieved to have Graci-An back with us. We managed to make it through her first visit, but that night turned out to be much more challenging.

She woke up screaming around eleven o'clock. Darryl and I jumped up and out of bed and ran to her bassinet. I picked her up and tried to calm her by patting her back.

The screams kept coming. I began rocking her in the rocking chair, and Darryl went and got a bottle.

She refused it. I felt her tummy, and it was as hard as a rock. Bless her heart. She was in pain.

We gave her gas drops, and they seemed to ease her pain somewhat, but the screams persisted for the next several hours.

I continued rocking her and praying. Had being with her biological mother earlier in the day affected her? Was she now having a physical reaction to the visit? Had the visit been stressful? Had it been comforting? Oh, if only she could talk.

I expected Micah to come into our room. He wasn't used to hearing a baby constantly cry in the middle of the night. But thankfully, he slept through the whole ordeal.

Finally, Graci-An's cries weakened to a whimper. She fell asleep in my arms around three o'clock in the morning.

All was well in her little world once again.

First Hearing

I pulled into the courthouse parking lot with time to spare.

The early morning heat had already become intense, not uncommon for the month of July in Florida. I rushed to the building, eager to get inside so that I could obtain some relief from the rising temperature.

After going through the metal detector, I asked a court officer where the cases for foster-care children were being heard. She pointed down the corridor with the black pen she was using to write on her clipboard. "Last courtroom on the left."

I maneuvered my way through several small crowds until I reached the end of the corridor. To my left was a small sitting area and a set of heavy, wooden double doors with the names of both Judge Rothman and Judge Anderson centered above them.

When I went to open the doors to go inside, another court officer jumped in front of me to block my entrance. I jumped back in response.

"Who you here for?" she snapped in a stern and perhaps overprotective voice.

"The case of Graci-An Gray."

Without cracking even a slight smile, she flipped through the papers on her clipboard. "Uh-hum. Mmm. Okay. Who are you?"

"I'm the foster parent. I was told I could come." I probably sounded a bit defensive.

The bailiff narrowed her eyes at me and tilted her head. "She's number thirty-eight on the docket. Step inside. No gum or mints. Turn off your beeper and cell phone. No reading books or magazines. No talking." And at that, she was kind enough to open the doors for me so that I could enter.

As soon as I stepped through the doorway, I found myself standing in a short aisle with five long, wooden, pew-style benches on each side. This area, referred to as the gallery, was where the spectators and participants sat.

The front of this section had a divider that resembled a solid wooden fence, complete with a gate leading to a larger area. Several feet past the "fence" stood a wooden podium on the left and several wooden podiums lined up horizontally on the right.

Straight ahead and beyond the podiums sat a raised and very large, ornate wooden desk, obviously the judge's bench. On each side of it were smaller desks. The desk on the left had a door behind it.

Court was not yet in progress. I sat down in the second row from the front and looked around. I didn't see anyone I recognized.

Before long, every seat in the gallery became filled. Each time the double doors opened, the thunderous chatter from outside the courtroom slipped in and disrupted the mandated silence. At one point, I turned and saw a mass of people peering through the opening and into the courtroom in anticipation. When someone left, someone else scurried in, looked around, saw the empty seat, and then hurried to sit in it.

Dear Lord, I thought, *what are we doing as a society to have such crowded dependency courtrooms?*

Several minutes later, a uniformed, heavyset man with a receding hairline stood at attention near the judge's bench and shouted, "All rise for the Honorable Alexander Anderson." All heads turned to the front of the courtroom as everyone got up from their seats.

A gray-haired man wearing a long black robe entered the courtroom through the door behind the desk to the left of the judge's bench. After he sat down at what I had correctly assumed to be his bench, everyone followed suit and sat back down in their seats.

For the next two hours, I listened to case after case being argued before the judge and acquired quite an education on the dependency system. From my vantage point, the biological parents and their attorneys stood on the left side of the courtroom, and the state and its representatives stood on the right. I was surprised to see that only one other foster parent out of thirty-seven cases had appeared on behalf of her foster child.

Finally, someone called Graci-An's name. I rose from my seat and saw Gretchen enter the courtroom through the big double doors. She walked past me and took her place next to the left podium.

I stepped hesitantly into the short aisle. The bailiff who sat in front of the doors came over and told me to stand between the state and the parents.

I then saw Julia, Graci-An's caseworker, walking to her designated spot next to the other state representatives. A familiar face, her presence provided me with some comfort.

The two defense attorneys announced their names. One stated that he represented the mother; the other stated that she represented the father.

The judge then directed his gaze at me and asked, "Who are you?"

"I'm the foster parent."

His voice softened. "Thank you for coming."

The door behind the judge's bench opened again. A court officer entered with a young man dressed in orange prison garb, handcuffs, and ankle shackles. The prisoner was tall and thin with dark hair and dark, deep-set eyes. The officer introduced him as the child's father, Jesse Cooper.

This was the first time I saw Graci-An's father, and admittedly, seeing him in this condition shocked me. Of course, it increased my plethora of questions concerning this case. What had this man done to be in jail?

The officer led Jesse to the left side of the courtroom. He stopped when he got close to Gretchen, his body tensing. He glared at her.

She stepped away from where he stood, stiffening in retaliation. She refused to look in his direction.

Now that all of the introductions had been made, the judge began the case, referring to the two defendants as the child's parents. He looked at the two attorneys standing next to Gretchen and Jesse. "Have both parents been given their case plan? And has the case plan been explained to the parents?"

Both attorneys answered yes.

Jesse Cooper spoke up. "Judge, I don't even know if I'm the baby's father."

Gretchen glowered at Jesse and pursed her lips.

The judge's eyebrows rose. "Okay, then I'm ordering a paternity test be performed."

He then set a date next month for everyone to return with the test results. The gavel went down, concluding the hearing. I'm sure we weren't up there more than five minutes, but it seemed like a lot longer.

On the way home, I called Darryl and told him everything that had happened. "I'm not quite sure what all of that means. Hopefully, we'll find out soon enough."

"Yep," he said. "Hey, I tried to call you, but I guess you had your cell phone off. Graci-An's been assigned a guardian ad litem named Paula. She dropped by the house while you were in court."

One more person assigned to this case, and one who spoke volumes, both literally and figuratively. From what I learned from Loren Dixon, the court appointed a guardian ad litem to represent only those foster children whose cases were considered at risk. Some guardians were volunteers; some were employees. Regardless, they pulled a lot of weight when it came to deciding a child's fate.

So, the comments and actions were accumulating: Mr. Berg saying that the baby would be in a bad situation if she stayed with her mother; Julia saying the case was pretty bad; Loren telling me that guardians ad litem were only assigned to those children whose cases were considered at risk; and the *alleged* biological father in jail.

Granted, we were new to this system, but it didn't take an expert to see what would have awaited Graci-An if the state had not intervened and taken her into foster care.

Unexpected Updates

"Graci-An's biological father's out of jail now."

Julia was merely warming up with the first of several unexpected updates during her next monthly home visit. "He contacted me because he also wants to have visits with Graci-An. I'll have to set up a separate visitation schedule for the father since the relationship with the mother's so volatile. That means you'll have to take Graci-An to the visitation center twice as often. I apologize, but I can't have both parents together in the same room." She shrugged and gave a half-smile. Overall, she seemed friendlier during this visit.

I asked, "Why does he want to have visitation if he's questioning whether the baby is his?"

She was again writing on that green form. Without looking up, she said, "I don't know. I didn't ask. In the meantime, though, I've set up a visitation schedule for the mother. It'll be every other Wednesday, starting next Wednesday, at the visitation center off Mays Road."

I closed my eyes, trying to remember if I had seen this street. "Where's Mays Road?"

Julia's directions made me realize that this visitation wasn't around the corner anymore. No, it was located on the other side of town, a good twenty or twenty-five-minute drive one way.

My confusion escalated. "Julia, why are the visits so far away from us when there are much closer visitation centers, including yours?"

"This location is closer to where the parents live." She then handed me the green form to sign.

Her explanation frustrated me. The parents had obviously done some bad things that caused their child to be removed, and I was taking care of *their* child and getting very little sleep. Regardless, I had to be the one exerting the most effort. Driving across town at almost three dollars a gallon for gas, an expense for which the state does not reimburse, didn't seem right.

Putting myself in the shoes of Graci-An's parents, I knew I would have driven across the country to see my child. It seemed that the state didn't want to inconvenience those parents who were responsible for this whole mess but had no problem inconveniencing those who tried to help.

When I returned the form to Julia, she gave me an encouraging smile.

Darryl leaned forward, forearms pushed down on the table. "Julia, why was the father in jail?"

"I can't share that with you right now." It was another abrupt response but this time softened by a half-smile and warm eyes.

Before Julia left, she gave us some more not-so-good news. "I need to let you know that I'm only going to be at my job here for another month. This is my last home visit with you. I'm taking a job elsewhere."

Despite the new visitation arrangements, her leaving made me sad because Graci-An would lose her as a caseworker.

Julia must have sensed my disappointment. "Hey, you're going to really like my replacement. She's very thorough. Oh, I also want you to know that I'm recommending the parents' rights be terminated in my report. I can't give you any details, though. I can only say that from what I've read and know, these parents should *not* get Graci-An back."

I respected her need for confidentiality and didn't ask any more questions.

Her words validated my trepidation, though, and provided some much-desired relief.

The Case Plan

Life as we had known it had ended.

By the time Graci-An was seven weeks old, our schedule got much busier. Perpetual activity replaced peace and normalcy as more and more people got involved with this case, thereby weaving themselves into our lives. I got to the point that I didn't know who would call next and why.

My calendar filled with appointments, all centered on Graci-An—standard psychological examinations for her, home visits by the new support specialist who had taken Sandra Curtis's place, the new guardian ad litem who had taken Paula's place, another pediatrician's appointment, and another biweekly visit with Gretchen that, much to my surprise, included Jesse.

He and Gretchen had obviously made up. The way they hung onto each other at that visit, gazing at each other with adoring eyes, you would have thought there had never been a problem between them. At least their reunion made my life simpler by eliminating the additional visits with him.

This flurry of activity came in addition to being woken up two to three times a night because Graci-An demanded a bottle. Of course, the extra fluids resulted in extra diaper changes. Frequently, she also woke up screaming from stomach pains.

She was my first colicky baby. Desperately, I gathered as much wisdom as I could from other mothers who had had colicky babies. We changed her diet, rocked her, and paced the floor with her, praying, until the pain dissipated, and she could go back to sleep. Sometimes I had to rock her for hours, crawling back into bed when some people were just waking up to start their day.

We considered the lack of sleep a small price to pay for having her in our lives. She was such a happy baby. It didn't take much to make her laugh and squeal with delight. I began to see her wonderful, fun-loving sense of humor coming out, even at such a young age. Each day brought us closer and tightened the bond growing between us.

Undoubtedly, our lives had been changed in so many ways. Thank goodness for my small support team of foster parents.

Loren Dixon called soon after that first hearing to see how everything went. I told her what had happened in court and how we had a new guardian ad litem named Erin Daniels and a new support specialist named Esther Martin. And oh, Graci-An would be getting a new caseworker too.

Darryl and I didn't know if all of these changes so early in this case were normal. Having a more experienced perspective might help.

Loren said, "Sometimes that happens in the foster-care system. I think there's a high turnover rate or something. I've never heard of Erin Daniels, but I do know Esther Martin. She used to be our support specialist. We just loved her and were so upset when we lost her. She got put into a new region, which is probably your area. Lucky you! She's absolutely great, though. You'll like her."

Her tone went from optimistic to serious. "But if you don't mind my changing the subject, was the bio-dad in jail for anything serious?"

"I don't know. No one tells us anything."

"Well, the reason he's in jail should be in the case plan. Did they leave that out?"

"I wouldn't know. I'm the foster parent, remember? We don't get case plans." Did I sound a little aggravated?

Loren's soft-spoken voice turned emphatic. "Oh yes you do. I can't believe you haven't been given a copy of the case plan. You're supposed to have a copy."

"I am? That would help so much in answering our questions. I keep hearing *case plan, case plan, case plan*, but I don't even know what one looks like. How can I get a copy?"

"You get it from the caseworker. You should have already gotten one. It'll also tell why the child was removed."

I processed this new information for a few moments. "If I'm supposed to get a copy, and if it gives the reasons why Graci-An was taken away from the bio-mom, then why has everyone been so hush-hush with me about this case? I assumed all foster parents were treated this way."

"Well, they're not, and I don't know why everyone's been so secretive with you. That doesn't make sense to me either. I wondered why you seemed to be in the dark so much when it came to the details of Graci-An's case. The only thing I can think of is that maybe they didn't think you'd have her for very long."

I stood up, unable to sit any longer. "That doesn't make much sense. Julia told me the case was pretty bad, and Mr. Berg told me they couldn't find any relatives. Why wouldn't she be with us long?"

"Good question. Maybe they just assumed you already knew most of the details, and maybe the caseworker meant she couldn't tell you the extra stuff that they don't tell foster parents. There are *always* things we aren't told that are considered too confidential. That's the only other thing I can think of."

I hoped Loren was right. It didn't make sense that Julia would hide information that would be divulged to us sooner or later.

As soon as Loren and I finished our conversation, I called Julia Harvey. She was still Graci-An's caseworker. She answered the phone on the third ring and didn't seem at all surprised at my request for a copy of the case plan.

"Yes, you do need a copy. I'm leaving my office now for an appointment, and I'll swing by and drop it off. I can't stay because I do have to be somewhere."

I didn't say anything, contemplating whether I should ask her why she hadn't given us a copy earlier. I wanted to know why she had been so secretive. At this point, the reasons were moot. We were getting a copy of the case plan, and Julia was leaving soon.

A few minutes later, while letting our dog outside in the backyard, the doorbell rang. I ran to the front door to answer it, and there stood Julia. She held out a brown manila envelope.

"Here's the case plan," she said. "Gotta go."

I was more than okay with her leaving. I was eager to see what the infamous case plan looked like. Taking advantage of Graci-An being asleep, I grabbed a bottle of water and sat down at our dining room table to review it.

I perused it from front to back, studying it like a textbook. The beginning of the plan had a section called "Reason for Removal," which contained a narrative of the complaint against the parents.

Although I won't disclose the details given in the case plan, I will say that Gretchen appeared to have a substantial history involving adverse behaviors and actions, and in some important areas. Like a chain of dominoes, one issue led to a whole stream of other harmful issues. Each problem was detrimental to a child.

None of these situations seemed like she had hit a skid mark in the road—rather, they painted a picture of someone who had made a lifestyle out of bad decisions and actions. Suffice it to say that DCF's investigation imparted enough probable cause to remove the baby from Gretchen as soon as she was born.

A list of standard "Service Tasks" directly followed the "Reason for Removal" section. Some of the required tasks could include taking parenting-skills classes; paying child support while the child was in foster care; and maintaining stable employment and safe and stable housing, both for a minimum of six consecutive months.

Other tasks may consist of undergoing drug testing, evaluations, and psychological tests and enrolling in a batterer's intervention program or anger-management class. These would be mandated based on the parent's specific issues.

Each task gave specific instructions on how to complete it and how it would be measured, as well as the target date of completion. It required each parent to successfully accomplish each task on his or her list within twelve months from the day of the child's removal.

This document provided a lot of information and gave us a better understanding of this case. Now we finally had some answers. Consequently, I felt a stronger sense of protectiveness toward Graci-An.

From what I could surmise from the case plan, Gretchen's issues went deep. I didn't know if she would be able to overcome them and be on the road to recovery in what would now be less than ten months. I thought she'd have to be highly motivated and focused.

But I do know that when a mother loves her child, she'll do whatever she has to do and jump through whatever hoops are demanded of her. It was too early to know if this described Gretchen.

And surely, the state wouldn't give a baby to someone who wasn't ready to care for her.

The Appointed Voice of the Child

I had missed them so much over the past six weeks.

We were all very excited about my older three sons' pending return from their summer visit with their father.

When the day approached to pick them up, Micah kept asking, "When are we going to get them? When are we going to get them?"

I just knew he would burst at the seams if he didn't see them soon. If not for his seatbelt on the ride to pick up his brothers, he would have been jumping up and down in the van.

The big smile and raised eyebrows refused to leave their positions on his face. When we arrived at the airport, his enlarged, expectant eyes searched the sidewalk for his brothers.

Then I saw them waiting with their father. I yelled out to Micah, "There they are!"

In the rearview mirror, I saw him straining his head in an effort to locate them.

Darryl pulled over and parked. When I stepped out of our van, I couldn't contain the big grin on my face. Devlin appeared to have grown a couple of inches, and Tristan and Liam had acquired beautiful tans.

When they saw me, their faces lit up. All three ran into my arms, and we hugged. Oh, it was so good to have them back. They all asked about Graci-An and wanted to know if Micah was with us.

"He wouldn't have missed being here to meet you," I told them.

Darryl put their bags in the cargo area while the boys got into their seats. Micah's smile grew, and he demanded to sit next to them.

When they saw Graci-An curiously watching them, they commented on how different she looked. I think they wondered if we had switched babies. I told them that she had changed since they left six weeks ago and that she would change even more over the next six weeks.

They accepted my explanation. The constant chatter as they described their summer exploits contrasted with the quiet we had experienced over the last month and a half. We were just so glad to have them back, we didn't care that life would get even busier as a result.

Of course, the system placed their share of demands on our time and then some. The next day, Erin Daniels, Graci-An's new guardian ad litem, was coming for her first visit.

I had cleaned the house thoroughly before picking up the boys. But do you know how much of a mess four boys can make within a twenty-four-hour time frame?

So, on that Monday morning while the children slept, I got up extra early. I tidied each room. Darryl pitched in and helped. By the time we finished, we once again had a presentable home.

We wanted to ensure that we made a good impression on the guardian ad litem because the court appointed her as the voice of the child. She represented the child and no one else—not the biological parents, not the foster parents, and not the caseworker. The fact that she had such an important role in the case made this meeting a bit daunting.

Then the doorbell rang. I glanced through the window and saw two young women standing on our front porch. Taking in a deep breath, I opened the door and welcomed them into our home.

Both women were attractive brunettes. The petite woman had short hair and fair skin. Her hazel eyes conveyed intelligence, and her posture was one of ease and confidence. She reached out and firmly took my hand in hers, shaking it. She introduced herself as Erin Daniels and the other woman as her supervisor and case coordinator, Alisa Gifford.

Alisa had darker skin and long hair. She was of medium height and had a slim build and beautiful blue eyes. She looked too young to be a supervisor.

Darryl held Graci-An. Both women looked at her with smiles on their faces. Still, the environment seemed tense and awkward.

In an effort to make them comfortable, I asked, "Can I get either of you something to drink? Water? Soda? Juice?"

"No, thank you," they said at the same time.

Alisa spoke with a soft, almost timid voice. "We would like to see your home. Do you mind showing it to us?"

Oh boy, here we go again ... another tour, I thought. Of course, I wasn't about to turn them down. Being new to the system, this request still took me by surprise since our house had been examined during the licensing process and viewed by the caseworker. Did no one look at the records being compiled by other divisions?

I don't recall Darryl mentioning that the first guardian ad litem, Paula, had also requested a tour of our home. Come to mention it, I don't recall being warned in any of the training classes that everyone who comes to your house for an initial visit will need to see the place in its entirety.

I had always believed that bedrooms were private, yet everyone was interested in evaluating them. Thank goodness we had straightened up the house at the last minute.

Darryl glanced up from playing with Graci-An. "Why don't you all go ahead, and I'll stay here with the baby and wait for you?"

Neither of the ladies said a word as I showed them our home, room by room, nor did their faces reveal any expression. At least Julia had nodded with every room she saw, making me think that she approved.

They peeped in the boys' rooms since they were still asleep. When I took them to Graci-An's bedroom, I did note a glance that passed between them, but again, no emotion. I thought that these two would make unconquerable poker players, or at the very least, wonderful bridge partners.

We returned to the dining room and joined Darryl and Graci-An at the table where we now conducted all of our foster-care visits. Erin and Alisa sat next to each other.

"We love the baby's room," Alisa said.

"Thank you," I responded.

Erin sat across from me. She placed her elbows on the table and clasped her hands. "I'm a volunteer guardian ad litem, and this is my first case. I asked them to give me a baby, and so they assigned me to Graci-An. Can you tell us how she's developing?"

I glanced over at Graci-An, who was shaking her rattle. "Well, the doctor says she's right on track, in the fiftieth percentile in weight and height. I think she's trying to sit up."

Darryl, the proud foster parent, jumped in with his comments. "You can tell she's a happy little girl." He gazed down at Graci-An, his smile reflecting his adoration. "All smiles and giggles."

Alisa and Erin followed Darryl's focus, and their eyes also landed on Graci-An.

I said, "I'll have an update next week when I take her to her two-month pediatrician visit. They keep changing so much at this age."

They glanced at each other, giving that same shared look as when they had seen Graci-An's room.

Erin leaned forward as if trying to reach me. She looked me in the eye and got right to the point. "What are your intentions with Graci-An should she become available for adoption?"

"We would adopt her without hesitation," I said without thinking.

Both Alisa and Erin smiled at each other. They thanked us for our time. We shook hands, and they left.

Erin's final question gave us more hope. We knew that these two women knew more about this case than we did. We took her question to mean that there was a good chance Graci-An would be available for adoption.

When that happened, they wanted to make sure she had a permanent home.

Allusions

Two days after the guardian's ad litem first visit, our new support specialist, Esther Martin, came to our home for her first visit. I met her at our front door with Graci-An in my arms.

Esther was in her late thirties, taller than average, and thin. She smiled constantly. I had already been looking forward to our meeting after hearing Loren Dixon's high praise of her.

I returned her smile. "It's so nice to meet you. I wish my husband could have been here, but he had an appointment he couldn't get out of. You'll be meeting him soon enough. I guess you know that we're new to the foster-care system."

"Yes, I do know that. So welcome!" she said with genuine happiness. She then asked to see our home.

I was gradually getting used to this request; evidently, I didn't have a choice. I had fulfilled it so many times that I was developing a strategy of how to show it.

After giving her the tour, we settled down at our dining room table. She asked me about the case. I told her everything we knew and the comments made by different individuals within the system, from Mr. Berg not finding a suitable relative to Julia's recommendation to terminate the parents' rights to the guardian's ad litem recent question.

She tilted her head slightly to the side as I spoke, and her unblinking eyes remained steady on my face, her smile unwavering. She gave me the impression that what I said and felt mattered.

"Esther, I know we're really green and inexperienced, but we're not idiots either. I mean, everything we're being told is pointing toward our being able to adopt Graci-An. It appears that the mother shouldn't have her back, and we haven't been told anything that indicates otherwise."

She patted my hand. "Well, I hope it works out for you."

I said, "I know we shouldn't get our hopes up, but considering everything so far, it's awfully hard to ignore the innuendos and comments."

She rose from her chair to leave. "Just continue to pray about it, Mrs. Clark, 'cause Graci-An sure does look bonded to you."

Induction into the Secret Society

The adjustment period had long since ended.

Graci-An settled into our family like she had been with us forever. As she got older, she required more interaction from us. No longer was it enough to leave her alone so that she could sleep. She demanded to be held, or she demanded that we speak to her.

When she got bored, she designated us to be her entertainment, which of course made sense. We were her world, after all.

While we played with her, she smiled and looked up at us as if trying to laugh. I called it the "silent laugh." Until those laughs were able to make their way out into the atmosphere for us to hear and cherish, Graci-An took advantage of the capability she had at that time—squealing with delight.

She still continued to wake us up several times throughout the night, making our adjustment to a disciplined routine for the new school year more taxing. In the mornings, Darryl started the coffee. I took on the task of waking up each of the boys and keeping after them until everyone was ready to head out the door. Either Darryl or I drove them to school, depending on our schedules for that morning. The other stayed with Graci-An, cherishing the solitude for as long as she slept.

The ups and downs of parenthood further strengthened the bond growing between Graci-An and us. When I held her close in my arms, she rubbed her face over mine. She studied me and smiled.

When I stopped whatever I was doing and just played with her, she responded with enthusiasm. At times, I found myself studying her, hoping and praying that she would always be with us.

We were so close. When I entered the room, and she heard my voice, she turned her head in my direction, all the while kicking her legs with total joy. She simply adored Darryl, her eyes twinkling with sheer delight anytime she caught a glimpse of him.

All four sons were crazy about her. They always had to hug and kiss her when they were around her.

Still, we had to contend with the foster-care system and all of its idiosyncrasies. I came to realize that being a parent to several children was easier than being a foster parent to one child. There were so many requirements and so many appointments to attend, all based upon the foster child and her needs. Admittedly, it all could be quite overwhelming.

Darryl worked most of the time, leaving me to take care of just about everything else. He joined in when he could, like driving with us to the lab so that Graci-An could donate her saliva for the DNA paternity test.

Additionally, each month brought with it another hearing for Graci-An's case. The second hearing produced very little, if anything, to report—a waste of time on everyone's part.

The third hearing was the pretrial. Finally, the case showed progress. The parents pled guilty as charged to the state's allegations and reasons for removing Graci-An and putting her in foster care.

Also, this same hearing divulged the results from the paternity test—Jesse Cooper was indeed Graci-An's biological father. The judge made a point of telling both parents that they had to live independently. He warned them that they needed to work on their case plan. Both of these issues went hand in hand.

Last but not least, the judge set the date for a six-month judicial review hearing a whole two months away. Next month would be the first month without a hearing.

These were only a few of the events that made our lives more complex. At first, we found adapting to the invasiveness of this system to be difficult. We have always cherished our privacy. The frequent visits from various social workers were bad enough, but their evaluating our home was almost demeaning. We considered ourselves mature and logical adults, and thus far, we had done pretty well with our four children.

But the state went behind us like we were children ourselves, checking to see if we had our laundry detergent and aspirin locked away in a box or cabinet. It was still debatable whether common bath soap needed to be locked away so that the children wouldn't be tempted to eat it.

So those who opened their home to fostering must also open up their lives and submit to the demands placed upon them by an all-too-often ungrateful system. We were scrutinized, not appreciated.

At one of the foster-parent association meetings, one of the powers that be told us that being a foster parent was a privilege, not a right. Basically, we could lose that "privilege" if we screwed up. There was nothing like keeping people walking on eggshells, making them afraid that anything they did could be misconstrued as screwing up, and then, "Off with their heads!" or in the world of foster care, "Give me your license and your foster children."

I strived to keep up with their influx of dictates while balancing my other obligations and not neglecting my sons. But the system took from you as much as it could get.

I appreciated the support from my sons, and Darryl did as much as he could to help. But they all had lives before we became foster parents, and they all had lives outside of the foster-care system. I think I was the only one in our family whose life *became* the foster-care system, or was it the other way around? I don't really know because we both blurred into each other, becoming one.

Despite the system's intrusiveness, our family remained close. We adjusted our schedules and made the best of the situation. I tried to fulfill the system's insatiable requirements while the boys were in school. Otherwise, I used their absence as a time to write, take care of the house, and other responsibilities or as an opportunity to spend time with Graci-An.

Once I picked up the boys from school, our home broke out into an atmosphere of frenzied activity. This was their time. Before anything else, though, they needed to do their homework. Afterward, they played outside with a couple of the neighborhood boys while I cooked dinner.

We dedicated our evening meal to family time. Sitting around the dining room table, the boys talked about how they were doing and how their days had been. They sometimes even shared their plans and dreams.

Micah always wanted to sit next to Graci-An. He gladly surrendered his position as the baby of the family and doted on her more than the other boys did. Graci-An could do no wrong in his eyes. He laughed at everything she did, describing it all as "cute."

Devlin, the academic, talked about his classes, school projects, and assigned homework. He shared what he was doing in school and how he was doing it. For instance, he went into detail about a science project he wanted to create, the supplies he needed, his reasons for developing it, and the results he thought he'd get. Or he talked about a history report he was working on or a story he was writing.

My favorite times were when out of nowhere, he would say, "Mom, let's you and I go talk." This was music to my ears. I never wanted to lose that closeness and degree of communication with my child. I assumed it would go on forever.

My next-to-oldest son and our thinker, Tristan, just listened. He usually didn't offer any input or share anything unless asked, so we would ask him. He was bright and an excellent student. The school described him as one of the most popular kids in his class, very well-liked and respected by all of his peers.

As soon as dinner ended, he paced on the back porch. I think he did his best thinking this way. Tristan and I were very close too, but he wasn't as open as Devlin in sharing his thoughts and emotions. I took what I could get from him and valued it like a precious gem.

Then there was Liam, the next-to-youngest, my laughing boy with the big, brown, mischievous eyes and enviable, thick auburn hair. Liam had a tendency to be so talkative that we had to remind him to let others have a turn to speak.

If he wasn't making a joke, he was drawing his comical cartoons, like the creature with the polka-dotted underwear. Or he was asking questions, most of which took you aback and made you think, like, "If Santa Claus gives everybody gifts for Christmas, then who gives Santa Claus gifts?"

Darryl and I would look around the table, happy and contented with our family. The boys all loved him.

Tristan had written a paper for school about his admiration for Darryl. According to Tristan, Darryl was fun and always shared his childhood experiences when the children confronted challenges. He was more of a teacher than a disciplinarian.

As for me, I was Mom, the teacher, the nurse, the cook, the maid, the chief launderer, the chauffeur, the cheerleader, the counselor, etc., etc., etc. I loved my family, and I needed them as much as, if not more than, they needed me.

We did lots of things together as a family, especially on weekends when Darryl didn't work. We valued our Christian faith and attended church on a routine basis. We had always instilled in the boys a love for Jesus, the "do unto others" tenet, respect for others, and the importance of telling the truth. I cherished the intimacy within our family.

The boys didn't question Graci-An's role in our lives and family, nor did they ever consider her an interloper. They didn't understand the foster-care system, but come to think of it, I don't think Darryl and I truly did either.

We had gotten to the point of not liking our roles as foster parents. We knew that if we were to adopt Graci-An, we would turn in our license. This system meddled too much, and it assumed even more.

With each unyielding directive given by the system came the expectation of submission, regardless of the cost. As I gave and gave, trying in vain to satisfy its unquenchable appetite, my initial perspective of the system became tainted. It was losing its idealistic and heroic posture as I saw how it callously used the foster parents like workhorses.

You would have thought that it was up to me to determine how much of myself I gave to it, but once inducted into this secret society, that wasn't as easy as it sounded. The system had us lock, stock, and barrel, and it was too late to turn back. The option to set boundaries no longer existed.

For us, it wasn't about being foster parents; it was about our love for a tiny baby girl who had stolen our heart.

Chapter Four

Once Was Not Enough

Graci-An had hands. Two of them, in fact.

And how marvelous to have discovered this glorious phenomenon. Her face filled with wonder as she watched her hands move and then with surprise at the realization that it was she who made them move.

We enjoyed seeing her expressions with every discovery she made. When she hit a benchmark, like rolling over for the first time, we got just as excited as she did (if not more so).

Of course, we still hoped she'd reach a developmental milestone during the night and let us sleep. Darryl was a night owl, so he woke up and prepared the first bottle, mixing the formula powder with distilled water. By the next one, the diaper needed replacing.

One night in the midst of changing her, I discovered the hard way that she hadn't finished taking care of business. As soon as I pulled off the heavy, almost dripping diaper, her thighs squeezed together so tightly that when she urinated, the stream went straight up and onto the carpet.

I jumped out of the way just in time, but not before screaming and waking up Darryl. He shot out of bed, completely disoriented. He then ran over to save us from whatever danger confronted us.

Once he realized the "danger" lay within some harmless pee-pee that had escaped, he crawled back to bed. It's a wonder we survived.

Graci-An still had very little hair and no teeth. No one cared. Her personality was becoming richer and more wondrous. We loved to hear her jovial laughter that now filled the air like silken strings of vibrant and brightly colored confetti.

She still kicked her legs excitedly when we got near her, signaling that she wanted to be held. She had us all well-trained.

We loved it when she laid her head on our shoulders in complete trust and contentment. We melted when she looked into our eyes with such love.

I talked to her about the most mundane topics, and she kept her gaze fixed on me, making me feel like she found every word I said interesting. I loved to sing to her and took every opportunity to do so when we were alone … or not.

I tried to imagine how Graci-An might feel about being a foster child, if she were old enough to understand. The foster-care system had engulfed her life from birth. She lived with us and visited Jesse and Gretchen every other week for ninety minutes. I wondered if she could comprehend who they were.

The revolving door of social workers who entered and exited this case was the norm for her. At any moment, another social worker would be walking through that revolving door. Graci-An's new caseworker, Katy Farrell, had scheduled her first home visit with us.

When she knocked on our front door, I opened it to find a woman almost as tall as Darryl. I already knew what she looked like because I had seen her at the last hearing, but we had never met face-to-face. Her natural beauty was more evident up close. Her fair skin contrasted with her dark, curly hair, which she had pulled back into a loose ponytail.

She was dressed for the weather in an orange cotton skirt and a sleeveless peach-and-brown cotton top. In many other places in the country, her attire would be considered out of season ever since October had proclaimed its arrival on the calendar. But in Florida, we regarded this month, although officially fall, as an extension of summer.

Her warm eyes supported her smile. "Hi, I'm Katy."

She came inside, and we began our conversation with small talk. Katy then asked if I had gone to the hearing.

"Yes. I saw you there. I think I understand what happened, but what did you think about it, Katy?"

She smiled again. "Well, the judge is quite aware of the bio-parents' lack of compliance. That's why he reminded them in this hearing that they had to pay child support, live independently, and so on. That's why he warned them that they could have their child removed permanently if they didn't finish all their case plan tasks in time. But they've got to get busy. It's been four months, and they still haven't done any of their tasks, although I think they did start the parenting class."

As she talked, her face and body were relaxed. "The next hearing will be for the six-month judicial review because Graci-An will have been in the system for six months at that time. So, they'll have to show the judge what they've done on their case plan and what they haven't done."

She closed her burgundy portfolio and then snapped her fingers with a quick shake of her hand. "Oh, before I forget. Jesse has requested that the visits be moved from Wednesdays to Tuesdays. He's got a seasonal job, and I think that the fall season is their busy time. I think Wednesdays are a hardship. Are you okay with that?"

I appreciated her asking how I felt. That was a first. "Sure. It doesn't matter to me either way."

"Great. I'll start working on changing it and let you know the details."

She rose from her seat and gathered her belongings. "By the way, it took me awhile, but I finally managed to go through all of the information in the file for this case."

She placed her hand on the doorknob, and then turned back to face me. "I can't tell you what was in it, but I can tell you that it's *really* messy."

Appeasing the Beast

I don't do well with last-minute exigencies.

My schedule had no wiggle room. So, when Katy Farrell called me on that following Tuesday afternoon, notifying me that visitation had been moved to Tuesdays—starting *that* day—I almost went into panic mode. When she told me that the time had changed to four o'clock, a mere three hours away, I think I did panic.

The switch in visitation days happened too quickly and without any heads-up to adjust our schedule. My mind reeled. How would I pick up my sons from school at three thirty, get on the road by three forty-five, and make that drive all the way across town in time? On a good day, it took about twenty-five minutes. But this time of the day was rush hour, easily adding another fifteen to twenty-five minutes. Four o'clock was out of the question.

I wanted to tell Katy that I couldn't do it with such short notice. However, I didn't want to risk upsetting anyone in the system who could remove Graci-An from us, even though the demand was absurd.

After several moments of silence, I acquiesced. "Okay, Katy. Let me see what I can do." I explained my predicament to her and that I wouldn't be able to get to the visitation center before four thirty. "It's going to be up to the traffic," I said.

"I really appreciate this. I just got word about this too, or I would've called you earlier."

Did I feel strong-armed into taking Graci-An to a visit across town at the last minute? Not by Katy, but by the system. What if we already had something planned that we couldn't cancel on our end? Would they still expect us to accommodate them with only a three-hour notification? Did they expect me to leave my children at school while I did their bidding? Would they hold it against us if we were late? Something within me told me the answer would be yes on all counts.

While I was wrestling with my dilemma, trying to figure out the best way to attack it, Darryl called. He had been away on a business trip and couldn't have picked a better time. I told him about Katy's phone call.

"Okay, I'm on my way home and should be there by three," he said. "You can then leave the baby with me and go pick up the boys from school. I'll take Graci-An to her visit."

The muscles in my neck and shoulders loosened. "Oh, thank you, Darryl. Thank you, thank you. I owe you one for this. Have I told you that you're my hero? You don't know how much of a load you've just taken from me."

I breathed a huge sigh of relief, knowing that we'd be able to feed the beast and appease the system after all, once again.

Sometimes, though, the beast can surprise you, not unlike a scary monster on a children's show that dumbfounds everyone by doing something kind.

When Katy Farrell called a few days later to tell me that she had moved the visitations back to her office, a mere five minutes from our home, I became more than dumbfounded. Exhilaration overcame me. Trying to fulfill the insatiable demands of the system had been taking its toll on me, which in turn had been affecting my family. Even saving an hour in commute time was a big to-do.

Of course, I thanked Katy profusely for considering us and getting this much-needed change. The visitation time hopefully wouldn't be a challenge—one o'clock on Sundays.

Thinking to myself, I tried to calculate what we might face when attending Sunday morning church service and then making it to the center on time. We would work it out; the benefit of the center's proximity far outweighed the fact that the visits were on Sunday afternoons, a time we traditionally used for family activities.

I did wonder how it would affect Jesse and Gretchen since they lived near the other visitation center. But then I came to terms with what I had perceived for quite some time—the system would do everything possible to ensure that the biological parents completed their case plans. This included having the taxpayers pay for most of the services they were mandated to attend and giving them bus fare so that they had transportation.

I recall being told that the system wouldn't pay for the batterer's intervention program, but some creative financing could be done so that the bio-parent wouldn't incur any out-of-pocket expenses. They'd tell the parent to let them pay for their electric bill, and the money the bio-parent would have used for that expense would then be used for the program. It was just a matter of shuffling money around.

Then sometimes the beast decided to maintain its status quo. Just a few days after receiving this incredible news from Katy, Erin Daniels came by for a visit. Her mouth was formed into a frown and the inner edges of her eyebrows were pulled down as she sat at our dining room table.

"I guess you know that the six-month judicial review hearing is coming up, and right now, I don't know a whole lot about Graci-An's case. I've been trying to get important and relevant documents and information, but no one's returning my phone calls. It's so infuriating."

I could only imagine Erin's frustration. Additionally, I felt disappointed that she couldn't give us a recent update. Every time she came for a visit, we could always count on her telling us about the parents' progress on their case plans.

But clearly, more information existed because she would say, "I wish I could tell you everything, but I can't. I can't even elaborate on what you do know. And what you do know wouldn't fill a fingernail. Suffice it to say that this is a very bad case."

She spoke with such passion, and I envisioned it oozing as she tackled the behind-the-scenes tasks and when she spoke before a judge. Maybe that's why no one returned her phone calls. Maybe they weren't used to so much zeal and directness, and she or he found it intimidating.

Darryl wrinkled his nose. "But you're Graci-An's guardian ad litem. Don't you have the right to get this stuff? I mean, c'mon. You'd think they'd want you to have whatever you needed so that you could do your job."

"Yeah, you'd think." She threw her hands up. "Well, all I can do is keep trying. I'll keep calling and bugging them 'til they give me what I need."

"Speaking of the six-month judicial review," I said, "what do you think will happen at it?"

Erin shrugged. "I've never been to a JR, so I'm not sure. But from what I understand, what the parents have or haven't done will be talked about. The last I heard is that the parents haven't done their case plan. It doesn't look good for them. I just don't know all the details. Are you going?"

Darryl and I responded in unison, "Absolutely."

I said, "It's going to be at the Cypress Boulevard courthouse, right?"

Erin nodded. "Yes, it is."

When she left that day, she promised to call us if she found out anything we should know.

The three of us were learning together. We had gone through our respective classroom trainings, and now we were all going through on-the-job training. Graci-An was our first foster child, and she was Erin's first case.

In addition to Erin being exceptionally intelligent, the compassion and thoughtfulness I saw in her consoled me. She had once told us that all she cared about was doing the right thing by Graci-An. She liked us, but she let us know that her feelings toward us wouldn't sway her recommendation. To her, it was all about Graci-An. That was all I could ask.

As much as we wanted to adopt Graci-An, we knew that if she would be better off living with her mother, then so be it. But from all accounts, that wasn't the situation.

When it came to Erin Daniels, her passion more than compensated for her lack of experience. Give me passion over experience any day.

Erin could always gain experience, but passion was a gift that couldn't be learned.

The Continuance

I pulled my raincoat around me like protective armor as I got out of my van to brave the wind and cold rain.

I wished the mid-November weather was brighter, sunnier, more welcoming to embolden us in our imminent endeavor—Graci-An's six-month judicial review hearing.

Darryl and I had decided to meet in front of the Cypress Boulevard courthouse due to time constraints. He had to come straight from work, and I had to drop off Graci-An at Loren Dixon's house. When I spotted him standing in front of the entrance, I ran over to him and hugged him.

I couldn't control my lips from shivering and my teeth from chattering. I didn't know if both were from the cold or from the butterflies that were growing in size and volume inside my stomach.

Darryl took my hand and gave it an encouraging squeeze. I held onto his hand, using it as a support post as we entered the building.

Shaking off the wet cold, we passed through the metal detector. We looked around but didn't recognize anyone we knew. Darryl asked a court officer where the case of Graci-An Gray would be held. The officer looked at his clipboard and pointed to the courtroom to our left. Just as we sat down in the waiting area, another court officer made his announcement.

"Graci-An Gray. The case of Graci-An Gray."

We followed that court officer through double doors and entered what appeared to be an oversized conference room with courtroom components. Compared to its downtown counterpart, this courtroom presented a less formal and less intimidating atmosphere with its lower ceiling, smaller judge's bench, and lack of wooden adornment.

Additionally, it offered no podiums for the parties to stand at, but instead provided each of the two opposing parties with their own large wooden table to sit at. Together, they filled the area in front of the judge's bench.

Like most courtrooms, though, a wooden fence-like divider still separated the hearing/trial area from the spectator section. This section happened to be completely empty.

Another difference included the magistrate, who presided over the hearings held in this court instead of a judge. A magistrate is an attorney and hears cases for a judge, and then gives his or her recommendations to that judge. The judge can agree or disagree before giving the final order.

The fact that the different hearing officers broke the chain of continuity concerned me. I didn't care who presided over the case; I just didn't like going back and forth between the two. Pick one or the other, and stick with it. How could either be as familiar with a case if both had not been present during all of the hearings?

The parties took their seats at their respective tables, pulling files from their formidable-looking briefcases. Erin, her supervisor Alisa, and Graci-An's caseworker Katy sat next to each other at the state's table. The attorneys for both the state and the guardian ad litem office sat across from them. At the other table sat Gretchen, her attorney, and Jesse. Surprisingly, I didn't see Jesse's attorney.

We didn't know what to do, so we sat down in the chairs in front of the spectator area. We waited for someone to ask who we were and to tell us to come forward and join the other parties.

The hearing commenced, and those present gave their names for the record, except for Darryl and me. No one even looked at us. We sat on the sidelines, invisible. We weren't acknowledged as a voice in this case, yet we were the ones who had taken care of this child in question twenty-four hours a day, seven days a week for the past six months.

Our presence may not have been recognized, but the magistrate did notice the absence of Jesse's attorney. She asked him if he had one to represent him.

Jesse responded, "She's not here. I fired her. I want a new attorney. And while you're at it, I want a new caseworker too. None of them have done anything for me."

He appeared to be putting all of the blame and responsibility on "them," as if doing his case plan tasks was their responsibility.

The magistrate ruled that the hearing needed to be continued so that the father could have legal representation. She then passed it to next month before concluding it. We had no control over the matter, and based on this hearing, we had no input either.

Disappointed, Darryl and I left the courtroom and stepped back outside into the blustery cold. The events of the hearing left me too numb to experience the full impact of the angry wind as it slapped my bare face. I felt drained and confused. How could the state insist on dragging out a case for parents who apparently were not willing to do what it took to get their child back?

While walking to our vehicles, we heard Erin calling behind us. We stopped and waited for her.

When she caught up to us, she rolled her eyes and shook her head. She then gave a half-smile. "I just wanted to personally thank you for your time in coming here today. I'm sorry nothing happened." The cold air turned her breath into vapor as the words left her lips.

I didn't know how to respond. Erin wasn't at fault. She had no control over the hearing either. My confusion, disappointment, anger, and many more things were directed at what had or hadn't taken place. We had all come here with a purpose and an expectation that were thwarted because one person didn't take responsibility for his indolence.

What could I say? "You're welcome?" No, that seemed too pardonable. "Yeah, it kinda blows that we took the morning off, and for what?" No, that seemed too bitter. The best thing was for me to say nothing.

Darryl, being the optimist, thankfully replied. He returned her smile, and his voice sounded cheerful. "Hey, that's okay. It's not your fault. We'll be back next month. Just for clarification, though, it's being held in the downtown courthouse, right?" He always did well speaking for us both in times like this.

Erin's face relaxed a little. "Yes, it is. I'll be there too. Hopefully, we can get it heard at that time." She smiled again and nodded, digging her hands deeper into the pockets of her tan coat, her body stiffening against the thrashing wind.

The smile then left her face. "I haven't had the chance to tell you, but I finally got some of the documentation I had been requesting. As far as I know, the parents have a long way to go to complete their case plan. They haven't even begun the big tasks. I don't see reunification happening, especially in reading all of the documentation I have. I wish I could tell you the details of what I know about this case, but I can't tell you anything. Again, all I can say is that what I've read doesn't look good for them."

About that time, Jesse and Gretchen walked past us, catching Erin's eye. Turning back to us briefly, she said, "Excuse me, I need to go."

At that, she hurried after them like a cat scurrying off after a mouse.

Will You Take Her Too?

The chill of an early winter had made itself comfortable, refusing to leave.

The boys started back to school after the long Thanksgiving weekend, only to begin gearing up for the Christmas holiday in a little over two weeks.

After putting the children to bed, Darryl and I began our wind-down for a meeting with Mr. Sandman when the phone rang. I glanced at the clock on my nightstand and saw that it read 10:10 p.m.

Placement came up on the caller ID. Why were they calling us? We had hit the state's maximum of five children per household. Theoretically, our home couldn't take any more foster children. I answered it, though, interested in hearing the reason for their call.

"Mrs. Clark? This is Nancy from Placement."

I looked over at Darryl, who was reading a book, and shook him. Pointing to the receiver, I mouthed the words for him to get on the other phone. He creased his eyebrows together in annoyance but complied anyway, getting out of his comfortable position.

Nancy continued, "We have a four-year-old little girl who needs to be placed in a home. DCF wanted to see if you would take her since you have her sister."

I tried to grasp the meaning of her words. Then it hit me. The case plan had mentioned that Graci-An had an older sister but that she lived with her former stepfather. I ran into the living room where Darryl stood with a phone to his ear.

To me, this was a no-brainer. Our precious Graci-An had a sister who needed a home. We had to take her.

Darryl, on the other hand, didn't appear to share my fervor. He had a frown on his face and was staring at the wall in front of him.

Several silent moments elapsed while I held my breath. Darryl spoke first. "Where's she at now, Nancy?"

"She's downtown in a building with the child protective investigator. I'm afraid there's nowhere else to place her on such short notice."

Darryl looked at me, cocking his head to one side and raising his eyebrows. His eyes seemed to silently ask if I *really* wanted to do this.

I envisioned this little girl: Graci-An, several years older. Oh, what fun we could all have! I nodded my head up and down with a huge smile on my face.

He closed his eyes before answering. "Okay, Nancy. Go ahead and bring her here. When can we expect her?"

"Oh, thank you, Mr. and Mrs. Clark. I would say that the investigator should bring her to your house within the hour."

I could sense Darryl needed some encouragement after our call with Nancy. I walked over and hugged him.

Leaning my head back, I stared into his worried eyes. "We can do it, sweetheart. She's a four-year-old little girl. And most importantly, she's Graci-An's sister."

I went to Graci-An's room, pulled out the twin bed from the love seat and put clean sheets on it. I then took a spare child-size toothbrush from our linen closet. I wanted to make sure she didn't lack for anything during her first night with us. Then we waited.

Small Voices Silenced

The much-anticipated knock finally sounded on our front door when the clock's hands reached the eleven-forty position. I opened the door to find a tall, pretty dark-skinned woman. Behind her, a slender little girl skipped toward us as if her world was carefree. When she bent down to pick up a leaf illuminated by the front porch light, I saw her face. She didn't look anything like Graci-An.

The lady spoke. "Mrs. Clark? I'm Glynnis from DCF, and Molly's the one picking up something off the ground." Her face looked tired, the outer edges of her eyes turned down. We shook hands, and then Glynnis looked over her shoulder and said to Molly, "C'mon. Let's get inside. It's cold out here."

I opened the door wide to make Molly feel welcome, not able to imagine what was going through her mind. She walked into our house without showing the least bit of intimidation, like she had moved from home to home a hundred times before in her young life.

I crouched down to her eye level. "Welcome to our home, Molly. I'm so glad you're here. Let me show you to your room."

I stood up and said to Glynnis, "Excuse me for a minute. I'll be right back."

Molly followed me down the hallway and into the corner bedroom. She didn't say one word, but she didn't appear scared. That surprised me. If I was four years old, taken away from my parents, and placed in a strange home with strange people in the middle of the night, I would have been terrified. Molly, however, appeared to be quite comfortable with the situation.

I said, "This is your room, Molly, and this is your bed."

She looked around without any expression. There was just nothing there—not fear, nor curiosity, nor sadness—nothing.

"Go ahead and make yourself at home. I'll be back in a few minutes." I wanted to talk to Glynnis without Molly present.

Darryl and Glynnis were talking about the cold weather when I came back into the room. I joined their conversation briefly before asking Glynnis why Molly had been taken into custody.

"Well, we found out that the mother wasn't supposed to have Molly at all, for one thing."

I was shocked. "You mean you took Molly from her mother? She was living with her mother? Why would Molly be with her mother? I thought Gretchen wasn't supposed to have any children living with her at this time."

"Yes." She handed me a bag and Molly's red folder. "Here are some clothes for Molly, and there'll be a number in the folder in case you need anything." She turned and opened the door, and then she was gone.

Clearly, Glynnis had no intention of divulging anything to me. I found this odd, especially since she knew I would obtain the answers to at least some of my questions sooner or later.

I took the bag into Molly's room and emptied it. Great: a nightgown, some underpants, a pair of pants, and two short-sleeved tops, but no toothbrush. Thankfully, we had what was missing.

I said, "Tell you what, Molly. Let's get you started with brushing your teeth. While you're doing that, I'll run you some bath water."

She followed me into the hall bathroom, still not saying anything. Was she capable of talking?

She climbed into the bathtub, her little body very slender—not skinny—and sat down. I then I heard a noise come from her … a whimper.

"What's wrong, Molly?"

She pointed between her legs. "It hurts. It hurts."

I looked down to where she was pointing. Red, angry skin greeted my eyes. I didn't know what was going on. I did know, though, that she was in pain.

She began to cry, and I took her out of the bathtub. Gently, I patted her dry with a towel and helped her get dressed in some clean clothes.

After getting her tucked into bed, I finally made it to my own bed. Darryl had already settled in and gotten back to reading his book.

I told him what had happened in the bathtub. I then shared my surprise at how calm Molly appeared to be in our home from the outset.

"It's as if being put in different people's homes is something that has happened to this little girl frequently."

Some Things Haven't Changed

I couldn't wait for them to meet Molly.

They had their introduction to her at breakfast the next morning. All four of my sons seemed to find her absolutely adorable, and understandably so. She had curly red hair, freckled, fair skin, and big green eyes.

She was so tiny that I needed to place a booster seat on a chair at the dining room table and buckle her in. She could then reach her food more easily, although she didn't eat much.

I then brought Graci-An over to Molly. Although they were sisters, they had never met each other.

"Molly, this is Graci-An. She's your little sister. Graci-An, this is Molly. She's your big sister."

Molly looked at Graci-An with a blank face. She just blinked and went back to delicately eating her cereal. I don't think I would have gotten less of a reaction if I had read the weather report to her. There was something missing. I credited her lack of ardor to being in a new place.

Liam began talking to her; he never met a stranger. Micah ignored her. I think he didn't know what to do. Tristan and Devlin kept looking at her with smiles on their faces. Graci-An just couldn't bring herself to fully wake up.

After I got the boys off to school, Molly and I went shopping to buy her some warm clothes. When the boys came home later, she loosened up some and began talking to all of us.

The following day, I took Molly to the health clinic designated for foster children. I had made an appointment for two reasons. First, the state required foster children to have physical examinations within seventy-two hours of entering the system. Secondly, and most importantly, the doctor needed to look at that rash or whatever it was that had caused her to cry while in the tub.

Upon checking in at the clinic, the receptionist handed me a large manila envelope that the CPI had left for me. I opened it and was relieved to see that it contained Molly's Shelter Order. The clinic won't see a foster child without that order because it provides the reasons for the child being placed into foster care.

I turned to see that Molly had found the play area and its toy box located on the left side of the waiting room. She emptied the contents of the plywood chest and didn't seem to care that the toys had seen better days. Many of them had missing or broken pieces.

She picked one up and played with it for several minutes before moving onto another.

I sat in one of the blue cushioned chairs next to the play area while we waited for Molly's name to be called. I took advantage of her distraction and read the report. Evidently, Molly had been with Gretchen for two weeks before an anonymous person called DCF to make a report against the mother.

The allegations revealed that Gretchen still exhibited the same unhealthy behaviors that had caused Graci-An to be removed from her six months earlier. Again, I won't disclose the allegations; the reasons why her children were removed from her are not important for the purpose of this book. The key point is that the mother's actions were serious enough for the state to step in and take her children from her for the sake of their safety and well-being.

I suppose I could make up some fictitious allegations, but it wouldn't be fair to "Gretchen" to accuse her of things she didn't do. We'll keep it to more of the same kind of critical concerns that led to the stream of other issues.

By the time I finished reading the report, my suspicions were confirmed. Gretchen's problems were created by a destructive lifestyle that she continued to lead. But Molly being in Gretchen's unsupervised care was still a mystery.

I looked over at Molly, who was playing peacefully and innocently with the toys. I thought about how Gretchen's decisions had affected her life. For one, they had put her in the system, something no child should ever have to experience. At least Graci-An hadn't known life with Gretchen, but Molly had. A child could not have escaped those kinds of circumstances untouched. But we had yet to see how much of an impact they had made on her.

Glancing at my watch, I saw that we had been waiting in that room for almost two hours. With nothing else to do, I studied my environment, thinking how the plain white walls could have been improved with a few animated characters or a picture or two. I found it odd that the only warmth this pediatrician's office offered its patients was the multicolored indoor-outdoor carpet.

Finally, a nurse called Molly's name. When the doctor examined her, he diagnosed her rash as being the result of very poor hygiene. He instructed me to teach her the proper way to clean herself. I wondered where her mother had been the last two weeks while she had Molly with her.

The doctor also told me that Molly was overdue on some of her immunization shots. He suggested having them administered when she came back for her thirty-day comprehensive physical examination.

By the time I left the clinic that day, I knew a whole lot more about this case than when I had first arrived. But I still had plenty of questions. For one thing, I couldn't help but wonder what else could have been neglected with this young child.

The Revolving Door

"The parents still have a lot to do."

This was one of the first things Katy Farrell reported to us during her next home visit. "They've done a couple of things on their case plan, but not a lot."

She sat with her hands folded in front of her on our dining room table, looking back and forth between Darryl and me with warm eyes. "For instance, Gretchen and Jesse are now living on their own. I had a home visit with them."

She squirmed once in her seat. "Jesse doesn't believe he should have to do some of the required tasks on his case plan. He wanted to argue with me about doing them." She tilted her chin up, her eyes steady. "I wouldn't give in, so he finally backed down. He said he'd do those tasks but that he *ain't* changing because he is who he is."

I sat up straight. "Sounds like he thinks everyone else has the problem, not him. Sounds like he doesn't want to accept responsibility for his actions."

Katy nodded. We then discussed the judicial review hearing and Jesse's requests for both a new attorney and a new caseworker.

I said, "Katy, I know the father can get a different attorney, but can he get a different caseworker?"

Katy held her head down for a moment before looking back up at me with a frown on her face.

My heart felt like it skipped a beat or two. "What is it, Katy? He can't get rid of you because he doesn't like you, can he?"

"Oh no." She smiled with her mouth but not with her eyes. "If that were so, caseworkers would be changed around a lot. Unfortunately, I will be leaving, but it has nothing to do with Jesse. Graci-An's and Molly's cases are being transferred to another agency. The structure of my agency and the type of cases we're going to serve are changing."

My eyes and mouth opened wide in shock. I couldn't believe what she had told me. She, too, was now leaving.

Gathering my thoughts, I asked, "When? When is this supposed to happen?"

Her eyebrows rose in the middle of her forehead. "In two days. I really hated to tell you. I'll still be around for a few weeks to help with the transition."

At the end of our conversation, Katy looked me in the eye. She then told me that she believed the best thing for these girls would be for Darryl and me to adopt them.

Then Katy Farrell left our home for the last time. Watching her drive away, I knew the girls were losing a true ally.

I guess I needed to learn to get comfortable with the constant changes, whether it be guardians ad litem, support specialists, judges, or caseworkers. But seriously—Graci-An had been in the system just over six months, and a third caseworker would now be assigned to her case.

I did regret losing Katy, but I didn't dread the arrival of another caseworker because again, I only knew what I had experienced. I didn't worry whether the next one would make herself as familiar with the cases as her predecessors had and see the same precarious environment that Gretchen offered the girls. I wasn't concerned as to whether she would allow Jesse to push her around.

After all, Graci-An had been blessed with two wonderful caseworkers who wanted the best for her. We assumed she'd be assigned another wonderful caseworker. Based on what we had witnessed, we knew that those horror stories about caseworkers were the exception to the rule.

After all, Katy's replacement could be even better.

The Changing of the Guard

I didn't know what to expect when I heard the knock on my door.

I mean, I knew *who* to expect, but my first conversation with her led me to be somewhat uncomfortable.

The *who* was Mara Damian. She had called the day before, introducing herself as a supervisor at the Community Children's Network, the agency now assigned to the girls' cases. According to her explanation, her position as supervisor required her to do all of the first home visits.

Her tone took me somewhat off guard—hard, haughty, and almost attack-like. She informed me that she would be at our home the next day and at what time.

I opened our front door to her knock. In front of me stood a short and heavy woman with short strawberry-blond hair and an acne-scarred face. She wore a smile that traveled only as far as her lips. I didn't know if the chill that rushed at me and permeated my sweater was from the mid-December air or from this middle-aged woman.

"Mrs. Clark? I'm Mara Damian from the Community Children's Network. We talked yesterday." The corners of her mouth seemed fixed in an upward position.

Darryl and I motioned her to the dining room table, where she took a seat.

Okay, I thought, *she seems like she may be nicer in person than on the phone. At least she has a smile ... of sorts.*

During her visit, she asked us questions from the green form. We asked her questions as well, such as if Molly would be returned to her former stepfather soon. Additionally, we wanted to know what to expect as a result of changes in caseworkers *and* agencies in the middle of a case plan. We asked how the upcoming six-month judicial review hearing would be handled. Since a caseworker hadn't been assigned yet, who would represent the girls? Would Katy be there?

Mara didn't have any of those answers but assured us that she'd go back to her office and get them. And she proved true to her word. That night, she called to follow up on her visit.

She assured us that the system had no intention of giving Molly back to the former stepfather. And yes, both the new caseworker and Katy Farrell would be at the six-month judicial review hearing.

She asked, "Oh yeah, guess who the new caseworker is?"

"Who?" I asked in return.

"Me. My supervisor told me that I had to take this case 'cause it was so messy."

Hearing that the girls had a supervisor for a caseworker was reassuring. From all of the information I had accumulated regarding this case, having just *any* caseworker wouldn't be enough. It needed someone very competent. Better yet, a supervisor would have the authority and additional influence to ensure that any actions required by this case would be done accurately and in a timely manner.

As for Mara, I honestly can't say I felt the warm fuzzies with her. That was okay because we didn't need a friend in this case, but the girls did need someone thorough.

Maybe she didn't have the best of personalities, but she made up for it in other ways, like getting back to us quickly with answers to our questions. I didn't want to prejudge her. After all, Julia Harvey had come across as kind of tough during my first conversation with her, but she warmed up to us.

Of course, I think Graci-An had a lot to do with that.

Twisted Truths

The gavel went down.

I stood there, disappointed. Once again, the six-month judicial review hearing had been passed to another date. No one could provide certain information that the magistrate and the judge had requested. In about three weeks, we would reconvene once again in the downtown courthouse for yet another try at this important and time-sensitive event.

Unfortunately, Katy would be gone by the next hearing date. Mara would have to fly solo. We didn't know if she would be familiar enough with the case and all of its nuances by that time. At least Erin would be there.

When I came home, I still felt deflated. Even the festive Christmas tree sitting in our living room couldn't alter my mood. Darryl greeted me with an encouraging hug and kiss before running out the door to an appointment.

I went in the kitchen and started making lunch for the girls. Graci-An woke up from her nap and started crying. The dog began scratching at the back door to go out. Then the doorbell rang.

I really didn't want any company.

Imagine my surprise when I opened the door to find Mara Damien on my stoop. I *especially* didn't want to see anyone from the system. Plus, she had just been here last week.

Mara announced, "I was in the neighborhood and thought I'd drop by and get a home visit done." She then lumbered inside and to the dining room table, where she plopped herself down in a chair.

I thought that she couldn't have picked a worse time to "drop by" and get a home visit done. What was I supposed to say? Come back later? That would have been a sin. You don't dare tell a caseworker you can't see her no more than you can refuse to pay your electric bill. You may disagree with both, but if you don't submit, you may find your home without electricity or your family without the foster child you've come to love.

I told Mara to make herself comfortable while I went to get Graci-An.

When I returned, I sat across from her. She looked briefly at Molly but didn't speak to her. She ignored Graci-An in my arms.

Forcing myself to be optimistic, I said, "I want you to know how excited we are that Molly and Graci-An have you for their caseworker. I've told everyone that they've got a supervisor handling their case."

Mara's face got red, and her eyes broke contact with mine as she looked down. She mumbled something before saying anything audible. "Well, I'm not really the supervisor. I'm the lead caseworker."

My eyes popped wide as my head jerked back. Why had Mara misled us regarding her title and position? My mind tried to rationalize her actions, but my heart told me differently.

I wanted to give her the benefit of the doubt. Hopefully, Mara just had a one-time "slip." But admittedly, she had been caught in a big "slip." Was her indiscretion a red flag? Often, if someone demonstrated the capability of being dishonest once, that person had a propensity to do it again.

Mara must have caught the shocked look on my face. I'm sure she hadn't expected me to mention her misrepresentation of the truth to anyone.

In an obvious effort to change the subject and end the visit, she handed me a yellow sticky note. "Here, Molly's former step-grandparents, the Pinkertons, called me. This is their phone number.

They asked me if they could talk to Molly but promised they wouldn't be pests. They just wanna talk to her every once in a while."

I took the note from her, my brow furrowed. "What are the rules for this, Mara?"

"It's up to you. It doesn't matter to me either way. I'll just leave this phone number here for you."

Mara got up and gathered her belongings. Her staying for such a short time made me wonder if she was anxious to leave. Did she want to escape the whirlwind of activity within our home, or was she embarrassed about being caught in a lie? Perhaps the next time she wanted to drop by for a visit, she'd let me know in advance.

And from now on, she needed to tell the truth.

The "Snatch"

I stared at the yellow sticky note, turning it over and over between my fingers the next evening.

Should we call Molly's former step-grandparents? Although the Pinkertons were not blood-related to her, they had known her for a couple of years while their son was married to Gretchen.

I discussed the pros and cons with Darryl. We decided that calling them might help Molly transition better into foster care.

Darryl agreed to make the call while I bathed Graci-An. I overheard him on the phone: "Mr. Pinkerton? My name's Darryl Clark, and I'm Molly's foster parent. Her caseworker, Mara Damian, gave us this number to call you."

He was on the phone with Mr. Pinkerton for quite a while before I saw him walk to Molly's room with the handset. Her part of the five-minute phone conversation consisted of short answers like "Uh-hmmm," "Yes," and "Okay." She didn't sound excited.

After putting the children to bed that night, Darryl and I climbed into our own bed. I pulled out my journal to write.

Darryl turned to face me. He glanced over at our closed bedroom door and squirmed closer to me in the bed and started whispering. "I had a very interesting conversation with Mr. Pinkerton. First, he gave me an earful about Gretchen. According to him, she wasn't supposed to have had Molly with her at all. She had taken her illegally. He said that Gretchen had walked into a crowded restaurant and snatched Molly while yelling obscenities at her ex-husband. And, according to him, Molly was screaming and crying the whole time."

He then relayed what else Mr. Pinkerton had told him about Gretchen and how she had treated Molly.

I wondered if some of the things that Mr. Pinkerton had divulged to Darryl were what Erin and the caseworkers were prevented from telling us. If so, then I had a better understanding of why they described this case as "pretty bad," "very bad," and "really messy."

A Christmas to Remember

Christmas was wonderful.

I made a big breakfast of sausage links, eggs, and buttered toast, but none of the children ate very much. The wrapped packages under the Christmas tree consumed their attention.

Once we cleared the table, Darryl and I made the much-anticipated announcement for everyone to come to the living room to open their presents.

Five eager children raced into the room, their faces filled with innocent expectancy. Graci-An, on the other hand, tilted her head sideways and watched.

Darryl then proceeded to pass out the gifts. The kids couldn't open them up fast enough, tossing aside ripped pieces of wrapping paper and empty boxes. By the time they finished, the room looked like a windstorm had passed through, and with it, an assortment of colorful debris.

Liam took his loot into his bedroom. Darryl helped Micah put together a robot. Devlin and Tristan took their remote-control cars outside. Molly took her dolls into her bedroom.

I straightened up the area while Graci-An played with the boxes. She appeared to be more interested in what held the gifts than the gifts themselves.

Realizing that Christmas dinner couldn't cook itself, I forced myself to go into the kitchen to prepare the turkey. The sound of my sons' laughter outside permeated the kitchen window, distracting me from my objective. I stood at the window and watched them play as a smile covered my face.

Who needed to hear Christmas carols when they could hear the beautiful music of a child expressing his or her delight? I thanked God for my family and for this time together. Then I prayed.

I prayed that this family would have many more Christmases together.

A Missed Opportunity

The afternoon imparted perfect weather for late December.

The warm front permitted the temperature to hover around the sixty-five-degree mark. Scattered throughout the blue skies were puffy white clouds that looked like big scoops of mashed potatoes.

My neighbors and I stood in my front yard, basking in squeals of laughter from the children. We watched Micah and Liam chase Molly and the neighbor's daughter. Right before the boys got within reach of them, the girls sprinted away.

Erin drove up and parked in front of our yard. She smiled as she got out of her car and joined us. I allowed myself a few more minutes of enjoying both the weather and the children before leading her inside our home.

She sat down at our dining room table, and we made some small talk. Then the smile on her face vanished.

Her eyes focused on mine as she got straight to the point. "I was disappointed that the judicial review hearing had been passed again. I had a lot to say. Now I can't be at the next hearing because I'll be out of town. My supervisor, Alisa, will be there, though. Also, I've already submitted my brief to the judge." She raised the corners of her mouth, but her eyes didn't match the intended purpose of her smile.

My hand reached for the back of my neck as I tried to comprehend her words. Something in my gut sensed that she needed to be at this hearing, especially with all of the recent changes.

No matter how optimistic Erin tried to sound, I knew her brief and her supervisor wouldn't have the same impact as her physically being present in court. When someone made a statement contrary to a fact, that statement could be disputed at that time in front of the judge. But a person needed to be present to know when and if anything needed to be disputed.

Besides Darryl and me, Erin was the only one who had been with this case almost from the beginning. She had spent a lot of time working on it. She knew this case better than anyone.

Furthermore, Erin impressed me as someone who'd have no problem speaking up if she disagreed. Somehow, I didn't anticipate Alisa having as much familiarity with the case as Erin and definitely not as much passion. And I couldn't foresee Alisa disputing any errors.

Erin then discussed the case plan. She shared that the parents should have accomplished a whole lot more than they had after seven months. The clock was ticking, yet they were far away from completing the required tasks.

From all appearances, the parents still weren't too motivated to do what was needed to get their children back.

Benchmarks and Concerns

Her independence was waiting for her.

At seven months old, Graci-An had successfully reached all of her benchmarks. If only she could master the art of crawling, she could possess the ability to propel herself to where she wanted to go, when she wanted to go. She was determined, though, getting on her hands and knees and rocking back and forth like she was revving up her motor. As she tried to pick up one hand and move it forward, she would fall headfirst on her face. The mishap didn't affect her. She got right back up with a smile and tried again.

Conversely, we noted some concerns with Molly, although we were surprised she didn't exhibit more problems. She had been with us about a month now, so we were just beginning to learn some of the things this little girl had experienced during her short life. I didn't know if we would ever have the full story.

Curiously, Molly always called her mother "Gretchen" and never "Mommy." She also displayed difficulties with social skills. With our children and other neighborhood kids, she came across as domineering. Her emotions toward them fluctuated from hot to cold.

We worked to help her improve her attitude. Fortunately, she seemed eager to please, and she listened to me.

Other behaviors were more concerning, such as her aggressive behavior toward our animals. Several weeks after she arrived at our house, my son Devlin complained that he had walked into the kitchen and caught her trying to stuff his two-month-old kitten under the oven.

I hoped that he had been exaggerating when he told me the story. But when I asked Molly if she had tried to put the kitten under the stove, she shrugged and told me yes. When I asked her why she wanted to hurt a tiny baby animal, she explained that the kitten was being bad.

We realized that Molly needed to be watched around animals and prayed that she would improve. I hung onto to the belief that she was still young enough to undo any unhealthy mindsets that had been established in her early, formative years.

Molly needed time and patience, and we were willing, ready, and able to provide both. We already loved Molly and wanted to adopt her along with Graci-An should they become available. From all reports regarding the bio-parents' inactivity with their case plans, a strong likelihood of that availability coming to pass grew stronger. Very soon, we'd learn just how much.

Supposedly, Molly's case would be heard when the court held its third attempt at the six-month judicial review hearing for Graci-An's case.

Chapter Five

Rules of Engagement

Something surely will be accomplished this time around, I said to myself as I entered the courtroom for Graci-An's six-month judicial review hearing.

I didn't see Katy, Graci-An's former caseworker, but I didn't expect to see her at this one. I knew Erin would be unable to attend. Only Mara and Erin's supervisor, Alisa, were there. I didn't have a good feeling about the girls' new "support team."

While waiting for the judge to enter the courtroom, Jesse sat next to me. He asked, "How was your Christmas?"

"Fine, and how was yours?"

"Oh, just great." His voice dripped with sarcasm. He folded his arms and had a scowl on his face. "Gretchen told me she was leaving me. She had another boyfriend." He then shared how she got physical with him during that conversation. "I had to call the police, and they made a police report."

He lifted his hips off the bench to pull a piece of paper from his front pants pocket and showed it to me. Underneath the police department's logo at the top of the page was a report that had been made against Gretchen Gray for domestic battery.

I could tell that Jesse needed to talk to someone, and I happened to be at the right place at the right time.

He looked straight ahead; his eyes were set and unblinking. "Yeah, we were planning to get married, but that's all gone. She's with someone else now." He sounded sad.

Compassion for his loss rose inside me. "I'm so sorry to hear that, Jesse. I know this must be hard on you, especially during the holidays."

"Hey, no big deal." His seemingly strained bravado, disingenuous smile, and the obvious pain exposed in his eyes contradicted his words.

Jesse sat beside me for the next three hours while we waited for the girls' case to be called. Finally, a court officer announced, "The case of Graci-An Gray and Molly Monahan."

Jesse looked at me, and we both stood up from our seats. I walked behind him until we took our positions in front of the judge.

First, the court arraigned Molly's case. The parties agreed to have the case plans for Molly and Graci-An combined so the mother wouldn't have to repeat the tasks.

The court then addressed Graci-An's case. The judge asked how the parents were progressing with their case plan. Both attorneys tried to make light of their respective clients' lack of activities.

The mother's attorney justified Gretchen's changing residences and paramours as trying to better her life. He blamed the state for Gretchen's lack of initiative with other tasks, alleging that the state had not given Gretchen the required referrals.

I specifically remembered Katy Farrell telling me that the mother had gotten all her referrals five months ago. Unfortunately, Katy wasn't there to dispute this allegation.

Perhaps Mara hadn't reviewed the file in its entirety because she actually apologized to the judge for the state's "oversight." The state looked guilty for not doing its job when indeed it had.

Now I knew the impact caused by changing caseworkers *and* agencies in the midst of a case.

Jesse's attorney highlighted the few tasks her client had completed, perhaps as an attempt to divert everyone's attention from the ones he had failed to even start.

Jesse and Gretchen had accomplished very little because from all appearances, they either chose to procrastinate or chose to ignore the requirements. The state did what it could by paying for the parents' programs and transportation, eliminating as many potential obstacles as possible that could prevent their compliance. But if the parents didn't want to participate in their case plan, the state couldn't make them.

The judge seemed to understand quite clearly what was occurring in his courtroom, maybe because he had heard the same excuses before from other attorneys. He looked directly at Jesse and Gretchen and warned them several times that their case plans must be completed by the expiration date. Otherwise, they could risk losing their children.

I kept waiting for someone to bring up the fact that Gretchen had illegally snatched Molly from her custodian and defied a court order. I kept waiting for someone to say that the mother had very recently displayed violence by beating on her former fiancé, and the police had to be called. I kept waiting, but no one said anything about either of these issues. It was like they had never happened.

Since I had never been involved in a judicial review hearing, let alone witnessed one, I didn't know protocol or what I could or couldn't say. I had been instructed to inform the judge *only* about Graci-An's development.

I waited for the judge to address me and ask me if I had anything to say. He never did. I wished Erin was there. She would have said something.

Regardless, why wasn't anyone saying anything? Weren't these events recent, negative, and important, painting a clear picture of the mother's character? Were they really thinking about putting a baby back into that mess? Didn't they want to look at *everything* to determine whether Graci-An and Molly would be safe if returned to their parents? Shouldn't they consider the best interests of these dependent and defenseless babies? In doing so, shouldn't they also be examining what the parents had been and were doing that reached outside the limited scope of a case plan?

Was this not the appropriate hearing to discuss these issues? Were they to be brought up during another hearing? Surely, if this was the hearing in which these matters were to be addressed before the judge, someone would have done it.

I consoled myself with the knowledge that there had been a hearing every month but one since the onset of this case. I planned to discuss these matters with the caseworker and guardian ad litem in preparation for the hearing that I assumed would be held next month.

This information needed to come from the workers, not the foster parent.

Then the hearing concluded. The state must have bought into the attorneys' excuses as to why the parents weren't doing their case plan. To my surprise, the state recommended reunification with the parents, despite the lack of progress and obvious lack of motivation.

The judge set the date for the next hearing for another five months away. This would be the big, twelve-month judicial review hearing that would seal Graci-An's and Molly's fate.

I felt as if I had been hit with a Molotov cocktail of confusion and panic. What happened to the permanency review hearing? My head reeled. These matters were significant and needed to be shared with the judge, but everyone kept silent as if they were keeping a secret. The hearing ended and so did the opportunity to disclose this crucial and relevant information.

Walking out of the courtroom and into the corridor, I saw Mara approaching Gretchen. While passing them, I overheard her ask Gretchen for her new contact information.

I must have been on autopilot on the drive home because I don't remember any of the trip. Getting out of the car, my whole body felt heavy. The leafless limbs protruding from the large oak tree in our front yard looked like necrotic, skeletal arms, ready to scoop me into an abyss. The overcast sky further accentuated my dismal mood.

I called Mara as soon as I got inside. "Mara, I'm confused as to why you didn't say anything about the domestic-violence incident and about Gretchen illegally taking Molly."

I could sense I caught her off guard. "Why didn't you say something if you thought it was important?" she replied.

I seethed. If I thought it was *important*? Didn't *she* think it was important? "Mara, isn't it *your* job to present *all* of the evidence?"

She didn't say anything.

My tone turned to pleading. "Please, Mara, help me understand what happened and why no one said anything about these two very concerning incidents. Was this not the appropriate hearing to bring these up before the judge?" I tried to find some logic.

Mara's silence continued for a few moments longer. Finally, she spoke. "No, it wasn't. This hearing was just to see where the parents are in completing the tasks. That's all. Well, the parents had done some things on their case plan. Since they had, the state had no choice but ask for reunification."

"I see. So, the judicial review hearings are *solely* to discuss case plan tasks and the progress on them. Nothing else outside of those tasks is discussed. Is that what you're telling me?"

"Yes, ma'am, they just stick to those tasks and nothing else," Mara said with what sounded like forced conviction.

I believed her because I didn't know any better at that time. I believed her because I needed to believe her. The alternative would have been more than I could stomach.

Looking back, I now know that Mara had taken full advantage of my naivety and had lied again. In fact, that hearing did provide the appropriate avenue for *her* to address those incidents. Now the judge would have to wait another five months to hear them.

Additionally, the state could have and should have pushed for concurrent goals of both reunification and adoption, especially considering the lack of progress the parents had made with their case plans. The state would have absolutely been within its rights.

The other dependency court judge ordered concurrent goals for some of the cases that came before him. Why didn't this judge? Shame on him!

At the time, I knew so little about the legal side of foster care. At the time, I knew so little about Mara Damian.

Soon, though, we would find ourselves becoming very familiar with both.

The Setup

Perhaps she could provide some clarity and sense.

When Esther Martin came for a home visit two days later, I unleashed on her as many of the details as I could remember from the hearing. I was desperate to understand what had happened.

She wrote on a pad as I spoke. She lifted her head and looked at me. "Did they combine Molly's and Graci-An's case plans in this hearing?"

I gave a quick nod of my head.

She leaned forward. A big smile emerged on her face, and she had a twinkle in her eyes. "They're setting you up, then. When they combine the case plans, the mother has to finish both of them at the same time. I mean, why not? Why should she have to repeat the tasks? She has to complete all the tasks for her case plan for Graci-An anyway."

She moved closer, adjusting her hips in her chair. "They know the mother's incapable of getting her children back, and they won't give Molly to Jesse since he's not the bio-father. And the state's determined to keep siblings together. So, if the mother can't get them, and even if the father completes all of his case plan tasks, he may only get Graci-An. However, they aren't separating siblings."

She slapped the table with the palm of her hand.

"You're getting the girls, Mrs. Clark."

What Did You Say?

The morning was cold, cold, cold.

Since January had only been around for about a week, we didn't hold out hope that the day would warm up very much, if any.

Molly was scheduled to go back to the clinic for her mandated thirty-day comprehensive physical. We stepped outside to run the few yards from our front door to the car.

Our feet couldn't move fast enough to escape the frigid wind from nipping at our bare faces. It reminded me of a mother swatting the rear end of a young child in an effort to get him to move.

Upon arriving at the clinic, only two other people were sitting together in the waiting room. Yet we had to sit for a couple of hours before being called.

When Molly got tired of sifting through the toy box, I found a book and read it to her. Before long, she lost interest in that as well. I've always wondered why pediatricians' offices made parents with young kids wait for so long. They, of all people, should realize that young children have short attention spans.

Molly's boredom got the best of her. She took off running down the hallway, and I after her. I brought her back to the waiting area and grabbed a toy kitten.

"Look, Molly. This looks like our kitten."

She laughed. "Yeah, I put her in my dresser drawer last night because she was bad and needed to be punished."

My head jerked up, my eyes got big, and I shook my head. "You can't do that, Molly. She's just a baby kitten."

I bit my bottom lip to keep from saying more because I needed to process this information. I'm an animal lover, and I get very upset when I learn that a helpless creature is being mistreated.

Then the nurse called Molly's name. The scale showed that she had gained four pounds since last month.

After the doctor examined her, he reported that everything looked fine, and her rash had completely disappeared. My persistence in teaching her proper cleaning habits had paid off. But I couldn't take all of the credit. Molly worked hard at making sure she applied the proper techniques to cleaning herself.

The nurse administered two injections and drew a vial of blood. I held Molly while she cried and screamed through it all.

On the drive home, she sat silently in the backseat. When she spoke, the tone of her voice exhibited no emotions but had an eerie calmness to it. "Let's go beat her."

"What did you say, Molly?"

She repeated it. "Let's go beat her."

"Did you say, 'Let's go beat her'?"

"Uh-huh. I want to go beat her," she said in an adamant voice.

"Beat who?" I asked.

"The woman that stuck me with the needles."

Dear Lord, what had this child experienced?

The Wrath of Molly

I wondered when, or even *if*, they would commence.

The upcoming Sunday would make six weeks since Gretchen had seen her children, despite Mara's numerous efforts to contact her to schedule a visit.

When Mara finally got a hold of Gretchen, she called to notify us that biweekly visitations were scheduled to start that Sunday. She said,

"Oh yeah. I asked Gretchen if she's still at the new address she gave me a few weeks ago at court, and she told me no. She done moved again. Can you believe that? I guess we're really getting to see a certain kinda side to her."

While I had Mara "sharing" on the phone, I told her about Molly's behavior, her mistreatment of our pets, and the comments she had made about the nurse when we left the clinic ten days earlier.

I said, "I think she's just a little girl who may have been picked on by bigger people, and she felt defenseless. Now she's the one doing the picking, and she's doing it to things smaller than her."

Mara didn't comment.

When Sunday came, Darryl drove Graci-An to the center for her visit with Jesse. Ninety minutes later, he drove Molly to the center to visit with Gretchen. After Jesse left, Graci-An joined Molly and Gretchen. Another ninety minutes passed, and Darryl left to pick up both girls from the center. This became our life every other Sunday afternoon.

When Molly came home after that first visit with Gretchen, her attitude took me by surprise. She walked into the house and refused to acknowledge me. She wouldn't even look my way.

"Hello, Molly," I said, but she continued to walk by me in silence with her nose tilted up.

Okay, I thought, *this is probably tough and confusing. Give her some space and time.*

A few minutes later, I had Graci-An sitting on my hip while Darryl and I talked in the kitchen. Molly passed through and stopped, apparently startled by my presence. She turned on her heel and spoke to me for the first time since her visit. Her stiff stance and the firm placement of her hands on her hips enhanced her hostile glare. The slight parting of her feet did more than ensure a firm balance. It demonstrated her unwillingness to be swayed physically and emotionally.

Molly spat out angrily, "Why you holding Gretchen's baby? She belong to Gretchen. I belong to Gretchen. We not belong here. We belong to Gretchen."

Darryl and I exchanged a bewildered glance before facing Molly's fury again. I had considered that she might be different after visiting Gretchen, but I hadn't anticipated her attacking me.

"Molly, Graci-An needs to be held. Gretchen isn't here to hold her, so I'm holding Graci-An for her."

She huffed and stormed off to her bedroom. We had not witnessed the last of Molly's wrath, though. She asked the same questions and made the same comments repeatedly for the rest of the day.

What had happened at that visitation?

For the next few days, Molly continued relentlessly with her insistence that she and Graci-An did not belong with us but with Gretchen. By the third day of listening to her mantra, I knew something needed to be done.

I sat across the table from her so that we could be at eye level. "Molly, you have to stop. This isn't good for you. We know Graci-An is Gretchen's baby. We know Gretchen is your mommy. You have to think on something else, like what you're doing tomorrow at school or playing with your toys. Do you understand?"

Molly nodded. She seemed to successfully grasp my words because she started talking about what we were going to have for dinner. As if a switch had been flipped, she dropped the subject, and it was never to be heard again.

The more time that went by after a visit, the more Darryl and I began to see Molly's conduct improve. But the progress only continued until the next visit.

A pattern had begun to develop. It consisted of a predictable two-week cycle hinged around visitations with Gretchen. Whatever was happening within this child would surface and amplify following those visits. This was the time when Molly's incidents of misbehavior peaked in frequency and intensity.

For instance, Molly would abuse our animals more. Two Sundays later, I caught her squeezing the trapped kitten with the laundry room door. She smirked as she watched the agony, fear, and pain she placed upon the defenseless animal. With each incident, she explained that she needed to "punish" the kitten because it was being "bad."

I believe she inflicted anguish upon the animals as a way to transfer her own torment. I didn't know what caused it. I could only stand my ground against this faceless enemy, pray, and let Molly know that I loved her.

By the second week of the cycle, Molly always turned back into a wonderful, happy, and obedient little girl. And then … there was another visit.

As time went by, the visits didn't seem to affect her as strongly. Although she came home with an attitude, we could at least see more glimpses of her sweet nature earlier in the cycle.

During one of Molly's bath times, she talked about her visit with Gretchen that day. She relayed several things that her mother had told her.

"Gretchen say she have a bed for the baby. Gretchen say she taking me back. She say I not belong here."

So, Gretchen *was* the reason for little Molly's obsessive remarks after that first visit. I thought, *She should know that she's not supposed to say those kinds of things to her child.* The monitors were supposed to make sure that no such commitments were made in case the promises couldn't be fulfilled. Otherwise, the children became confused.

Afterward, I sat on the edge of Molly's bed to tuck her in. She seemed preoccupied.

Placing the blanket under her chin, I said, "Penny for your thoughts."

She looked at me with tear-filled eyes, her bottom lip trembling. "I not belong with Gretchen. I belong with you. I want to stay here with you, Mommy."

Not This One Too

The advent of spring had begun its descent upon Florida, although we had barely left the month of February.

The weather at this time of year challenged me when I tried to decide what the boys would wear to school each day. The cool, sometimes cold mornings evolved into warm and even hot days within a few hours.

This time of year also marked the debut of the birds' musical performances. The beauty of their songs sounded like operas that had been rehearsed throughout the winter.

When Erin came for her next visit, the volume of their chirping escalated as I opened the door. She appeared pensive and distracted from fully appreciating the concert going on around her.

She smiled when she saw Graci-An, but her usual confident and graceful stride had stiffened into a robotic amble. Her smile vanished as soon as she sat down.

She didn't waste much time in informing us that she would be out of town again for the twelve-month judicial review hearing. My muscles tensed. She just had to be there. This hearing would be the grand finale that would determine the lives of these two little girls. Graci-An and Molly needed her passion to fight for their best interests.

Erin assured us that she had been trying to get the hearing date changed. My muscles relaxed somewhat because I knew it shouldn't be a problem. After all, the magistrate had rescheduled the six-month judicial review hearing once she discovered that Jesse didn't have an attorney present. The children had just as much right for representation. The girls needed a mouthpiece, and Erin more than adequately fulfilled that role.

At that time, we had no reason not to be optimistic. Surely, the court knew the importance of having the guardian ad litem involved; otherwise, it wouldn't have assigned one.

When the Walls Came Tumbling Down

The doorbell rang.

It must be Mara since she had scheduled a home visit this morning. I hoped she was bringing more upbeat news with her than Erin had when she visited last week.

When I opened the door to let her in, the smell of impending rain rushed to my nostrils. While taking in its fresh scent, I noticed the black sky behind Mara. It acted like a frame around her silhouette as she stood on our front porch.

Despite the bleak forthcoming weather conditions, Mara wore a big smile. She stepped through our doorway, almost with a skip, and sat down at our dining room table. She glanced at Graci-An in my arms but didn't say anything.

Molly walked into the room to find out who had come to see us. Mara gave Molly a quick glance. As usual, she didn't say one word to Molly either and turned her attention back to Darryl and me.

Her smile reappeared. "The parents aren't making much progress on their tasks. Neither one of them is in compliance. And I don't see how they're going to be in compliance by the next judicial review. It's less than three months away. I guess they're going to lose their parental rights since they aren't working their case plan."

Darryl and I looked at each other. His fingers touched his open mouth. He mirrored my surprise.

I asked, "Are you saying that we'll be able to adopt the girls?"

Mara smiled and nodded. "Yes, ma'am."

I couldn't speak. I couldn't move. In my mind, I thanked God for his goodness in blessing us with Molly and Graci-An. If I had been able to express my exuberance out loud, I would've come across as a giddy, silly girl.

Darryl grabbed my hand and squeezed it, which would have to suffice for a pinch to make sure I was awake. He said, "Mara, that's wonderful! What happens now? What's the legal process of terminating parental rights, and what does the legal process involve for us to adopt Molly and Graci-An?"

Mara took the time to explain both in detail. "First, there will be a hearing to determine if there are sufficient reasons to terminate their parental rights, or to order the TPR on the girls. If the judge agrees, he terminates their rights. Jesse and Gretchen have thirty days to appeal. If they don't appeal, then their rights are officially terminated.

"I'll give you an adoption packet, and you got to complete the paperwork and give it back to me. You're going to have to be fingerprinted again and go through another investigation. Once your paperwork has been processed and approved, we set a date for the adoption hearing, and it's done."

Her eyes darted back and forth between Darryl and me. "Now, if Jesse or Gretchen appeals, you're going to have to wait until the court hears back on that verdict. Sometimes appeals can go on for up to a year, so you may have to wait awhile. Then we go from there. If the appeal is denied, and most of them are, then we start the adoption process."

I could have done backflips. We were discussing actually adopting these precious children. I had been hoping and praying that if the parents were unable to work their case plan, then we could make Molly and Graci-An permanent members of our family. Now that the opportunity had arrived, it felt surreal.

Bringing myself out of my dreamy state, I wanted to make sure there wouldn't be any major surprises. When I found my voice, I said, "Thank you, Mara. This is beyond exciting. If the state terminates their rights, then we'll adopt Molly and Graci-An in a heartbeat!"

Mara continued smiling. Darryl continued smiling. My smile disappeared, and I shifted in my seat. Time for a reality check.

I said, "I'm sure you can understand, however, that Darryl and I can't afford to get all excited and then have something unexpected happen where the girls end up going back to their bio-mom. We cannot, *cannot* have our hearts ripped out. This is too important. With that said, do you think the judge will give them more time? I mean, from what I understand and from what I've been told, parents must complete their case plan by the expiration date, unless there are what's referred to as 'extenuating and extraordinary circumstances.' Is that true?"

I already knew the answer because I had been doing research on the dependency system and reading the state's statutes; I had them almost memorized. I wanted to hear what the caseworker had to say about my findings to see if we were on the same page. I also wanted to remind her of the statute in case she had forgotten.

Even with this wonderful news, I questioned Mara's competency, especially after that last hearing. I wanted to make sure that nothing went wrong during the adoption process and that she would be able to see it to fruition. If I needed to remind her of laws and statutes to ensure they were being followed, then so be it.

Mara nodded her head. "Yep, that's right, unless there are extenuating and extraordinary circumstances."

Darryl asked, "Do you see *any* extenuating and extraordinary circumstances for either the mother or the father that would qualify for an extension by the court?"

Her emphatic response encouraged us. "No, Mr. Clark. There are *none*."

When Mara left on that glorious day, Darryl walked over to me and gave me a tight hug. "Honey, Graci-An and Molly are going to be ours forever."

And just like the walls of Jericho when the trumpets were blown, the wall that I had erected to protect my heart came tumbling down.

In the Best Interests of the Child

Over the next week, our excitement grew as the reality of Mara's words sunk in. From all appearances, we were on our way to adopting Molly and Graci-An.

Even the calendar agreed with our upbeat mood, showing that spring had officially sprung. It also reminded us that the case plans expired in two months and a few days. According to Mara—not to mention logic—the parents didn't have enough time at this point to complete a twelve-month case plan.

We had been looking forward to Mara's home visit, even if it was a week early this month. We couldn't wait for the next update and were eager to get more of our questions about the adoption process answered.

When she sat across from us at our dining room table, we unashamedly stared at her, our eyebrows raised in anticipation, grinning from ear to ear. Mara appeared relaxed, her shoulders hanging loosely.

Then she informed us—bluntly, using the same tone she would probably have used to tell us that she needed to cancel a beach party due to rain—that Gretchen was now compliant with her case plan.

Our mouths opened simultaneously. I looked at Darryl, and he stared at Mara with his eyes widened and fixed. Three weeks ago, Mara had sat in our dining room, and we discussed the process we would go through to adopt the girls. Three weeks ago, Mara emphatically reported that there was no way the parents could be compliant with their case plan in three months. Now suddenly, this same mother had become compliant with a twelve-month case plan in only three weeks? What a miraculous undertaking.

Darryl's asked a question that my shock had prevented me from voicing. "What are you saying, Mara?"

"I'm saying the mom is now in compliance with one of her major case plan tasks."

I swallowed hard and tried to make sense out of what she just said. Cutting through the emotional haze, I found myself articulating my thoughts. I pointed out that Gretchen needed to complete *all* of the tasks in the case plan to be compliant, not just one. I reminded her of the numerous reasons why the state had removed the girls from Gretchen and how nothing had changed.

I surmised that this must be a joke. Mara couldn't be serious.

She continued to smile as if she expected us to accept her news as inconsequential. "Well, when a parent isn't doing her case plan tasks, sometimes the state's gotta step in to make sure the parent's doing what they're supposed to do. Sometimes that means giving the referrals again. I like to see my parents get their kids back."

Oh yes, she was serious indeed.

Heat rushed throughout my veins. "But what about those situations where it's not in the best interests of the child to be put back with a parent who isn't any different from when the child was removed?"

Mara squirmed a bit, and her chin jutted forward. "You can't predict the future. Gretchen could turn her life around over the next several months. Plus, we'll be supervising her after the children are returned to her."

My eyebrows popped up. "Mara, are you kidding? Gretchen has had a *lifetime* of bad decisions and behaviors, and now she's going to turn it around in three months? Based on her past, do you believe that *you* can predict the future? Regardless, change doesn't happen that quickly, especially with problems that have manifested themselves for many, many years. I mean, you just admitted that you needed to give her the referrals again."

Darryl jumped in. His eyebrows were slightly pushed together. "Is it in Molly's and Graci-An's best interests to be returned to someone who hasn't had the motivation to do what's needed to get them back? Until recently, all she had done was dabble in her case plan, and abracadabra, all of a sudden, she's on the road to glory as a parent?

The only thing she's accomplished is to show that she's not ready for two little girls. I'm concerned for them."

He took in a deep breath, and then forcefully pushed it back out. "By the way, Mara, isn't there supposed to be a meeting where everyone involved in this case determines whether the children should go back to the parents or placed for adoption? When is that meeting going to be held?"

Mara's smile returned. "Yep, you're right. The permanency review staffing meeting. It'll be held sometime next month. I don't know the date yet, but I'll let you know if you want me to."

Darryl nodded. "Yes, we would like for you to notify us because we'd like to be there."

Mara recoiled as her smile vanished. She shook her head. "You can't go. Foster parents aren't allowed to go to the permanency review staffing meetings."

I asked, "What about the guardian ad litem? We were told she needed to be there."

I witnessed a hint of arrogance in Mara when she said, "Don't worry. I'll let the guardian ad litem know when it's going to be."

Darryl stated firmly, "For the record, Mara, we want it known that we're strongly against reunification under these circumstances."

Mara said nothing in response.

I couldn't wait until she left. I felt sick. I didn't want that woman to set foot in my home again. Unfortunately, I knew I would have no other choice but to allow her inside.

How could she do this to those children? Was she actually planning on returning Molly and this precious baby to a mother who would be considered unfit by most people's standards? I say "most" because I now questioned the standards of fitness being used by this caseworker. Surely, the judge wouldn't concur with her. Surely, he would see the injustice in this matter and the harm that more than likely would be perpetuated upon these young girls.

We didn't know what to do. We didn't know where to turn. No one had ever discussed the possibility of something like this happening—something like being told you were going to adopt children because the parents were noncompliant in their case plan, and then being told that they would be returned to the imminent danger from which they had once escaped. No one told us what to do if you had a caseworker who allowed the interests of biological parents to take priority over the best interests of their children.

The breath had been knocked out of us. Denial set in. We optimistically reasoned that if Mara had so drastically changed her mind in the past three weeks, then she could change it again over the next three weeks. What she had told us was asinine; we knew she had to come to her senses.

At this point, we didn't want to do anything drastic or alienate her by going over her head. We had to calm down.

Nevertheless, I couldn't get over the callous way Mara had given us this news. She had witnessed our excitement when she informed us that we'd be able to adopt these girls. She had to know how much we loved them.

I found comfort in knowing that Erin didn't agree with reunification in this case. We had heard many people say that the guardian ad litem carries a tremendous amount of weight in the court's decision concerning a child. I prayed that would be the situation here. Erin told us that she had submitted several briefs to the judge conveying her concerns. I felt confident that he would strongly consider them and their source.

If the mother had demonstrated a sincere desire to change and had been working at doing just that, we would be cheering her on to the next level. But she hadn't.

And Graci-An would be the one who would suffer the most.

What about the Children?

What perfect timing.

A few days after Mara gave us the most upsetting news we had heard since being involved in the foster-care system, I attended a dependency system legal training workshop.

It just so happened that I had been in the right place at the right time several weeks ago. I met one of the managers for the area's lead foster-care agency, and she invited me to attend this event.

When I entered the large conference room, I stopped abruptly. All of the chairs lined up in multiple rows were filled, leaving some of the attendees without a seat.

The lady sitting at the registration table reported that about 175 people had signed in. Looking through the list for my name, I noticed that everyone worked for the state except for me. The audience consisted primarily of caseworkers, supervisors, and child protective investigators.

I didn't know why I had been invited. Whatever the reason, I intended to take full advantage of being there and gather as much information as I could.

While waiting for the training to start, everyone was talking to a friend, colleague, employee, or supervisor—well, everyone but me. I didn't know anyone.

Finally, the thunderous chatter came to a hush when someone came and stood in front of the podium microphone. Then the sound of rustling papers resonated throughout the room as everyone sat in their gold-cushioned seats.

I listened to attorneys and other experts speak on different legal topics, but the most enlightening and revealing statements came from a judge. He said, "It's our job to reunify families, and then we can all save some money."

I thought, *Save us all some money? But at what cost? That of a child? Is this what the dependency system has been reduced to—money?*

The more I thought about what appeared to be the priority, the more outraged I became.

Were we in for a fight? I didn't know. I hoped that money didn't govern the pervading attitudes of those involved with Graci-An and Molly's case. I prayed that these parties would consider the welfare and best interests of each child over and above any financial benefit for the system.

My opinion of his lecture didn't improve with the judge's light-hearted remark about "veteran parents"— those whose children were repeatedly taken away from them.

I wanted to jump up and shout, "But what about the children? Does anyone care how they're affected by being removed and returned to their parents time and time again?"

Everything began to add up as I considered the stories I had heard, the workshop lectures, and our experiences thus far with Mara.

If these girls were returned to their mother, I suspected they would more than likely go back into the system. Gretchen would then become one of their "veteran parents."

In the long run, it would cost everyone money, but more importantly, it would cost Molly and Graci-An a great deal more.

The Rumor Game

We no longer looked at time in terms of when we would be able to adopt the girls. Rather, we looked at time in terms of how much we had left to fight for them.

With March displaying just one more day on the calendar, we knew we had a little over two months before the final hearing.

The Pinkertons called again to speak with Molly. Before giving her the phone, Darryl told them about Mara now reporting Gretchen as compliant with her case plan.

They shared their surprise and concern over this latest news. They agreed that Gretchen was in no way rehabilitated enough to take care of two young girls.

That night, Molly sat on her bed and cried, saying she felt lost and didn't know where she belonged. Referring to her earlier conversation with the Pinkertons, she said they were telling her that she would be coming to live with them soon.

To make life more complicated for little Molly, Gretchen had also been telling her at the visits that she was coming home to live with her. Molly wouldn't be living with both Gretchen *and* the Pinkertons, so somebody had been making promises that couldn't be fulfilled. While these adults tried to satisfy their own needs and desires, a little girl was becoming more perplexed.

Darryl emailed Mara and then Erin with what Gretchen and the Pinkertons were telling Molly and their effect on her. He asked Mara to talk with both parties and convince them to discontinue these unacceptable statements. After all, Mara should have known that these types of promises were considered serious enough for the state to suspend or terminate a parent's visitation rights.

Several hours later, I walked into our home office and saw Darryl sitting at the computer. He turned to me and said, "Sweetheart, Mara responded to our email. I think you need to read it."

I didn't give his request much thought because I had my mind on other things. I walked over to the computer, still mulling over what I needed to accomplish for the day. I leaned over his shoulder to read Mara's email response.

The first few sentences addressed our complaint about the Pinkertons. She threw the ball back into our court and told *us* to talk to the Pinkertons about their improper remarks to Molly. She ignored the same complaint we had about Gretchen.

Then out of the blue, she ended her email with, "The girls will be returned to the mother since she is almost finished with her case plan."

Evidently, Mara still insisted on reporting Gretchen as compliant, refusing to amend her most recent proclamation. She was moving forward with her plans, and she had put it in writing.

Terror started to rise from within me as this absurd reality smacked me between the eyes. The room spun and I with it. Were we really losing the girls just like that? Were they really being returned to a situation that was just as dangerous as it had been when they were first removed?

I tried to make some kind of sense out of that last sentence. How could she say Gretchen was almost finished with her case plan? She had only begun seeing a professional for issues that had evolved over a lifetime. Where were the words "evaluated and determined fit" that should come from a professional?

In addition, she had only lived in the same residence for a little over two months, yet the state required a *minimum* of six months. What about the numerous other tasks that hadn't been addressed?

I stared at Mara's email, reading it over and over as if at any time the content would change. The words were stubborn, refusing to submit to my unspoken plea, and they became blurred. I realized the blurriness was caused by my tears.

I desperately turned to Darryl. Surely, he knew something different that would contradict those words. My heart plummeted further when I saw his drooped head and downcast eyes.

My tears were no longer enough, so I allowed myself to wail. The possibility of losing the girls forever pierced my heart like a razor-sharp sword.

I envisioned Graci-An as a preteen, thick black mascara and eyeliner smeared under her pale-blue eyes. I pictured her walking around a high-crime area and being exposed to dangerous situations and risky behaviors like drugs and sex at a young age.

"I can't stand the thought of never being able to hold her in my arms again, Darryl," I managed to get out in between moans.

He wrapped his arms around me and allowed me to cry until I couldn't cry anymore.

After I calmed down, Darryl forwarded Mara's email to Erin. She called us right away. Darryl answered the office phone, and I picked up the kitchen extension.

Erin's voice revealed concern. "What's going on, guys? What are you talking about?"

Darryl relayed the recent conversation we had with Mara to the best of his ability.

Erin said, "I don't know what she's talking about. There's no way Gretchen can be considered compliant. She's not even close. She's only got two more months. I don't know what planet Mara's on to give this kind of report. As I've told you, I can't share details, but I will tell you this much. In my opinion, what I know about the bio-mom is putrid. I've told Mara that she has got to get in touch with reality if she thinks this mom is capable of having these girls returned to her. I've also told her that these girls will be returned over my dead body. Let me make a few phone calls and see what I can find out."

Her words provided a relief of sorts. At least Erin agreed with us, realizing how perilous it would be to reunify Molly and Graci-An with their mother.

I again researched the legal definition of "substantially compliant." Perhaps I had missed something when I read it the first five times. I pulled up Florida Statute 39 and scrolled down to section 39.01—"Definitions."

The list of words being defined was in alphabetical order. I didn't find the word *compliance*. I could only find *substantial compliance*. I would assume that meant the law didn't recognize the word *compliance* unless attached to its modifier, *substantial*.

According to Florida Statute 39.01(71),

> *"Substantial compliance* means that the circumstances which caused the creation of the case plan have been significantly remedied to the extent that the well-being and safety of the child will not be

endangered upon the child's remaining with or being returned to the child's parent."

Everything about this case contradicted this definition. Gretchen hadn't *remedied* anything, let alone *significantly*.

Did anyone bother reading these legal definitions, or were we looking at those in power playing what we used to call "The Rumor Game?" This is the game that involves you telling someone a secret, who then tells someone else that secret, who then tells someone else, and so on. By the time it gets told to the last person, the secret isn't anything like the original one, because all along the way, each person added his or her own interpretations and desires.

We began to see that the Florida Statutes weren't being adhered to, based on their legal definition. Instead, they were constantly being twisted, misconstrued, and misinterpreted to achieve personal and professional agendas. Although the law's initial intentions focused on protecting children, by the time it got "told" to the last person, it wasn't anything like the original one because all along the way, each person added his or her own interpretations and desires.

From all appearances, the welfare of the children was negligible.

Protector, Corrupted

Mara called.

She wanted to schedule her next home visit. After we set a date and time, she brought down the sword, reopening the wound. "As it looks now, the mother's actively participating in her case plan and has almost completed all her case plan tasks."

I could practically feel the blood oozing from my pierced heart. I knew each task on Gretchen's case plan. With most of them, I knew what she had and hadn't done to complete them. There was no way she could be remotely compliant in any of them but the parenting-skills class.

This fact didn't stop Mara from proceeding. "I'm going to combine some of the stuff together, like all of her different residences, so that she'll be able to hit the different benchmarks. That way, the report can show that she is compliant with the six-month housing stability requirement."

Listening to her creatively manipulate data by twisting the law around the circumstances hurled a shudder of shock up and down my spine. I gripped the phone and took a deep breath. "Are you sure you can do that?"

Mara's tone was confident. "Oh yes ma'am, I can."

When I questioned her again, she insisted that she could use her method of reporting. I didn't back down. After a few minutes, she must have gotten tired of debating this issue with me and went to ask her supervisor, putting me on hold.

Darryl was working out of our home that day, so I walked into the office and told him what was happening. He picked up the other extension.

When she got back on the phone, I said, "Mara, Darryl's joined us on the other line, and I explained our discussion to him. So, what did your supervisor tell you?"

Her tone sounded defeated. "She says I can't do that."

I wanted to ask her how long she had been a caseworker. Instead, I asked, "Okay, so what are you going to report for Gretchen in the twelve-month judicial review report?"

"I guess I now have to say she's partially compliant."

This was another wrong answer. Those endless hearings I sat through all of those months were paying off. I remembered one of the attorneys stating that a parent could no longer be reported as "partially compliant." They were either "compliant" or "noncompliant," kind of like "pregnant" or "not pregnant." Furthermore, the statute appeared to only consider *substantial* compliance.

I decided not to argue the point with Mara. *Choose your battles*, I thought. *The court can pick up on this one and handle it from there.*

I couldn't help but wonder if Mara was reporting other tasks as compliant when in fact they were not. If so, who would catch those discrepancies? Either she didn't know her job very well, or she knew her job better than anyone realized. Both scenarios were chilling. At the very least, she knew how and where to manipulate her data.

Darryl had been listening in on the other line. "Hi, Mara, this is Darryl. Let me ask you a question. Would you feel comfortable placing your children in this woman's care temporarily, let alone permanently?"

After a couple of moments of silence, I realized Mara had no intention of answering Darryl's question. I then asked, "What about the domestic-violence incident involving the police that had occurred recently during her case plan? Shouldn't that be a factor?"

Mara casually said, "Yeah, I know about it, but I don't think anything came from it. Gretchen's going to a professional, so she'll be getting help to stop her from doing the stuff she's been doing in the past, so the girls will be safe."

I rubbed my temples, exasperated with her devil-may-care attitude. Why was she discounting this incident? "Is she making any progress with this professional? How is she doing with her other tasks?"

Her optimistic tone returned. "Well, I hadn't gotten any reports with how Gretchen is progressing in those areas. All I know is that Gretchen started those tasks."

Mara made it sound as if Gretchen only needed to begin the case plan tasks to be compliant. Whether she finished them successfully, understood what she had been taught, and could apply the lessons appeared to be insignificant.

I reiterated, "Gretchen has only *begun* her tasks." I picked up my printout of the Florida Statutes and flipped through the pages.

She sounded annoyed when she spoke again. "I know what she has or hasn't done 'cause I never forget anything about my parents."

Darryl joined in. "Mara, we're concerned for the girls."

She said, "It's my job to see if the parents have completed their task, and that's it. I just look at if they're compliant or noncompliant."

I felt nauseous. "But Gretchen hasn't *completed* any of the major tasks."

Darryl began to pace. "Shouldn't your job also be to consider and care about *everything* that could affect these children? Otherwise, you could be recommending that young children be placed in potentially harmful conditions. Mara, I can't stress how important it is to us for all of the facts to be revealed."

After finding the applicable statute in my printout, I said, "Mara, I've heard from more than one person what Judge Rothman said in his courtroom. I heard how he announced to everyone that he wished caseworkers would quit telling parents they had twelve months to complete their case plan, because they don't. They have to *work* their case plan *for twelve months*. This isn't something that Judge Rothman or I made up. It's the law.

"Let me share with you some of the research I've done. Florida Statute 39.806(1)(e) says,

> 'the failure of the parents to substantially comply for a period of 12 months after an adjudication of the child as a dependent child or the child's placement into shelter care, whichever came first, constitutes evidence of continuing abuse, neglect, or abandonment unless the failure to substantially comply with the case plan was due either to the lack of financial resources of the parents or to the failure of the department to make reasonable efforts to reunify the parent and child.'"

I put the statutes back on my desk, my nervous energy forcing me to stand. "I don't think we can argue the point that the state goes above and beyond making 'reasonable efforts' to reunify. Based on this law, if the parent isn't substantially complying *throughout* the twelve-month case plan, then that child is still in the same situation from which he or she had been taken. I can't see anything that gives the okay or pardon for beginning the case plan during its last three or four months. Mara, the parents don't have twelve months to *start* their case plan tasks. They have twelve months to *work* them."

I gripped the phone tighter. "To go a bit further, we've also heard from other credible sources that all of the case plan tasks should be *completed* by the tenth month. Otherwise, reunification is *not* an option. The operative word is *completed*, not *just beginning*."

Mara said nothing in response, and her cheery disposition vanished. "I only look at if they've completed the case plan tasks. I'm going to tell you, though, that the baby's father's no longer in the picture. He hadn't begun the major tasks. He doesn't have enough time now 'cause he's only got less than two months left. There's no way he can complete a six-month task in two months. Otherwise, I'm for children going back to their parents."

Darryl added, "*If* it's in the best interests of the children."

In spite of our personal feelings for Graci-An and Molly, we knew that the mother was not ready emotionally, mentally, and physically to take on the challenge of caring for two extremely dependent children. Who was Mara really trying to help?

My heart didn't break any less than if I had been told that my child had a terminal disease with only a few months to live. I tried to maintain my composure while on the phone with Mara, even though I felt as if my blood was boiling.

We couldn't believe our ears. After nine months of being told that the children would more than likely be available for adoption, we were now being told with certainty that the plan to return them to their mother had been set in motion.

The rug hadn't been pulled out from under us; it had been yanked.

Chapter Six

Falling through the Cracks

We unofficially designated Erin to be our conduit to make right what had gone very wrong.

As soon as our phone conversation with Mara ended, I sent Erin an email informing her of everything we had discussed.

We didn't know what else to do but go to Erin. Our lack of knowledge of the foster-care system impeded our ability to address this situation in the most effective way without any serious repercussions. We sensed that we had to tread lightly. Otherwise, if we came across like gangbusters, Mara had the power to remove the girls from us before we had a chance to tell what we knew ... and before we had a chance to fight.

Erin's inexperience with the system allowed her to advise us on just so much. She had yet to learn the shortcuts and little secrets.

In my email, I further emphasized the importance of her attending the twelve-month judicial review hearing, especially now that we knew Mara's unyielding agenda. Erin fully understood what the risks would be if Mara's plans became successful.

In the meantime, the girls needed her at the permanency review staffing meeting. I also let her know that Mara had assured us that the guardian ad litem should already be aware of its date.

Erin responded. She told us that she had been in contact with both Mara and the guardian ad litem office, and no one had told her anything about a permanency review staffing meeting. She would be there, though, if she received notification of the date and time.

Erin didn't display much optimism about having the twelve-month judicial review hearing moved but encouraged us not to worry. She said her absence shouldn't be a big hindrance because she would submit her very long, in-depth judicial review report with lots of supporting documentation to the court. She would include her concerns about not attending the hearing. She would also express her willingness to go to the courthouse or to the judge's chambers to discuss anything further and make up for her absence.

I tried to reassure myself. It wasn't over yet. Mara had a couple more hurdles to jump before her aspirations became a reality. She would have to convince those involved with the permanency review staffing meeting as well as the judge that she had sound reasons for reunification, and she was only one voice.

The guardian ad litem still had a voice, and regardless of what had happened in the past, we were determined to have our voice heard too.

Jesse Is Now Compliant?

Although we were a few weeks into spring, I felt as if we were now entering summer. The temperature increased faster than we would have liked, and the flowers had long since bloomed.

Speaking of blooming, Graci-An's development progressed perfectly, and we witnessed improvements with Molly all across the board. We thought that much of Molly's breakthrough could be contributed to stability.

She didn't seem as angry because she no longer felt fearful. Molly knew what to expect and when to expect it. There were rules, and she not only had become familiar with them, but she had memorized and applied them.

Molly also learned how to deal with frustration and anger. She didn't hit as often. Now when she became angry, she stated that she was angry and that whatever the offender had done was "not nice."

Watching the girls grow and flourish was rewarding. But Mara's quest to put them back into an unhealthy environment loomed over us like a dark cloud.

Then to make matters worse, we received word from a credible source that Mara was now reporting Jesse as compliant. I should have expected this and gotten used to it, especially after her being wishy-washy about Gretchen's compliance. Still, it did surprise me.

Mara wanted to see her "parents get their kids back" so much that she completely disregarded the part of her job that required her to help the children.

Being their caseworker placed her in an excellent position to manipulate the system so that she could achieve her goal.

Duped Again

The revolving door continued to turn.

Jill Moseley replaced Esther Martin, making her our third support specialist within the past ten months.

She came to our home for her first visit. Jill appeared to be in her late thirties. She was of average height and thin, and she had long, wavy dark hair. She held her shoulders back and her chin up. Her countenance reflected strength.

We invited Jill in and directed her to our dining room table. We didn't hesitate to tell her about the girls' case, and in particular, its latest occurrences.

Darryl said, "We wished we could go to the permanency review staffing meeting, but the caseworker told us that foster parents aren't allowed."

Jill jerked her head. "No, no, that's not true. Not only are you allowed, but I encourage you both to go. It's your right as the foster parents to attend those meetings." She rolled her eyes and shook her head, apparently agitated over this news.

Darryl and I looked at each other. We were both dumbfounded by Jill's adamant correction and by the fact that Mara had lied to us yet again.

It seemed that she didn't want us at that meeting. I wondered if she had underhandedly tried to keep us away, afraid of what we would reveal.

We had been swallowing Mara's behavior and comments thus far because we simply didn't know what our options were. We were too afraid to do anything. We had heard stories of how caseworkers retaliated against foster parents by removing their foster children from their homes.

She had gone too far. We wouldn't take it anymore. We realized we couldn't wait any longer to go over her head. Evidently, this problem wasn't going to fix itself no more than Mara was going to change her mind about the reunification.

Her behavior proved to be so egregious that surely her supervisor, Carla Mendes, would intervene and stop this foolishness. So, when Jill left, we emailed Mara and copied Carla.

Our short and simple e-mail stated, "Mara, other workers within the system have not only encouraged us to attend the permanency review staffing meeting but have informed us that it is our right to attend. Please advise us as to the meeting's date, time, and location."

We had no intention of debating this one. We were going to be there.

The Sins of Omission and Commission

The weather did an about-face on us.

A cold snap had enveloped the city. Normally, I'd rather stay in bed and allow the blankets to envelope me.

I couldn't do that today. We had the permanency review staffing meeting this afternoon, and no rain, sleet, nor snow would keep me away. However, I couldn't help but wonder if the overcast, dreary day represented an ominous forewarning.

At noon, Darryl and I drove through the misty rain to the Community Children's Network for the one o'clock meeting. Both of us sat in silence as we looked out the car window. In a little over an hour, a group of strangers would decide the recommendation for Graci-An's and Molly's futures.

Erin pulled into the parking lot as we were getting out of our car. We walked over to where she parked. After closing her door, she turned and gave us a half-smile.

I couldn't miss the sarcasm in her voice when she said, "Mara finally notified me of this meeting in an email today, sometime during the early morning hours."

Thank goodness we had notified Erin weeks earlier, and she didn't have to wait for Mara. I wondered if Mara hoped Erin wouldn't look at her emails until after the meeting had started ... and ended.

Darryl, Erin, and I walked into the building together and sat in the reception area. My stomach churned with anxiousness and anticipation.

A tall, slender woman with shoulder-length dark hair walked into the waiting room. She appeared quite cheerful. The smile never left her face as she came over to greet us.

"Hi, my name's Carla Mendes. I'm Mara's supervisor. Won't you please come with me?"

We all stood up and followed her and her lively personality down a short, dark hall and into the last doorway on the right. Upon entering the small white room, I noticed several people sitting around a table. Carla showed us to our seats and introduced each person.

To Darryl's immediate left sat Irene Linberg, deputy director of Community Children's Network. Whereas Carla supervised Mara, Irene supervised Carla.

To Irene's left sat Neal Santoya. Across the table from Neal sat Trent Taylor. Both Neal and Trent were attorneys for the Department of Children and Families.

To Trent's left sat Dionne Kincaid, a representative from Family & Children Connections, the area's lead foster-care agency. Next to Dionne sat Carla and then Mara. Erin sat to Mara's left. I sat between Erin and Darryl, completing the circle.

Darryl and I were prepared with our notes in hand. We opened with our concerns regarding Jesse. Since we had been told that Mara supported his compliancy, I wanted to make it clear to this group that he was in no way compliant.

As I spoke, they all nodded their heads, appearing to understand and be in agreement with everything I said. I wondered if they would've taken Mara's word and deemed him compliant if we hadn't said anything.

Next, we shared our concerns about Gretchen. We had compiled what we read in her case plan with what we had witnessed over the past ten months and then subdivided all of this information into speaking topics. We explained the negative impact each particular concern would have on the children if they were returned to her.

We brought up the subject of Gretchen receiving help from a professional who *might* eventually help her with her problems. We believed some of her issues were so serious that it would take years of intensive professional help before she would be able to handle parenthood, though. Of course, any progress depended on her acknowledging her problems and wanting help.

We had done our research and only stated facts, omitting any emotion. Those sitting around the table again nodded their heads in agreement.

Okay, I thought, *we're on the same page.*

Looking around the small group, I noticed Irene Linberg's face. Her open mouth, big eyes, and raised eyebrows told me that our information surprised her. She interrupted and asked with alarm in her voice, "The mother has *those* kinds of issues?"

Had they not read the documented allegations which had led to the girls being removed, or were they accepting Mara's apparently incomplete and biased version?

Darryl and I were just as shocked at the fact that Mara hadn't said a word about Gretchen's needs for a professional. The caseworker must apprise everyone about *all* of the issues. She couldn't pick and choose what she wanted the staffing members to know. That undoubtedly took caseworker power and control to a whole new level.

Mara conveniently couldn't produce a report and recommendation from the professional. She also didn't convey whether a report would be forthcoming.

The attendees assigned to make the recommendation for the girls' futures seemed totally unaware of any concerns that necessitated a report from any type of professional. This report should have been vital in notifying them of the parent's level of participation and if she had progressed to the point of being fit enough to have her children returned.

At first, I presumed that the intentional withholding of information proved Mara's incompetence and that she had committed an act of omission. Then I realized she had also perpetrated the act of commission, which in my mind confirmed a lack of character and integrity. No wonder she had deliberately tried to keep Erin, Darryl, and me from attending this meeting.

Irene's lips were pursed, and she looked apprehensive. Did she now feel a little off balance? I hoped she did, enough so to compel her to learn more. I caught her looking at Mara with flaring nostrils and eyebrows sloping inward.

Mara hung her head and had a sheepish look on her face. Neal's furrowed brow made him look concerned and confused as he kept flipping through the pages of a document in front of him.

The other attorney, Trent Taylor, didn't refer to any notes or documents. He just nodded with everything we said as if he was eagerly receiving all of the information and holding it captive in his brain.

About twenty minutes into our presentation, Neal cut us off. He asked Erin if she had anything else she wanted to add.

Erin held up a four-page report she had prepared specifically for this meeting. She stated that she supported everything the foster parents had said. She then asked Carla to make copies and distribute her report to everyone in the room.

Erin went further and added, "I fear for the lives of these two little girls if they're returned to their mother."

Her statement couldn't get any stronger, especially coming from the guardian ad litem. Surely the group before us would at least take notice and investigate some of *her* statements and remarks. After all, the court had appointed her to represent the best interests of the children.

Dionne Kincaid didn't look pleased. I got the feeling she hadn't been pleased since we walked through that door to attend this meeting. She had been silent up until then.

She looked at us and asked how long we had been foster parents.

I thought, *what does the length of time of our being foster parents have to do with the cost of tea in China?* In other words, what does the length of time of our being foster parents have to do with paying attention to the safety and welfare of these children?

Ms. Kincaid told us we had to understand that the goal for all cases was reunification. According to her, Gretchen would receive a six-month extension on her initial twelve-month case plan. The clock would start over from the time she (illegally) took Molly. Gretchen now had eighteen months to do a twelve-month case plan.

This was the first time I had heard this interpretation. I didn't recall hearing this creative twist discussed or even brought up during the six-month judicial review hearing when they had combined the two case plans.

Evidently, crime does pay. Dionne tried to justify this gross action by explaining the concept of a parent giving birth to a baby during a case plan with another child. She told us that this birth mother got a whole new twelve months to do her tasks from the date the baby was born.

I almost asked Ms. Kincaid how long she had worked for the foster-care system. Her version conflicted directly with the Florida Statutes and to the cases of other foster parents I personally knew. When the biological mothers had babies in the midst of their case plans, the expiration didn't change from its original date.

Furthermore, her example compared apples to orangutans. Since when did having a baby become illegal and comparable to the unlawful snatching of a child? Was Ms. Kincaid trying to let us down easy? If so, she needed to work on her game plan a bit more. She came across to me as almost hostile.

Hundreds of thoughts ran through my mind while I tried to find even a hint of logic in her words. According to her self-defined laws, you get one child removed from you. Six months later, you illegally take another child from her custodian. This same child goes into foster care within a few weeks of this explosive event. During the process, you have defied a judge's ruling and a court order, committed a crime, and your consequence is, "Bad girl. We're going to show you. We're going to punish you by giving you more time to complete your case plan." I'm sure the mother's response would be, "Oh no, anything but that."

Clearly, Ms. Kincaid needed to stop playing the Rumor Game before providing this same ludicrous explanation to someone else. She needed to familiarize herself with the very law she claimed to represent and read Florida Statute 39.001(1)(h):

> "To ensure that permanent placement with the biological or adoptive family is achieved as soon as

possible for every child in foster care and that no child remains in foster care longer than one year."

I don't feel that the laws were written in some kind of gibberish that prohibited the typical layperson to clearly understand its intent. I believe it's just the contrary. The simple, straightforward wording omitted any need for guesswork.

I guess their plans excluded Graci-An's rights in this matter. Little did I know, but Graci-An had absolutely no rights regarding her own destiny.

The group dismissed us, and Carla thanked us for our time. She promised that Mara would call us that afternoon to tell us the group's decision.

Walking out with Erin into the wet, bitter cold, I could sense she was deep in thought.

Breaking the silence, I said, "Well, Erin, I think we gave a good argument. What did you think?"

"Yeah, we did. However, are you asking me how I feel the meeting went? There's corruption here. I think that our being here was a total waste of time."

She looked up and directly into my eyes. "Sherrie, they had already made up their minds before we walked in there."

An Unfulfilled Promise

Hopefully, Erin had analyzed the meeting incorrectly.

Hopefully, the permanency review staffing group would take our information and look more closely into our allegations before coming to a decision.

I couldn't help but feel anxious. We sat on pins and needles all afternoon, wondering. When five o'clock came, Mara had yet to call as her supervisor had promised.

I picked up the phone and dialed Loren Dixon, another foster parent who had been through two permanency review staffing meetings. She said, "The caseworkers for my foster children notified me of the recommendation right after each of the meetings. It happened the same way for other foster parents I know."

Then why hadn't Mara called?

By ten o'clock that evening, we still hadn't heard from Mara. Since it was Friday night, we knew we wouldn't hear the decision before Monday morning.

Her failure to notify us could simply have been a matter of carelessness on her part, but something inside told me different. I sensed that she may have resented our presentation of the facts, which made her look negligent and incompetent to her peers and bosses.

I wondered if her silence might be a form of revenge meant to make us suffer through what would now be a long weekend.

Deceit's Impact on Destiny's Plan

The lack of response had really gotten out of hand.

Over the past week since the permanency review staffing meeting, Darryl called or emailed Mara every other day to inquire about the outcome.

At first, I thought the staffing team had perhaps heeded our words of warning. As a result, they were investigating our concerns, and a decision had not yet been made, so they had nothing to tell us. But as time went by, I realized that could have been communicated. We weren't going away, and we most certainly had a right to know what had been decided.

Exactly one week after the meeting, Darryl tried emailing them again.

Carla responded almost two hours later, apologizing for not getting back to him sooner. She offered no reasons or excuses for the "delay" in returning any of Darryl's previous phone calls or emails, nor did she hint at the group's decision.

Three hours later, Mara finally responded in an email. I assumed she did so because her supervisor prodded her. I wouldn't doubt Carla saw that we'd be leaving messages for her until someone told us about the recommendation.

We shouldn't have had to call her once, let alone several times over the course of a week, just to be told the results. We deserved an answer when they concluded the meeting, just as Carla had promised.

Mara began by apologizing for the late notice, stating that she had been out of the office, and when she returned, she had "many tasks to complete." Why didn't she call us last Friday afternoon after the meeting? Was she "out of the office" immediately after the decision was made?

Shaking off my anger at Mara, I weeded through the rest of her email and discovered that my fears had been confirmed. The permanency review staffing team recommended "to continue with reunification and to maintain and strengthen placement with the mother." The reason given for this decision? Gretchen's "compliance with her case plan."

Mara had cleared that first hurdle spectacularly.

Insurmountable grief overcame me. I collapsed on the floor and cried.

Darryl grabbed me and said with strong resolution in his voice, "It's not over yet. Remember, this is just their recommendation. We saw firsthand how Mara withheld information from those at the meeting. She's probably going to do the same thing during the hearing, but we'll be there. We'll have our say in court as well. The judge needs to know this stuff before he makes his decision."

He held me while I cried for several minutes.

Then anger overcame my grief. I thought about the group supporting Mara's recommendation, even after we had provided them with enough facts—not opinions—to demonstrate the existence of identifiable risks. Shame on them!

Next, I became angry when I thought about what Mara was trying to do. Her plans didn't consider the children's best interests. These girls merely represented a case number to her. Mara had never tried to get to know them.

Mara had never touched, smiled at, or talked to the baby the entire time she had been Graci-An's caseworker. She had never said one word to Molly. Mara had definitely kept her distance from both girls, yet the state looked to her as the expert in these children's lives.

I was disturbed at the image of placing a happy and confident baby into the care of a mother who hadn't overcome the issues that the state initially thought could harm the children. More importantly, we knew Graci-An would be traumatized if removed from us. We were all she knew. There were others who shared our apprehension.

One of those was Julia Harvey, Graci-An's first caseworker. I ran into her a few days later when I took a friend's foster child to a visitation as a favor. Julia was working as a part-time monitor at that center.

She smiled and asked how we were doing and if we had adopted the baby yet. My face must have revealed my feelings because Julia's smile disappeared. "What is it, Mrs. Clark?"

"Well, things seemed to have gone awry," I said. I then told her about what had occurred with the case. "They're planning on sending the girls back to their mother."

Julia shook her head. "I'm sorry to hear that. I'm surprised. If I was still the caseworker, this case would have ended a long time ago. That mother should not be getting that baby back." She continued to talk about how she felt the parental rights should have been terminated and how she didn't understand why they hadn't been.

I valued her opinion because she knew more about this case than we did; she had read reports that weren't disclosed to us. I assumed they were the same reports Erin had referred to when she said, "In my opinion, what I know about the bio-mom is putrid."

I thought, *If only Julia hadn't left. If only the girls hadn't been transferred to another agency. If only, if only, if only.* Instead, the luck of the draw had resulted in the girls getting a corrupt caseworker.

From all appearances, no one was looking out for them. Erin, although passionate about this case, was immersed in other commitments and obligations. She wouldn't be available until about two weeks before the hearing. By the time she got around to investigating anything, it'd be too late. Time was of the essence.

No professional had sanctioned reunification in this case. It boiled down to Mara making plans to return these girls without any recommendation but her own. The fight-or-flight response kicked in, and we knew flight was not an option.

We still didn't have an answer as to whether Erin was successful in getting the hearing rescheduled. For months, she had been telling us that she had contacted several people to see about changing the date, but no one had responded to her requests. If Erin couldn't be there, then someone must speak on behalf of these children.

We resigned ourselves to the possibility that the entire onus might fall upon us, and we might very well be their *only* voice.

Holding On by a Thread

This case consumed our lives; we could think of little else.

In less than one month, the hearing that would determine the course of Molly's and Graci-An's lives would occur. It was as if we could feel the ground quivering beneath us, preparing to collapse and make victims of those standing too close to the fault line.

I found myself on edge and obsessing about the case, even when performing everyday tasks like brushing Molly's hair, preparing Graci-An's bottle, driving home from taking the boys to school, cooking dinner.

During those family times when we were all together, I would fall into deep thought as I watched the children. Each one was special in his or her own way, and each brought something unique to our family tapestry. How would the girls' precious, silken threads be removed without damaging the very texture of our fabric?

While in public places, I watched people with children and wondered if they had ever felt threatened that the little ones they loved would be taken from them. I found myself wishing I could trade places with them, although I didn't know what that place was; I only knew it had to be better than the place I was in at that time.

I daydreamed about taking all six children and running away somewhere ... anywhere. I felt overwhelmed and frustrated.

We forced ourselves to remain optimistic that something would rise out of the muck and reveal the errors of their ways. I prayed and prayed for God to expose the truth to the decision makers.

I called Loren Dixon, but all of her adoptions had been successful, so she didn't really know how to advise me. I called a dependency court attorney who assured me that a child should not be returned to her parent if identifiable risks existed. Unfortunately, plenty of obvious identifiable risks presented themselves, all of which we had shared with the decision makers. No one seemed to care, though.

We had assumed a burden that no one else wanted or could handle. A battle awaited us, and we sharpened our swords in preparation. We were struggling to hold onto our family and to these girls' right to be safe.

Darryl emailed Mara and Carla again. Maybe, just maybe, they had gotten a report from one of the professionals who provided court-ordered services to Gretchen. If so, then surely that professional would tell them that Gretchen wasn't ready to take care of two little girls. He also asked about getting our copy of the twelve-month judicial review report.

That afternoon, Carla, not Mara, responded to Darryl's inquiries. In her email, she said that Jesse would be reported as noncompliant, that Mara was still working on the judicial review report, and that they had not gotten a response from any of the professionals. She assured us that the recommendations would be forwarded to Erin's supervisor.

This seemed strange. Why wouldn't they forward the report directly to Erin?

At that time, we had no idea what the powers that be had in the works.

This is a rancorous system, and those who try to question it should beware.

Erin Believes the Reunification Status Is Illegal

It was three weeks and counting before the hearing.

The children were still in school, although it would be ending soon for the year, signaling the beginning of summer vacation. As far as I was concerned, summer had already settled in. The temperatures were reaching into the high eighties.

I decided to take the afternoon and pay bills in our office. Darryl sat at his desk and worked on a client letter. As soon as I placed a stamp on the last envelope, Erin called.

I answered the office phone, and Darryl picked up the kitchen extension. She wanted to inform us that she had a new case coordinator named Celeste Poole.

Erin shared with us how she had told Celeste all she knew about the case, including the reasons why she believed the reunification status to be against the law and what she thought should be done about it. She added that Celeste should be coming to our home soon.

Erin said, "Tell her everything, all of your concerns, situations, etc. Also, make sure you give her copies of your documentation."

Darryl assured her we would.

"By the way," she said, "I honestly don't believe they're going to change the twelve-month judicial review hearing date. I am, however, submitting an extensive report for the trial, and that paper is as good as what I'd verbally express if I were present but with more detail."

Again, I knew that a written report couldn't compare to the powerful impact she would have by being physically present. A report couldn't stand in court and argue against the discrepancies that probably would arise.

Toward the end of the call, she encouraged us to attend the hearing and speak on behalf of the girls. I told her we had every intention of being there. We were preparing to reveal everything; especially what Mara was hiding.

After we finished talking, I pictured myself handing Graci-An over to Gretchen for the last time. I imagined what life would be like for her. Bile rose in my throat, and I wanted to throw up. My heart began to beat fast, and I paced nervously around the room. I told myself, *Breathe deep, slow and deep. It's not over ... not yet.*

I then envisioned myself standing before the judge in a courtroom full of people, telling the side of the story that wasn't being told. I didn't look forward to the daunting mission of butting heads with the system.

Then Graci-An's and Molly's faces reappeared before me. As I saw their eyes trusting and innocent, I realized that any fear I had experienced until then had suddenly become trivial.

Sacrificial Lambs

My eyes opened slowly from a sleepless night.

I looked over and saw Graci-An sleeping soundly in her crib. She looked so peaceful lying there, her eyes closed, her breathing steady, and her lips puckering and making a sucking motion.

Then I remembered how the state wanted to take this peace from her, and Mara came to mind. I tightly gripped the sheets when I recalled that she was coming to our home today.

The thought of seeing her made my head hurt. Even the marvelous sight of the sun trying to rise and welcome another beautiful spring day didn't detract from my negative feelings about her.

I tried not to despise Mara, but I unashamedly despised what she was trying to do. The person and her actions did go hand in hand and couldn't be separated.

Every time I thought about the possibility of reunification, I felt as if I were watching a horror movie. This was the scary part where you hid your face so that you didn't have to see it. I couldn't bear to picture Graci-An being torn away from her family; she had become too bonded. By now, reunification for Graci-An would be inhumane. But the system did it all the time.

Glancing at the clock, I saw that I didn't have to wake up the children for another two hours. Even though exhaustion prevented my body from getting up to make a cup of coffee, my mind raced.

Usually, I pace when thinking, but my feet couldn't move. Even while lying in bed, they felt like they were encased in concrete. I allowed myself to continue my musings.

My thoughts went to how Mara had blatantly ignored the meaning of the statutes. She had her own aspirations, and she refused to let anything, including the law, get in the way of her reaching them.

Personally, I believed she wanted to get a pat on the back with an "atta girl" and show herself to be a sacrificing member of the system who could turn a life around. I got the impression that she needed praise and acknowledgment, and that for her, the end always justified the means.

I forced myself to climb out of bed, praying to God that he would have mercy on Graci-An and Molly, and I prayed that his will be done. I've often found this prayer a difficult one to think about, let alone speak.

Occasionally in the past when I had prayed his will, my prayers felt as if they bounced off the ceiling. It wouldn't be until much later before I understood why—God's will didn't match up to my own. I frequently forget that in the end, he only wants what's best for us.

This time around, though, I couldn't imagine my will being any different from his.

The Clash between Destiny and Deceit

Looking out our front window, I saw Mara's car pull into our driveway.

I could see her staring out her driver-side window and toward our front door for a few moments before giving a big sigh and opening her car door. Her shoulders sagged, and she dragged her feet as she walked to our house. After what we had brought up in the permanency review staffing meeting, she had to know we were watching her like hawks closely watching a field mouse.

Darryl answered the knock on our front door and smiled at Mara. I couldn't bring myself to welcome her into our home, let alone produce a smile.

As soon as she stepped inside, the atmosphere changed to an almost suffocating tension. Darkness hates the light, but you can always count on the light to overcome the darkness. With Mara, I'm sure she felt as if the spotlight of truth was being shined upon her.

Darryl didn't waste any time and got right to business. "How's it going with Gretchen working with a professional each week?"

Mara responded, "Well, the mom had to change professionals 'cause the other professional could only see the mom every other week."

I hadn't expected that one. "So, for the past three months, Gretchen's only been seeing a professional *every other week*? I was under the impression she was supposed to see one at least weekly."

This news revealed a situation that was worse than I had imagined. Gretchen's progress and the time needed to make an accurate evaluation had been cut in half.

Mara wore a false smile on her face. "Well, that's why she had to switch professionals."

I asked, "Has she seen the new professional?"

She still had that same smile. "Not yet."

My eyebrows creased together. "There are two little girls at stake here, Mara. To make matters worse, the frequency of help that should have been at least weekly was reduced to every other week. And now, she's not seeing anyone. As it stands, Gretchen has seen a professional for a total of what, about *five hours*? How can that help someone with issues like hers?"

Mara stared at me and then shook her head and looked down. "Mrs. Clark, all I can say is that as long as a parent works her case plan, I'm going to recommend reunification." She wouldn't look at us. She kept her head down and eyes fixed on the table in front of her.

Darryl asked, "But what if working the case plan isn't enough? What if the parent still hasn't learned anything and continues with the same old behaviors? We've heard how the state keeps returning the children to the biological parents, and then they have to remove them again from those parents. And why? Because the parents didn't get it the first time around."

I kept my eyes on Mara while speaking to my husband. "That's just it, Darryl. Whether or not the parent actually learned something and is able to apply what he or she was taught has nothing to do with her recommendation. Whether they are able to be good or even better parents has nothing to do with her recommendation. It all boils down to a checklist, or the list of tasks on a case plan. Am I correct, Mara?"

SMALL VOICES SILENCED

She nodded without lifting her head. How could she look at herself in the mirror? She could be placing children in danger all the time. Clearly, her crusade didn't involve parents learning lessons so the children who were returned to them would be safe. With Mara, it was all about that checklist, and in Gretchen's case, an incomplete one.

I thought about my children and how I gave them checklists for their chores. One of my sons swept down the middle of a room and didn't touch the corners or sides but marked it off as completed on his chore checklist.

Just like my son, Gretchen was sweeping down the middle and not touching the sides or corners where mounds of dirt were piling up. Yet she too checked off the task as completed even though dirt remained, dirt that would soon be dispersed back onto the cleaned areas. The difference here was that my son was held accountable and made to do the job correctly.

Darryl asked, "Why didn't you tell anyone in the permanency review staffing meeting about Gretchen's issues, and especially the major ones that would certainly place young children at risk?"

She jutted out her chin. "I didn't need to tell them 'cause you all did." We couldn't believe her response.

Darryl jumped in, stopping the tongue-lashing I was about to deliver. He must have read me like a book because he spoke exactly what I thought, but more calmly. "Mara, wasn't that *your* job to inform them? In other words, you're saying that if we hadn't said anything, no one would have known about the more serious problems. Is that it?"

Mara mumbled her reply. Darryl and I gave each other a quizzical look before realizing that neither one of us had the ability to decipher her words.

I asked for clarification. "Mara, we just don't understand why you wanted to hide that information."

She raised her head and pushed her chin up in a defiant manner. "It wasn't about hiding. I just didn't think it was important to discuss."

Darryl's voice reflected the shock on his face. "Important? These are serious issues. You had admitted that this professional would help her so she wouldn't continue to do the things she had been doing so the girls would be safe. Do you remember telling us that? Why wasn't the professional's report included in the decision making?"

"Well, there wasn't a need for that kind of report for this kind of meeting."

Looking over at Darryl, I refrained from reaching over to pick up his jaw from where it had just dropped. I could tell he was trying to make sense out of what she just said.

Her words took me just as much by surprise, and the anger rising within me prevented me from being silent. "Just like the six-month judicial review hearing wasn't the right time to tell the court about Gretchen's domestic-battery report and her illegally taking Molly." My eyes narrowed as I stared directly at her. "I've gotten to be a big girl since then, Mara, and you and I both know that was precisely the right time to tell the court."

Darryl managed to compose himself. "Why wouldn't there be a need for that kind of report? This involved some of the major reasons Graci-An and Molly were removed from Gretchen and probably the root of all of her other problems. You just decided the fate of two innocent little girls, and you did so without seeing if the mother had improved in these areas."

Mara clasped her hands and held them close to her chest. She kept her chin jutted upward. "Yes, sir, Mr. Clark, it wasn't important. The decision could've been made without any report or recommendation from a professional."

I began to feel my stomach churn, a feeling that had become too familiar when dealing with Mara.

The atmosphere became thicker, but the temperature of the discussion cooled down. Mara put that fake smile back on her face. "Mr. and Mrs. Clark, Gretchen will continue with services after the girls are returned. We'll be checking on her for six months after the reunification."

Her last few words hit so hard they left me breathless. It was one thing to talk about returning the girls, but it was another to talk about having actual plans *in place after* the girls left us.

Darryl's tense jaw belied his calm voice. "You're talking about returning the girls, but you haven't even gotten a report or recommendation from the professional saying whether or not Gretchen is able to take care of them."

A smug look appeared on Mara's face. Her shoulders rolled back, and she sat upright. "The professional told me she's okay with unsupervised visits."

Darryl tilted his head to one side. "Do you mean that you finally got the report from a professional working with Gretchen?"

Mara looked at Darryl. "Well, I didn't exactly get a report, but I did get a verbal okay that we can start them."

Darryl wrinkled his forehead. "That's it? You don't need a report? The court doesn't require anything in writing?"

"Nope. A verbal okay is fine." Her shoulders relaxed as her hands released their grip on each other.

I said, "I guess I'm a bit confused now that we know Gretchen has only had about five hours of working with one professional, and no time at all with the other one. How can the professional who saw Gretchen a few times provide an accurate evaluation to support even the idea of young children being put with a mother who has such issues? As for the new professional who hasn't met with Gretchen yet, surely he or she didn't even try to give a verbal okay."

Darryl looked at me; Mara looked down. We waited for her to respond, but she didn't. What could she say?

Darryl took his attention back to Mara. "That's a good point. So, my next question is whether the professional said he or she agrees with reunification or only with unsupervised visits."

Mara squared her shoulders a little bit more. "No, she didn't say anything about reunification. Also, the guardian ad litem is agreeing to the unsupervised visits." She added the last sentence as if to prove a point, and a smug smile resurfaced on her face. Talk about the confusion level being raised to the nth degree.

Darryl's eyes darted to me and then back to Mara, his eyebrows furrowed. "The guardian ad litem? No, Erin is very much against unsupervised visits, let alone reunification."

"No, not Erin. The guardian ad litem. What's her name?" She looked up at the ceiling and then back at Darryl. "Oh yeah, Celeste Poole."

Darryl's mouth opened in obvious confusion. "No, Erin's the guardian ad litem. Celeste is her supervisor. Erin spoke to us very recently and didn't say anything about her not being the guardian anymore."

"I'm telling you, Erin wasn't at this hearing. Celeste was there. Erin's just a volunteer. Anyway, it was Celeste in court as the guardian on this case."

The more she said, the more confused I became. "Mara, I was at the last hearing. It was held over four months ago. Alisa Gifford was Erin's supervisor then, not Celeste. Alisa stood in for Erin, but I know that she's no longer there. And I know Celeste wasn't there."

Mara shook her head. "No, the hearing we had last week."

Darryl and I looked at each other. A swarm of flies could have had their choice of which mouth to fly into since both were wide open in complete and total bewilderment. We asked in unison, "What hearing last week?"

Mara's eyes grew large, and her face turned red. Apparently, her disclosure had been a slip of the tongue. She looked down and mumbled, "The hearing with the Pinkertons."

Darryl asked, "Why was there a hearing with the Pinkertons?"

Mara shrugged and scratched her nose. "Um, the Pinkertons wanted to get a home study done. They want the children placed with them, just in case it didn't work out with Gretchen."

Darryl's face darkened and his lips stiffened. "Shouldn't the children be placed back with us?"

My face started getting flushed, and the churning in my stomach intensified. The Pinkertons wouldn't know Graci-An if she fell from the sky in front of them. As for Molly, she had never lived with them; she just spent time with them sporadically. They were as blood-related to those girls as we were. In an apples-to-apples comparison, we were way ahead of the game.

I had a difficult time believing Mara and suspected that she wasn't telling us the whole story. Since when does one go to court to get a home study done? It didn't make sense that the court took valuable time for something they were counting on not happening. If they placed these children back with the mother, they were stating she was fit to take care of them.

Mara said, "Gretchen was at the hearing and said that she didn't want her children being placed with the Pinkertons."

All right, then the mother had attended the hearing, but I didn't hear anything about Jesse, Graci-An's father, being there. If he were, he'd have definitely said something against it. After all, it would have affected his child, which would have affected him. Considering how outspoken Jesse was, I would have heard him yelling across town if he knew about a hearing to discuss his baby going to live with his ex-fiancé's ex-husband's parents.

Darryl surprised me with what he said next. "Mara, is there something you're not telling us? I mean, you've been lying to us from the beginning."

"Now, I have never lied to you, Mr. Clark. Never." She pulled her shoulders back and blinked several times.

"No?" He gazed up and stroked his chin. "Let's think back." He looked straight into Mara's eyes. She looked down. "You lied when you told us you were the supervisor, when you were actually the lead caseworker. You lied when you told us that we weren't allowed to attend the permanency review staffing meeting. And we were. You just didn't want us there. You lied when you told us that you'd inform the guardian ad litem about that very same meeting. Shall I go on?"

"Now, you hold on a second, Mr. Clark." Mara clutched her hands again, interlocking her fingers. She looked toward Darryl, but not directly into his eyes. "I never told you that you couldn't attend the staffing meeting. And I did inform the guardian about the meeting. So, I never lied to you."

Darryl placed his palms on the table and leaned forward. "Yes, you did lie to us, Mara. You sat right in that seat, and I asked you if we could attend that meeting. You flat-out told us no."

I sat there nodding my head emphatically in support of my husband and added, "Yes, Mara, you did. I specifically remember you telling us no. And you're right. You did tell Erin about the permanency review staffing meeting ... after midnight *the day of* the meeting."

Mara squirmed in her seat. We had nothing to lose at this point. She had already made her decision.

After Mara left our home, I began to feel panicky.

Darryl looked at me and said, "That went well."

He immediately sent an email to Erin to ask about the unsupervised visits. Again, Erin must have been at her computer because she called us immediately.

"Mr. Clark, this is Erin. What were you talking about in your email?"

Darryl told her about Mara's home visit and her informing us that the guardian ad litem supported unsupervised visits with Gretchen. He wanted to know if she knew anything about this and why it was happening.

He said, "The last time we spoke to you, you were still adversely opposed to the mom being with these children."

Erin said, "I still am. Mr. Clark, I know nothing about this. If I had been there, I'd have told them no. I'll call Celeste and ask her what's going on. I had a long conversation with her last Friday, you know, the day after the hearing. She didn't say anything about the unsupervised visits. It may not be a bad idea for you to contact her. The more she knows, the better."

I wondered why Erin didn't tell us about the hearing with the Pinkertons and why Celeste didn't tell Erin about the unsupervised visits. It appeared there was a lot of not telling going on.

Darryl emailed Celeste that evening. We were drowning and clutching onto any piece of floating debris within our reach.

Early the next morning, Celeste responded to our email. She told us that she would very much like to meet with us as well. She explained her very busy schedule and that she wouldn't be able to come to our home. We set a time to meet at her office at one o'clock on Thursday afternoon, two long days away. By then, we wouldn't even have twelve days left before the big hearing.

Darryl and I put together some points that we considered imperative to this case. Surely, since she held the position as a supervisor at the guardian ad litem office, she would listen and be alarmed too. They were supposed to look after the children's safety and what was in their best interests.

Maybe things would now look up for the girls.

Chapter Seven

Is Anybody Listening?

Darryl and I had been looking forward to our meeting with Celeste Poole. On the drive to the guardian ad litem office, we were confident, convinced that we had put together a list of facts and talking points that should alarm anyone. We knew that once she heard what we had to say, she'd be up in arms, ready to slay the dragon alongside us.

After parking our car, we walked through the asphalt-covered lot to the tall brown building that held several different government offices and agencies. We increased our pace, eager to get out of the harsh humidity before our clothes wilted completely onto our bodies. Clearly, May wasn't about to bow out to June before providing us with a vicious taste of what to expect in the summer months ahead.

We reached the glass doors and stepped into the air-conditioned lobby. The blissful relief of the cold air distracted me from the dreariness of the interior's dark walls covered with wood paneling and the gray-tiled floor worn down by many feet throughout the years.

The security guard sitting at a desk asked for our identification. He then picked up a beige desk phone and called the guardian ad litem office to announce our arrival.

A few minutes later, a young man stepped off the elevator. He introduced himself as Jim from the guardian's office. We got into the elevator with him and rode up several floors.

The mechanical steel doors opened up into an expansive room full of furnishings but void of people. A few paintings hung on the white walls, and a closed door stood at each side of the room. Numerous blue chairs filled the waiting area as if they expected a multitude of visitors all at once.

Jim instructed us to take a seat and added that someone would be with us shortly. Darryl and I picked two chairs somewhere in the middle of the room and sat down, not sure which door we would be going through.

Within a few minutes, a petite Asian woman with short black hair entered the waiting area. She walked toward us with her hand extended.

"Hi. Mr. and Mrs. Clark? I'm Celeste Poole. Won't you please follow me?"

We shook her hand. She led us down a nondescript hallway and into a small room with a large brown conference table. She sat on one side of the table. Darryl and I sat on the other.

She started our meeting by telling us a little bit about herself. She apologized for not knowing much about this case.

I thought, *I don't know if I'd admit your ignorance about this case after you just agreed to let a mother, whom you "don't know much about" have unsupervised visits with two small children.*

I hoped that when we left her office that day, she would have more than enough information to effectively represent the children in court in less than two weeks.

Darryl asked her about the hearing last week with the Pinkertons.

Celeste stated, "Oh yeah. I was there. The Pinkertons petitioned the court to have the girls removed from you immediately and placed in their home. Once they realized the children were being returned back to their mom, they went ahead and agreed with the reunification and backed out graciously. In the meantime, though, they did want the girls moved into their home. The court didn't see any reason to remove them from their current residence and out of foster care."

No one saw the importance of telling us about this hearing because … why? Even if we couldn't have attended it, we absolutely should have been notified about it. If the court had granted the Pinkerton's petition, that decision would have had a tremendous effect on Graci-An and Molly and our family. Furthermore, we were denied the opportunity to have our say-so about it.

Darryl shook his head. "That's bull. The Pinkertons don't agree with the reunification any more than they agree there's a cow on the moon. Let me tell you, Celeste. We've talked to the Pinkertons a lot, and they've been adamant about not wanting the girls to go back to Gretchen. In fact, they told us they'd fight to keep them from her."

Celeste simply looked at Darryl and didn't speak. He then proceeded to tell her what we had heard, seen, and experienced with this case plan during the last year. She took notes and asked many questions.

Lifting her eyes from her notepad, she said, "You've definitely raised some red flags here, but I've gotta be honest with you. There's not much time left to investigate these concerns before the hearing."

Her eye contact with Darryl didn't waver. "Unfortunately, the state doesn't look at which home is better and who the better parents are. The state only requires the minimum of parenting skills. I'm sorry, but as it stands now, this case is positioned for reunification. With that said, I want to encourage you both to prepare for the girls going back to the mother."

Was this her way of telling us that she didn't intend to do any more work on the case? I felt like I had just been told by a doctor that I would be dead in two weeks, and that the disease had every right to infiltrate and destroy my body, so I just needed to go home and get my affairs in order and then lie down and die.

To add salt to the wound, we learned once again that Mara had lied to us. We suspected that she hadn't told us the real reason for the hearing with the Pinkertons. We didn't know what we were and were not being told.

Leaving the guardian ad litem office, Darryl told me he needed to go straight home and begin to work on an outline of what to present in court. "Right now, with Celeste standing in for Erin, it looks like we're all these girls have. She sounded like she didn't have much hope. Celeste sounded like she may even be okay with reunification."

The Twelve-Month Judicial Review Report

Better late than never.

Mara finally handed Darryl the twelve-month judicial review report when he picked up the girls. Gretchen couldn't make it to the Sunday visitation, so Mara offered to conduct the visit at her agency. That following Tuesday happened to be more convenient for Gretchen.

After Darryl came home with Graci-An and Molly, he told me he had a chance to observe Mara with Gretchen and the girls. He had arrived early at the Community Children's Network.

The parking lot was out of their line of vision, so they didn't see him. The whole time, Mara smiled and treated Gretchen like they were the best of friends.

I suppose that Mara may have felt proud of herself for rescuing a soul from the jaws of a lion. But did she even consider that she was sacrificing two little girls to that same lion?

We had to do everything we could to keep those girls out of harm's way, to keep them from going near the lion's mouth. Our rescue attempts were now focused on the upcoming hearing. We didn't have much time, though. In exactly one week, arguments would be heard by the judge. We'd have to work extra fast to review the report since it would be a major component in what we would have to present to that same court.

As soon as Darryl handed me the report, I sat down to review it. The front page stated the names of the children and their dates of birth and gave the court date and time of the hearing.

Thank God for Loren Dixon. She explained how the report never indicated the hearing location in terms of an address. The location could only be deduced by the hearing's time. If the time stated "9:30," then the hearing would be at the downtown courthouse. If the time stated "9:32," then the hearing would be held at the Cypress Boulevard courthouse on the outskirts of downtown. Perhaps those who compiled these reports were so busy that they instituted this method to kill two birds with one stone. Four keystrokes, and *bah-da-boom*, the reader's informed of both the time and the location.

Our copy of the judicial review report read "9:30." According to the established code, this judicial review hearing would be held at the downtown courthouse, which made sense. All of Graci-An's hearings had been held at or passed to that facility.

I continued reading. It didn't take long before I saw the need to make notes. The first mistakes were minor but revealed a lack of attention to detail. Throughout the report, Mara kept giving the girls a wide range of different ages. Alarms went off, and I wondered what other details had been slapped down incorrectly in this vital document.

She only listed the reasons for Graci-An's removal from Gretchen, using verbatim the language given in the case plan. Nowhere did she list the reasons for Molly's removal, although additional concerns and issues had been raised at that time.

Obvious inconsistencies existed when it came to addressing the individual tasks for each of the parents. Both Gretchen and Jesse seemed to have made the same amount of progress, or lack thereof, on the same tasks. Whereas Mara reported Jesse as "noncompliant," she reported Gretchen as "compliant" in those tasks

Then if what Mara had reported didn't infuriate me enough, discovering what she *hadn't* reported outraged me. She didn't include our concerns under the section entitled "Substitute Caretaker Input." This part provided us, the primary caretakers, with the opportunity to give our opinion about reunification. We had always been open with Mara about what we thought of the girls being returned, yet in this same section, she only wrote that we were good foster parents.

She again withheld information, and this time, she withheld our information. Her denying us a voice in this legal document made us question that much more the veracity of the whole report.

Mara's omission of what we thought about reunification would make a big statement to the judge—either we didn't care enough to say anything at all, or we agreed that Molly and Graci-An should be reunified with Gretchen at this time.

I found yet another discrepancy toward the end. Mara reported that she had notified us about the hearing on the same date of her last home visit two weeks earlier. This was not true. We had already known the date from my being at the six-month judicial review hearing in January. Never had Mara discussed the time, location, or anything else regarding this hearing during that visit or at any other time.

Mara's report would have been entertaining if it didn't make me so livid. It consisted of many contradictions and omissions. Her numerous errors could be dismissed as careless mistakes, or they could be perceived as a cunning manipulation of information.

Whatever the reason, her supervisor and the attorney for the state had agreed to its contents by signing off on her report. I understood that both had many cases; however, their signatures sanctioned Molly's and Graci-An's fate, placing little importance upon their lives.

Mara's never-ending deception motivated Darryl and me to work diligently. We began preparing a thorough and accurate presentation to the court.

I took all of my notes and the documentation collected over the last year—Gretchen's and Jesse's case plans, the six-month judicial review report, and Mara's past documented statements—and compared them to the contradictions I found in this report. I then made a chart showing the discrepancies for each case plan activity.

If the case plan was going to be what determined Gretchen's state of fitness, then I would use the same case plan to demonstrate her state of unfitness.

Is Anyone Paying Attention?

Time showed no mercy as it approached the biggest hearing of the case. We had only three business days left to prepare our argument.

Carla Mendes sent Darryl an email. She let us know that the guardian ad litem office had asked for the professional's report and recommendation. Furthermore, they requested that it be sent directly to Celeste Poole.

Darryl didn't pay any attention to this reiterated detail, but it alarmed me. The fact that they felt compelled to repeat these logistics made me speculate as to their underlying objective. Maybe they just did things that way. Since Celeste would be the one attending the hearing, perhaps everyone believed she should be the one to receive the report.

Erin already had a meeting scheduled with Celeste and the guardian ad litem attorney that afternoon to discuss the case. I was sure she'd get to the bottom of why they had instructed the caseworker to send this report to someone besides her. Erin needed to at least review it. Her guardian ad litem duties didn't disappear because she couldn't attend this hearing.

Still, no one had this report, and the hearing was days away. We were beyond frustrated. Darryl and I couldn't understand why no one paid attention to the events taking place with this case.

We had been involved with it for a year now, and we knew it pretty well. Did no one take our concerns seriously? Critical information was being intentionally withheld. Other information was not given accurately. Deceit played a huge role in the recommendation.

We felt as if we were doing everyone's job for them. We felt as if we were pushing on a stubborn mule that only bellowed at us in return.

We were sounding the alarm, but no one was listening.

Erin's Last Response

Friday morning arrived, giving us a total of two more business days to work on our information. Darryl accessed his email inbox first thing and saw that Erin had sent us an email.

The first sentence stated that she'd had a meeting on this case the previous day. The second sentence told us that if we had any further questions, we were to contact the guardian ad litem attorney or Tonya McCallister, upper management in the guardian's office.

A wave of nausea came over me. Darryl walked away as if Erin had told us she was doing her laundry. Hopefully, my experience with the system was causing me to overreact, and Erin meant nothing by her short and simple response.

Still, I couldn't ignore my uneasiness. "Darryl, do you think everything's okay? I mean, why would Erin do that? Has she been kicked off the case or something? She made it sound as if she couldn't reveal anything. Her email seems so final."

He shrugged and turned on the other computer. "Nah. I think it's because it's Friday, and Erin's getting ready to go on her trip next week. She probably referred us to them because she won't be available anymore."

I wanted to believe him. I did. But I had this nagging suspicion that there was more to it. "I don't know. I don't have a good feeling about this. My gut is throwing me some warning signals. Shouldn't we reply to her email and get clarification before she leaves for her trip?"

Darryl decided to listen to my gut and sent Erin an email. He asked if what she had written meant that we weren't supposed to speak with her any further about this case.

Erin didn't respond to Darryl's question for several hours. When she did, her short and simple yes perplexed and concerned us. What did she mean by that?

Darryl immediately called Tonya McCallister at the guardian ad litem office to find out what had happened. Tonya called back within the hour. I got on the other extension. The guardian ad litem attorney listened in on their line.

Darryl asked, "Has Erin been removed from the case, and if so, why?"

Tonya said, "Yes, she has. It's because there've been allegations made that Erin breached confidentiality and was showing bias."

Darryl's eyebrows were raised. "Do those allegations have to do with us?"

"Yes."

Darryl used a firm voice when he spoke. "Just to make everything perfectly clear, Erin hasn't told us anything that could even be remotely construed as confidential, and she's never shown any kind of bias toward us. Erin's decision and recommendation has nothing to do with us at all. In fact, she had said as much and was adamant when she told us that her concern was solely based on the children's safety."

Tonya said, "I understand. Let me explain our policy. When an allegation's been made that has any hint of bias or confidentiality breach, then we have to remove the guardian for the sake of appearances, even if the allegations are untrue."

This didn't make sense. Only one more business day remained before the biggest hearing of the case. Erin had rolled up her sleeves for a year and poured well over 170 hours into finding the facts, all of which brought her to her unbiased conclusion. No one else had taken the time to know this case like Erin had.

Since when did agreeing with someone's stance, particularly when it involved the best interests of children, make one biased? Erin wasn't the first guardian ad litem, nor would she be the last, who agreed with foster parents.

I had a strong feeling that Mara might be behind these allegations against Erin. No one else had a motive. Without Erin there to dispute her recommendation, Mara had the freedom to attain her personal goal.

Mara had worked this system long enough to know what to do and say. I was sure she had become familiar with the guardian's ad litem policies. Making allegations against a guardian ad litem ensured that guardian's dismissal from the case.

And hey, making this allegation just a couple of days before the biggest hearing of the case offered a bonus. What were the chances of a replacement getting truly knowledgeable about the case, at least enough to do an adequate job representing the children in court?

Even though Celeste would be standing in as the guardian ad litem, she wasn't Erin. She didn't know the case like Erin did. She didn't seem to have the same passion and drive to fight for the girls' best interests. Sadly, she appeared to be just fine with the reunification.

Why didn't the guardian ad litem office look into the facts of the allegations before going to the extreme of dismissing someone from their job? What does this say about our guardian ad litem office, whose main concern should be the children, not whether or not they're perceived as being politically correct?

I believed the system was overworked, and no one had any more room on their plate for the additional efforts an investigation would require.

With this in mind, reunification remained the priority.

Proper Protocol

The impending hearing had become more important than ever.

All weekend, Darryl worked on our presentation to the court. I took care of the children, entertaining them so that he could work without distractions.

On Sunday, I spoke to someone who worked in the dependency system. I told her what had been transpiring with the girls' case. She suggested we call the lead foster-care agency on Monday and ask that its Quality Assurance Department conduct an audit.

We didn't know this option existed. Apparently, it was a well-kept secret. Otherwise, someone would have told us about it sooner.

After the kids went to bed that night, Darryl and I stayed up late and worked more on the presentation. Still, we woke up bright and early on Monday morning so that we could get a lot of things accomplished. Fortunately, adrenaline acted as a stimulant, picking up the slack created by the lack of sleep.

We had one more day to do whatever we could to prevent the train wreck that was "positioned" to happen tomorrow. The kids were now out of school for the summer, so we needed to work fast before they woke up.

Darryl called Family & Children Connections and asked for the Quality Assurance director. The receptionist transferred the call. After two rings, we were greeted by a deep and husky voice that introduced its owner as Edward Long, Q.A. Director.

After briefly explaining our concerns, Darryl then asked him to perform a quality assurance review, or an audit, on Graci-An and Molly's case.

Mr. Long said, "You need to follow protocol if you want to have this done. First, talk to the caseworker."

We didn't tell him that we had talked and talked with the caseworker. The problem existed *because* of the caseworker. We didn't respond to his suggestion. We didn't know who we could trust.

After a couple of moments of listening to our silence, he gave another suggestion. "If talking to the caseworker doesn't get you anywhere, then talk to the caseworker's supervisor and keep going and work your way to the top of the agency if you have to. Now, if you still aren't getting any results or satisfaction, then come back to me. Even if the children are returned to their mom, you should feel better knowing that the caseworker will be watching the mother for six months afterward."

He must have believed his words encouraged us. Darryl and I just shook our heads and rolled our eyes.

After our phone conversation with Mr. Long, Darryl then called Mara's agency and asked to speak to Carla's supervisor, Donna Gieren. She didn't answer, so he left a message.

He immediately went back to charging full speed ahead on our presentation. Speaking with Edward Long had wasted precious minutes.

We didn't hear back from Donna Gieren until just before the close of business. She seemed distracted. Darryl relayed what Mara had been doing with the case and gave her our concerns.

Donna came across as kind, if nothing else, and encouraged us to talk with Mara's supervisor, Carla Mendes. Then, if we still needed her help, she invited us to call her back.

Basically, Donna Gieren handed this whole debacle back to Carla. I guess that was part of "protocol."

By the time we finished speaking with Donna Gieren, the business day had ended. First thing in the morning, the court would hear Graci-An and Molly's case.

We had done everything we knew to do.

What Memories Are Made Of

We gave Graci-An a small birthday celebration that evening.

I taped a few balloons here and there in an effort to add color to our dining room. The kids helped me set out the presents, the birthday plates, and the cake. Well, actually, the cake was constructed of several cupcakes placed together in such a fashion that it formed the shape of a teddy bear.

Darryl and I wanted to spend time alone with the children, so we kept the guest list limited to immediate family only. We knew that tomorrow morning, the judge might rule to send the girls back to Gretchen. For him and me, the undercurrent of this festive occasion was the fear of losing the girls, not knowing if this would be the last celebration for all of us together as a family.

We decided not to say anything to the kids until we knew something definite either way. Plus, we didn't want to ruin the mood of the celebration.

The children simply immersed themselves in the excitement of the party. They all stood around Graci-An with huge grins on their faces.

I put one candle on her birthday cupcake and placed it on the tray of her white high chair. At first, she didn't know what to think of this small mound covered in red. But after putting a little bit to her mouth, she must have decided it merited further investigation. By the time she finished eating it, she, her high chair, and the dog had red icing all over them.

Darryl stood next to me while I played photographer. He smiled as he watched the interaction among the children. Enjoying this event seemed to be his only focus.

Micah hugged her and said, "I love you so much, Graci-An." She returned his words of endearment with a smile.

Tears flooded my eyes as memories flooded my thoughts. I reflected on the past year and how she had grown. She had come to us as a tiny six-pound baby, but she had developed into a healthy, twenty-two-pound little girl who did a lot more than sleep in an infant car carrier.

We had come a long way as a family, and we had all grown together as well as individually. Like a movie called *This Is Graci-An's Life*, I had flashbacks of each of us with Graci-An: Devlin rocking her and gently caressing her small head covered with very little hair; Tristan playing with her; Liam trying his best to mix the formula for her bottle; Micah constantly loving on her; Molly's beautiful smile when she kissed her baby sister's head; Darryl holding Graci-An with such tenderness; and me dancing with her as she grinned from ear to ear.

My heart overflowed with love for this child. She had become such an important member of our family. At least I had tonight. Nothing and no one would rob me of the pleasure of being with Graci-An for her first birthday.

I looked around at my wonderful family enjoying this celebration, taking in every moment and detail. More memories were being made right before me, and I knew I wouldn't need a camera to recapture them in the years to come; they would be forever embedded in my mind.

For the first time, I felt my heart fill with joy while simultaneously breaking into a thousand pieces. I tried my best to hold onto the joy part, but ultimately, I couldn't help but wonder if this was Graci-An's first and last birthday with us.

The Showdown

I woke up especially early.

Blood started pumping through my veins at a rapid pace when I remembered that the girls' fate would be decided this morning. I didn't have a good feeling about this hearing. I couldn't explain it, but my gut was "talking" to me again. I tried to downplay this ominous feeling, rationalizing it as the result of my nerves working overtime.

Faith Mead came to our home to watch the kids. She held Graci-An while we gathered our personal notes and the documents we had so carefully prepared to present to everyone at the hearing. We were as ready as we possibly could be for something in which we had neither experience nor training.

Driving to the downtown courthouse, I still didn't have peace. We parked in the court parking lot. The car clock indicated that court wouldn't start for another thirty minutes.

Darryl wanted us to go into the building and wait, but I believed we had plenty of time. I had attended too many of these hearings and had waited for hours before the girls' names were called. My nervous energy would make sitting and waiting in a crowded courtroom unbearable. So, we prayed, and I felt some calmness but not peace.

About twenty minutes later, we finally walked into the courthouse. I held Darryl's hand tightly, my stomach doing flip-flops. I was sure that our walking down the corridor to the courtroom felt similar to walking a plank. Both led to shark-infested waters.

I found the docket and looked through it, but I couldn't find Molly's or Graci-An's names. I looked again to no avail.

Turning toward Darryl, I stated, "I don't see their names in here. Today is Tuesday, isn't it?"

Darryl grabbed the docket and inspected each and every page. When he got to the end, he looked at me, his eyes were big, and his eyebrows were raised.

I tried to keep the panic from rising. "I don't know what to say. What do we do? Their hearing is scheduled to start in eight minutes."

Darryl frantically looked around. He saw someone who looked official simply because he wore a uniform. It could have been a pilot's uniform, but he didn't have time to be picky. He must have figured anyone knew more than us right at that time.

Darryl asked the uniformed man, and to my surprise, quite calmly, "Excuse me, sir. We're supposed to attend a hearing today for our foster children, but we can't find their names on the docket."

The man stopped. Fortunately for us, he wasn't a pilot but a court officer. He asked for the names of the children. After we told him, he looked through the docket. "No, I don't see them here. Maybe they're with Judge Rothman today instead. I'd check his chambers if I were you."

Darryl and I scurried away like two rats that had just spotted a triangle of cheese. We almost ran into Judge Rothman's chamber reception area. Another court officer sat at the only desk in the room.

He eyed us suspiciously as if we were people with whom he should take precautions. I couldn't say I blamed him. I could only imagine what we must have looked like, spilling through those reception room doors. Still, he tried to help us by looking through some pages on his desk after we gave him the girls' names.

"No, don't see 'em here. Did you check in Room 103?"

"Room 103? Which way?" Darryl quickly blurted out, already turning his body toward the door so that he could make a quick dash in whichever direction given.

The court officer pointed to the right. "Just down the hall."

Darryl and I ran out of the reception room and down the hall to Room 103. We saw a few people talking to some of the attendees, but thank God, not enough to form any lines. We ran up to the first available person we saw. The attendee gave us a sincere smile.

Darryl said, "We were told there was a hearing here today for our foster children. We can't find their names on the court docket. Judge Rothman isn't hearing the case today either. Could you please tell us if perhaps there's been a continuance that we weren't notified about, or if not, where the hearing is being held?"

Darryl then told the woman the names of the girls. I pulled out our copy of the judicial review report so that she could have the case number.

The attendee typed all of the information into her computer. "Hmm. I don't see anything. I do see that there was a hearing about three weeks ago but nothing else. Here, let's check under both names." She typed in Molly's name and came back with the same results.

She seemed satisfied with her search but sympathetic to our concerns. "I'm sorry. There's nothing in my computer. I checked both names, and I checked both court locations. Maybe there's been a continuance, but the date hasn't been entered."

We thanked her and walked out of Room 103. "What now, Darryl? I don't know what's going on."

Darryl bit his lower lip, looking upward at nothing in particular. "I think we should run by the Cypress Boulevard courthouse, just in case."

He looked at his watch. Court had started two minutes ago.

"If it's being held there, we may still be able to make it if the case is further down on their docket. Let's go," he said over his shoulder, cueing me to run and keep up with him.

As soon as we got into our car, Darryl called the guardian ad litem office on his cell phone, but he got their voice mail. He asked me if I knew Carla's phone number. I dug my phone book out of my purse and dialed her number on my cell phone. I then gave my phone to him, and he left the same voice message for her that he had for the guardian ad litem office, informing her of the situation and asking for the hearing's location.

There was no one left to call, so Darryl drove like a madman on a mission. He was on a mission. The fate of two little girls, whom he had come to love as his own, might be decided at any moment. We were the only ones speaking for their best interests; we were their only voice.

When we got to the Cypress Boulevard courthouse, Darryl hurried and parked the car. We ran to the front door and rushed inside.

We didn't see anyone who looked familiar. Darryl and I walked over to an elderly court officer standing near the closed courtroom doors. He must have anticipated our plans to enter because he stepped protectively in front of them.

Darryl told him that we were foster parents and that we needed to find out if the hearing for our foster children was taking place. The court officer checked the docket on his clipboard for their names.

"No, there's no Graci-An Gray here," he told us as he looked up from his clipboard and over his glasses. "Do you have any paperwork with you? Maybe I can help direct you."

I pulled out the twelve-month judicial review report. The court officer looked at it briefly. "Oh, here's the problem. The hearing isn't here. See, it says 9:30 for the time. That means the hearing's downtown. You're at the wrong place. If the hearing was at this location, then it would say 9:32 for the time."

"Yes, sir," I said, taking back the report. "We know that. We've been to the downtown courthouse already this morning, and they don't have any record of the hearing being there either. Can you see if her sister, Molly Monohan, is listed on your docket?"

He looked back down at the papers on his clipboard. "Molly Monohan? Yep, it's right here." He pointed to Molly's name at the bottom of the page.

The court officer looked over and saw Darryl peering through the courtroom door windows. He pulled his shoulders back and pushed his chest forward. "Sir, you need to step back, please." He rushed over to resume his guard position in front of the doors.

Darryl moved slightly to the side, pointing to the doors and said with excitement in his voice, "That's them. That's them in there. The hearing's already in progress. Please let us go in."

The court officer looked at Darryl as if he was pondering his plea. He must have believed Darryl and that we shouldn't be considered a threat. He stepped back, opened the courtroom doors, and wished us luck as we entered.

Once inside, Darryl and I didn't know what to do or where to go. We decided to sit in the front row of the audience section to wait for an opportunity to speak.

I saw Gretchen but not Jesse. He had attended every hearing, so why wasn't he at this one?

We barely got settled into our seats when the general magistrate slammed down her gavel. The hearing had concluded. It was like someone had slammed that gavel into my chest.

I felt so lost. What happened? We wouldn't be able to speak after all? Graci-An and Molly had had no one in this oh-so-important hearing to speak on their behalf. We had poured untold hours into preparing all of this information, and for what?

This couldn't be happening. Oh my! This could *not* be happening!

We were like runners who had prepared for a marathon and arrived at the starting line late, missing the gunshot that began the race for the other runners. This was the first hearing I'd missed, if you didn't count the one that the Pinkertons had requested last month. To have to walk away without knowing what had happened left an indescribable void within me.

Everyone rose, gathered their papers and briefcases, and began to leave the courtroom. Darryl and I stood, immobilized in front of our seats. Celeste Poole passed our row but refused to acknowledge our presence. She made a point of looking the other way once she caught a glimpse of us out of the corner of her eye. She didn't seem happy.

We stared at the marching band of representatives exiting the courtroom. I couldn't watch anymore. Their final walk reminded me of a funeral procession.

I looked over and saw the same elderly court officer observing us. He must have seen the expressions on our faces and sympathized. He walked over to Darryl and me.

Speaking softly, he asked, "Why don't you talk to the caseworker and find out what's happening?"

His kind words must have slapped Darryl out of his paralyzed stupor. He turned to look at the court officer as if seeing him for the first time. Darryl thanked him, and we also left the courtroom.

Mara stood outside in the waiting area, and she appeared to be looking for someone. We walked up to her, and I asked her point-blank, "Mara, why didn't you tell us the hearing was at this location?"

Mara tilted her head and glared at me. "Why didn't you email me and ask me where it was? With all the emails you sent, it looked like you could've asked."

Darryl said, "But you don't answer our emails."

Mara put on a fake smile. She appeared to be somewhat embarrassed with our confronting her in the presence of others, including her peers and superiors.

She started looking around as if trying to find someone or something that could rescue her. With more people standing close by and watching, she had no choice but to try and save face.

"After seeing all those emails you sent, I decided I was done with you and turned you over to my supervisor," she said with a snarl.

I couldn't believe she had said that. She was "done with us"? She turned and walked away as if she truly were "done with us."

Evidently, she didn't quite understand how much she had upset us. We weren't backing off. We wanted answers, so we followed her.

She stopped at the courthouse doors and spun around to look. I didn't know if she was still searching for the same person or looking to see if she had gotten rid of us.

If it was the latter, I'm sure she must have been disappointed to see Darryl and me standing there. We were determined to pick up the conversation where she had dropped it.

"Mara," I said as if trying to talk to a child about doing what's morally right, "you were supposed to tell us the correct location."

Mara looked away and then turned her face back in our direction but didn't make eye contact. Her voice dripped with contempt. "Haven't you ever been to a JR hearing before?" She tried to put the blame on us.

"Yes. A six-month one," I said.

She jutted her chin toward me. "And where was it?"

"Downtown," I said with a smug smile on my own face. "We've never been to a twelve-month judicial review hearing. This was our first, and you knew that."

Darryl's hands were on his hips. His eyes drilled into Mara's. "Whose responsibility was it to inform us of this hearing and its details?"

Mara's face turned red. She looked down like a child ashamed for getting caught cheating on her math test. Obviously, her ploy of blaming us wasn't working. She started mumbling about something else, trying to change the subject.

Darryl's anger made him relentless. "Whose responsibility is it to inform everyone about the details of these hearings?"

She looked away and then held her head down, mumbling, "Well, either the caseworker or the attorney."

I rolled my eyes. "C'mon, Mara. You know that the attorneys don't communicate with the foster parents. So, who should've told us?"

Mara wouldn't answer us directly. She did, however, glower at me with her chin extended forward again. "Didn't I give you a copy of the judicial review report?"

Darryl said, "Yes, just last week. In fact, it was exactly one week ago today."

Mara tilted her head in defiance as if saying, *Then what is your gripe?* "Well then, consider *that* your notification."

This time, my roll of the eyes was supplemented by my head shaking and a sigh of exasperation. "Mara, the JR report said the hearing was downtown. If you notified us one week ago today via the

J.R. report, then why did you state in that same report that you notified us weeks earlier during your home visit?"

Darryl's eyes were squinted, and his face was red. "Obviously, that notification never happened because we didn't know the right location."

What could she say?

I looked around and saw that we had the attention of too many other people, so I suggested that we all go outside and finish this conversation. By now, Mara must have realized we weren't going away, and she'd have to face the piper. We followed behind Darryl as he led the way to the parking lot.

He had always been the calm one. No matter how bad something appeared to be, he would remain unruffled. I've come to rely on his quiet strength.

Now, his intense concerns about the future of our Graci-An and Molly triggered the eruption of a volcano. He had spent countless hours, neglecting his job to prepare for this hearing so that they would have a voice.

Darryl's body language revealed his anger with his wide and staring eyes, hands on hips, and chest thrust out. He clenched his teeth, and I could tell that he was striving to keep his voice at a normal volume. "I want to know why you omitted our information and input and concerns about the reunification in the judicial review report. Why did you withhold that information?"

"I gave them your input," Mara said, her feet together and body slightly turned away from us.

Did she really think we were going to fall for that after knowing we had read the report?

Darryl continued. "Mara, it's us. Remember? Two of the few people who actually know the *real* truth. We know exactly what you did and didn't put in that joke of a report. You *didn't* tell them what we thought about the reunification. They asked for our input and *in our own words*. You denied us the opportunity to be heard in that report, and then you denied us the opportunity to be heard in court today. When you robbed us of our voice, you silenced the voices of Graci-An and Molly."

I reminded her about Gretchen illegally taking Molly and the domestic-battery incident that happened during her case plan. "You never did disclose them to the judge and the permanency review staffing team," I said.

Mara said, "And Gretchen did a lot of other stuff too."

Her spontaneous admission surprised me. "What other stuff, Mara?"

She looked away, then back at me, and then her eyes darted between me and the parking lot as if looking for an escape.

With perfect timing, Jesse ran over to us from the back of the parking lot. He appeared to be rushing to go somewhere. He looked back and forth between Mara and us with a perplexed expression on his face.

He asked, "Am I too late? Has the hearing started yet?"

Mara didn't even give him the respect of turning to address him. She put her narrowed eyes back on us and kept them there. She said over her shoulder, "Yep, it's done. You got here too late."

His eyes opened wide. "What happened?"

"Call me at my office, and I'll fill you in," she replied. This time, she didn't even bother to talk over her shoulder. She kept her back to him and continued to face us.

After a few moments, she turned around to Jesse, and in doing so, completely turned her back on us. Her action would have been understandable if she had said something first, but she apparently was "done with us" once again.

That was fine by me because I figured we were now done with her.

Deceit's Impact

When Darryl and I got home, I grabbed Graci-An and hugged her tightly.

I didn't feel optimistic, especially knowing that she and Molly hadn't had anyone there to speak on their behalf. Their small voices had been silenced throughout this case plan.

At least Molly had lived with her mother in the past and knew her. She recognized Gretchen as her mother.

Graci-An didn't. In her little mind, Gretchen was someone whom she saw occasionally, only to come home to us—her family.

Darryl went into the office and sent emails to the guardian ad litem office and to Carla Mendes. He wanted to give them an explanation as to why we didn't attend the hearing, especially after we had made such a big fuss about the various issues.

He explained that we were given the wrong location. By the time we arrived at the Cypress Boulevard courthouse, the hearing was concluding. He requested that someone inform us of what had occurred and what had been decided in the hearing.

We could do nothing else at that time but wait.

That evening, I noticed I had some messages on my cell phone. I listened to them and discovered that Carla Mendes had left one.

She had responded to Darryl's voice message from that morning when we were trying to find out about the judicial review hearing. Since his call had been made on my cell phone, Carla must have redialed my number, which would have been displayed on her caller ID.

She said, "Mr. Clark, I'm returning your phone call regarding the hearing. I'm sorry there was a mix-up. I'll call you tomorrow about it." She didn't say anything else.

But a *mix-up*? Well, Carla Mendes was certainly naive … or very creative.

Mara's Strategy

We still didn't know what had transpired in yesterday's hearing and its outcome.

We went through the day trying to make it as normal as possible for the sake of the children. By the end of the close of business, no one had yet responded to us. We knew everyone had busy schedules, but the lack of communication made us feel almost like we were being exiled. Was everyone else "done with us" as well?

For now, I had to be "done with" them, if only temporarily. It was Devlin's birthday, and I wanted to focus on him. Although we had big plans for a celebration on Saturday, I cooked him a special dinner in recognition of his actual birthday.

Sitting around the dining room table, I wondered if it would all end soon. It seemed as if we had always been a family. I couldn't imagine having two fewer seats at mealtime.

Afterward, we took the family to church. The children knew even less than we did about what had taken place the day before.

The boys knew that we were fighting for Graci-An and Molly. We had also made them aware that we could lose them. Even if we wanted to give them an update, we didn't know what to tell them.

Walking through the main doors of the sanctuary, I can't say I felt comfort of any kind. A part of me understood that this might be the last time we would be all together at church. But not one inch of me accepted it.

Sitting in the pew, my mind couldn't focus on the sermon at hand. I speculated on what we could anticipate now for the girls. What would be the next steps? Again, no one had prepared us for something like this.

I prayed silently, begging God for mercy. Then somehow, peace finally came.

When we got home around nine o'clock, I discovered that we had a message on our home voice mail.

"Darryl, you need to hear this." He put his ear up to the receiver portion of the phone. I replayed the voice message back for him.

"Mr. and Mrs. Clark, this is Mara. My supervisor, Carla Mendes, asked me to call you in regard to tomorrow's unsupervised visitation with the mom. Gretchen's going to be here at my office at ten o'clock in the morning to pick them up. They'll be done at five. My supervisor left you a message yesterday about this visitation, but since you're refusing to return her call, she asked me to call you for her."

Darryl clenched his jaw and stormed away to the office. Fortunately, he had listened to Carla's message last night since it had been meant for him. He knew Mara's message was a complete farce.

I listened to it a second time, and her words "unsupervised visit" upset me even more than her contrived accusation. No one would be watching Gretchen with those babies. I pictured Graci-An wandering off by herself—no one would know.

So much for the peace I had felt earlier, I thought.

I went in the office and found Darryl composing an email at the computer. He sat erect with his body stiffened, his jaw still clenched, and his eyebrows sloped downward in the middle as he stared at the screen.

Admittedly, Mara had nerve. She knew that we knew she lied. Carla's message had nothing to do with any visitation tomorrow, next week, or next year; she had simply responded to Darryl's voice mail concerning the missed judicial review hearing and nothing else. We didn't even know a visitation had been scheduled, supervised or unsupervised.

Carla's message clearly stated that she'd call us the next day, as in, "Don't call me. I'll call you." She never asked us to call her back.

"Darryl, I think Mara's trying to set it up and make it look like we aren't cooperating with the visitation. If she can do this, then she can have grounds to remove Graci-An and Molly from us now."

Darryl stared at me for a moment. He spoke in a soft, almost whisper-like voice. "Do you mind looking this over for me?"

I read his email. In it, he clarified Carla's voice message and reminded them about its content. He added that if she had requested we call her, we most certainly would have welcomed the opportunity; we wanted to talk to someone anyway about the hearing. He assured them that we would gladly bring the children to their agency tomorrow morning at the scheduled time. Next, he asked if someone could tell us what had happened at the hearing yesterday.

After I told him his email looked fine, he sent it immediately to Carla and copied Mara.

I started pacing around the office. I couldn't stop thinking about the girls being alone with Gretchen tomorrow, and for seven hours. I wanted to scream.

I've never been a physical kind of person, but now, throwing something across the room would have felt good. The fact that I couldn't do a thing to protect these girls frustrated me beyond what words could describe.

After all, we were merely the foster parents. Technically, we were no more than fifteen-dollar-a-day babysitters.

Carla Believes

The next morning, we woke early before the alarm clock went off. I'm not quite sure I went to sleep.

Exhaustion only exacerbated the anxiety. The girls would be spending an unsupervised day with someone whose only proof of rehabilitation was the word of a caseworker, one we considered biased and unscrupulous.

I let all of the children sleep late. When the girls woke up, I fixed their breakfast before picking out their clothes. I dressed Graci-An in a pink jumper with red strawberries and matching bonnet. Molly dressed herself in a yellow-and-green dress. They looked so beautiful.

Darryl then left with the girls to take them to Mara's agency. At that point, we didn't know where Gretchen would take them.

I took all four boys to the pediatrician to get their annual physicals. This year, I welcomed the distraction it offered.

Afterward, I took them to the video store. Darryl called me on my cell phone while I was trying to choose which video to rent.

He told me that he was with Carla Mendes in her office. He wanted to put me on speakerphone so that I could be included in their conversation. I agreed, although I wondered how much good it would do.

He said, "After Gretchen picked up the girls, I came to Carla's office to ask about the outcome of the hearing. She said that the girls are being reunified with the mother."

My throat got dry, my heart raced, my stomach churned, and I became extremely hot. I couldn't speak.

Darryl allowed me a few moments of silence before continuing. "I've been talking with her for about forty-five minutes now, telling her the history of the way this case has been and is being handled. She didn't have any idea about any of the things I told her. She admitted that at first she believed we were trying to interfere with reunification like Mara wanted her to believe. Just the little bit I've shared with her, she now no longer believes that. She now understands what's going on and the motives behind our actions and that we've been looking out for two little girls.

"I've also told her that we found several discrepancies in the judicial review report. I thought I'd let you go into more detail about that. Oh yeah, Carla was surprised that Mara didn't include our concerns about reunification in that report because she said she knew better."

Although my input might no longer help this case, Carla needed to know about the devious actions of her employee. I had no problem educating her. I calmed myself down and took a deep breath.

"Carla, thank you for taking the time to listen to us. It's very much appreciated." I walked to the back of the store and found a deserted area to talk. I proceeded to tell her about some of the report discrepancies.

I then said, "Mara's told us that as long as the mother works her case plan, she'll recommend reunification. This is despite any other conditions or concerns that may not be in the best interests of the child. She told us that it was up to the guardian ad litem and the foster parents to show anything outside of the case plan. As you know, neither of us got the opportunity to do that."

Darryl said, "Carla, we see a number of issues, concerns, and identifiable risks which we believe are ongoing."

We gave several examples of Gretchen's misdeeds, including her illegally snatching Molly and the domestic-violence incident that required police involvement. Both of these could threaten the children's safety and welfare. She confirmed that Mara never disclosed either of these events to her.

We told Carla about Gretchen not working her case plan until the ninth month, except for attending the parenting class. We also told her about the disconcerting behaviors she continued to engage in throughout her case plan.

Darryl went into detail. He laid out a logical and sequential account of the major issues which no one seemed to know existed.

He asked Carla, "Knowing what you now know, what would be the one piece of paper you'd want to have with you when you went into that permanency review staffing meeting?"

Without any hesitation, Carla said firmly, "The professional's report."

Darryl said, "Right, yet we were shocked to see that we were the only ones to raise those major issues of concern. Mara obviously and intentionally omitted them. She hadn't even requested this report for this meeting. In fact, she told us that it wasn't needed for that meeting. Reunification was determined without it. Mara knew she could've been intentionally placing these children in harm's way by excluding it."

Carla sounded sincere when she agreed with our concerns. "I had no idea all of these issues were involved. I'll have to admit that I've been worried about Mara's job performance lately." She also told us that she felt Mara was getting sloppy in her work.

Darryl asked, "Knowing what you know now, do you think the decision and recommendation for these girls would be different?"

"Yes," Carla said. "I think that it could very well be different."

Darryl said, "I think about all of those times when Mara looked the other way or justified the actions and behaviors of the biological parents. We're afraid that if these children are reunified, Mara will continue excusing the mother's behaviors, even when they threaten the safety and well-being of the children. It frightens us to know that this caseworker will be the eyes and ears for these small children."

Carla said, "I agree after talking with you. What I'll do is have another caseworker in addition to Mara do pop-in visits. That way, there'll be two sets of eyes."

"Thank you, Carla," I said, breathing a sigh of relief. "I've seen nothing but deceit and incompetence from your caseworker." I shared with her some of the lies in which we had caught Mara.

Carla said, "Ever since we became privatized, the quality's just not there anymore."

Darryl said, "Evidently, Mara withheld information from you as well. She withheld information from that important permanency review meeting. To make matters worse, she kept us from providing this information to the court by not giving us the correct location of the hearing. The reports Erin submitted to the judge were probably thrown out based on Mara's false allegations of bias and indiscretion. We were the only voice those girls had. This isn't good, Carla."

Carla said, "No, no it's not. I'll tell you what I'll do, although I'll probably get a lot of grief from the guardian ad litem office. Write all of this information you told me in a letter, and I'll give it to the judge. I'll be honest with you, though. It's not going to do any good for the girls now, but your concerns will be on record."

We told her we'd think about it. Then Darryl asked, "No one's told us what to expect with the unsupervised visits and reunification process. How's that supposed to go, Carla?"

She said, "Well, the girls will have a series of unsupervised day visits with their mom for a few weeks. I like to give the day visits about two to three weeks and see how they work out. If those are determined to be successful, then we'll move to unsupervised overnight visits for about three weeks. If these are determined successful, the next stage is unsupervised weekend visits.

"Reunification's the last stage, and that's *only* after we've assessed and determined that three successful, unsupervised weekend visits have occurred. The mom may discover that she just can't handle these girls."

In my mind, I calculated how many weeks that would take and how much longer we'd have Graci-An and Molly *if* they were reunified. I came to the conclusion that the girls would be with us for the next eight to nine weeks.

But when Carla told us that the visits must first be determined "successful," I regained a small thread of hope. Her last statement thickened that strand. We knew Gretchen wouldn't be able to handle the girls.

When Darryl got home, I told him I didn't agree with Carla's suggestion that we write a letter to the judge. "Why would we want to spend precious time writing him a letter when Carla's already told us that it isn't going to do any good? Anyway, seeing it on paper isn't the same as hearing someone speaking with passion and concern.

"Why would this judge, who has a reputation of being the most liberal judge for this kind of stuff, reconsider this case simply based on the foster parents' concerns? Erin should have had a lot of weight in this case as their guardian ad litem. She had already written this judge letter after letter and brief after brief and pages upon pages informing him about her concerns about the reunification. What she had written would clearly have more weight than anything we could write. Look where it got the girls. All of her communications to the judge didn't seem to make any kind of impact on this case."

I started to feel that familiar nausea again. "Anyway, I'm sure if Mara hasn't yet vilified us to the judge, she will after he receives this letter. We may not have much time left with Molly and Graci-An. I don't want to spend it writing a letter that's not going to help them.

"Carla's not offering us an opportunity to be heard. She's offering us the opportunity to clear her conscience."

Chapter Eight

Preparing Lambs for Slaughter

What a relief!

The girls had their first unsupervised visit with Gretchen. Nothing seemed out of the ordinary when Darryl brought them home at the end of the day.

Molly came in starving, so I was glad I had dinner ready. Graci-An grinned when she saw me. She held up her chubby arms for me to pick her up.

That night, while bathing Molly, I asked her if she had a good time with her mom. She just shrugged and said, "Yeah."

I remained silent, sensing that Molly wanted to say more. She did. "I met my new grandma. She was nice, but I miss my grandma with the short hair."

Mrs. Pinkerton, the mother of her former stepfather, was the grandma with the short hair. The new grandma was Gretchen's new boyfriend's mother.

"I'm so sorry," I said. "Hey, what fun things did you do?"

"Gretchen got us hamburgers for lunch. Then we just stayed around my new grandma's house."

I then explained to Molly that she would be visiting her mother again soon. She didn't say anything either way. I hesitated to tell her more. What if it didn't work out with her going back to Gretchen?

Plus, I suspected I didn't need to tell her anything at all about the upcoming visits; Gretchen had probably filled her in. I can't say I blamed her.

If the state bent over backward to return my children to me, I would be ecstatic and tell everyone, and in particular, my children.

Taking Power to a New Level

After Darryl returned from taking Graci-An to the visitation center on Sunday to visit with Jesse, he relayed to me what he had learned.

First, Jesse told Darryl that he didn't know about the unsupervised visits until he ran into Gretchen when he cashed his paycheck. While he was walking to his ride, she came running after him and told him that she now had unsupervised visits with Graci-An and Molly. She told him in a way that was like, "Nah, nah, nah, nah, nah. I've got unsupervised visits, and you don't. Nah, nah, nah, nah, nah." He felt like she was bragging and doing so to rub it in and make him angry.

Jesse said he asked her, "Why are you telling me this? Are you trying to upset me or something?"

Jesse then disclosed that Graci-An's unsupervised visits with Gretchen concerned him because they, referring to the system, didn't know the real Gretchen.

She also told Jesse that he was no longer Graci-An's father. He shared a few other things with Darryl as well.

Jesse then talked about the judicial review hearing. According to him, Mara didn't inform him of its location either. When he asked Mara why, she told him that she didn't think he wanted to come because he had gotten so far behind in his case plan.

She had no right to make that choice for him. This again took caseworker power to a whole new level.

Mara had a legal obligation to inform Jesse of this hearing, and Jesse had the legal right to attend it. Florida Statute 39.502 (1) states:

> "Unless parental rights have been terminated, all parents must be notified of all proceedings or hearings involving the child."

Whether or not he wanted to attend was *his* choice to make. Apparently, he had wanted to be there because he did appear, but like us, he showed up too late.

Mara's admission to Jesse confirmed that she had been capable of intentionally keeping others away from this hearing. Of course, if anyone made an issue of it, she could always come back and discount what she had put in the judicial review report as a mere "mix-up."

Jesse also confirmed my suspicion about Mara's bias toward Gretchen. How strange that Gretchen had attended both the hearing with the Pinkertons and the twelve-month judicial review hearing, and we hadn't because Mara never notified us.

Had the caseworker intentionally provided the mother with different and more complete information than what she had provided to the father and foster parents?

In addition, Mara broke at least one federal law. The Adoption and Safe Families Act of 1997 not only required her to give the foster parents notice of any review or hearing involving the foster child, but an *opportunity to be heard*. Evidently, Congress must have thought the court needed to hear what the foster parents had to say.

Instead, the state's decision for Graci-An and Molly had been derived from a big slab of ignorance sandwiched between a thick slice of deception and a sizable slice of manipulation.

Allegations Against Us

"There have been some allegations made against you and your husband, that you're causing some problems," reported Jill Moseley several days after Gretchen's unsupervised visit.

I held the phone in my hand, not knowing how to respond. Her statement rendered me speechless.

She asked, "You know that the guardian ad litem on this case has been dismissed, don't you?"

"Yes, Jill, we're quite aware of that. However, we didn't know about any allegations made against us, although I shouldn't be surprised."

Evidently, someone somewhere had been very busy catching Jill up on his or her version of the events that had occurred since we saw her a month ago. I could already tell that whatever was being told about the case and us didn't include the complete truth.

She said, "Well, the allegations are that she was dismissed because she gave you and your husband confidential information, and that she's shown bias. I also need to warn you that you're in jeopardy of having those girls taken away from you because you know too much and because you're too close to this case. There's also the concern that you may be interfering with reunification."

"Seriously?" My sudden anger stopped me in my tracks. This had gone too far. "Let me tell you what's going on here, Jill. We know too much because we've done everything a foster parent is encouraged to do. We've read all of the documents given to us by the caseworker. We've attended every hearing we were notified about. We've taken the children to each and every visitation and even to the paternity test. In the course of all of this, the biological parents have spoken to us unsolicited each and every time we've come in contact with them."

I needed to do something to unleash my frustration. Looking around my kitchen, I grabbed a pan and began scrubbing. "And the former in-laws, well, that's another story. Suffice it to say they called into our home weekly, and the caseworker pushed us into facilitating visits with them and Molly. Doesn't anyone realize that former in-laws talk a lot, and we don't need to ask one question?

"We didn't need the guardian or anyone else to provide us with any confidential information. We're smart enough to pull together all of the information we acquired by legitimate means, connect the dots, and come to our own conclusions. Evidently, our conclusions must have been pretty accurate."

Realizing that I could benefit from my pent-up aggravation, I attacked the counter with my sponge while I continued venting to Jill. "As for 'interfering,' all we've done is question actions. We must have different definitions of the word. I don't see how trying to make sure these girls aren't at risk is considered interfering, especially when we have valid and justifiable concerns that we can prove. We must be ruffling some feathers." I told her about our recent conversation with Carla Mendes regarding the interference-with-reunification issue.

I again relayed to Jill that Erin, the guardian ad litem, had been nothing but professional with us and very careful not to give us any confidential information. I then proceeded to tell her some of the other details of what we had experienced, witnessed, and documented throughout this case plan.

Jill listened. She admitted to me that she hadn't known any of what I had just shared with her, and she was now concerned for the girls as well.

"Mrs. Clark, you can be assured that I'll check more into these allegations, especially after hearing your side."

"Thank you, Jill. But I'd like to know who it was that made those allegations."

"Let me see." I could hear her rummaging through some papers over the phone. "Hmm. I believe these allegations came from the guardian ad litem office, but I'll get everything verified by the time I see you on Monday. It looks like they sent over to us a copy of every email you sent them. I'll get as much information as I can before I see you."

"Thank you, Jill. I'm beginning to feel that the foster-care system is nothing more than a despotism. There are consequences for those who dare to question. Things look as if they're getting uglier."

"Well, let's hope not. Give me some time to see what I can come up with," Jill encouraged as we ended our call.

After drying my hands, I immediately called Darryl and repeated my phone conversation with Jill. We had sent emails to only three people at the guardian ad litem office: Tonya McCallister, Erin, and Celeste Poole.

I was sure Tonya hadn't made the complaint because we had sent her just one email that contained an overview of our concerns. I was sure it wasn't Erin since she herself had been dismissed as a result of complaints against her. Celeste Poole appeared to be the only person capable of this. Darryl had copied her on a few of the emails he had sent to Mara. We felt tricked, betrayed, and upset.

We were fighting for the lives of two little girls. Instead of looking into our concerns to protect these children, people talked about us behind our backs and made allegations and threats as if we were doing something illegal.

As for interfering with reunification, we had been overly accommodating in making that happen—more so than most foster parents would be, considering the string of last-minute demands placed upon us.

We'd just have to wait until Monday when we saw Jill. Hopefully, she'd have more information for us. We'd then have a better idea of what needed to be addressed and to whom.

In the meantime, at least I had a clean kitchen.

When Someone Takes Time to Listen

They had come to love them like sisters.

As the boys prepared to leave for their summer visit with their father, they hugged the girls with solemn looks on their faces. Yet I don't think they completely grasped the idea that when they returned, the girls could be gone. They had gotten used to Molly and Graci-An being a part of their lives. I don't think their maturity level gave them the capability of imagining life without them. For that matter, I couldn't imagine life without them at my maturity level.

Fortunately, by the time the boys saw their dad, they had smiles on their faces. Their obvious happiness seemed to have pushed the thought of losing Molly and Graci-An out of their minds. I wished I had something that would have the same effect on me.

Once home, I walked into Devlin and Tristan's bedroom and sat on their bed. I looked around at their toys, placed haphazardly on shelves, and felt a strange emptiness.

We were such a busy, active family, and our house was full of energy and life. Now, half of my children were traveling a thousand miles away, and two more were in danger of being ripped away forever. The two situations had one distinct difference—I knew I'd see my three older sons again in six weeks. But once the girls were reunified with Gretchen, we would never see them again. Fear joined the emptiness, creating a poisonous concoction that was difficult to stomach.

The next morning, we welcomed the interruption that Jill's visit provided. We were eager to see her and to hear what she had to say.

Darryl opened the door to let her inside. Jill walked through our doorway, rolling her eyes and commenting on how the day already felt muggy.

They joined me at the table. We talked about how hot the month of June had been. July was just around the corner, and the temperatures would get even higher then.

We asked Jill to tell us what she had found out about the allegations.

Jill interlocked her fingers and placed them in front of her on the table. "Mr. and Mrs. Clark, my information shows the guardian ad litem office as the one who made the complaints about you and about Erin's alleged breach of confidentiality. I believe they could have been the very ones who threatened to remove the children."

Darryl and I looked at each other. We both had our eyebrows pushed together in confusion as we tried to figure out what in the world Jill meant by her report.

Here we go again with the allegations against Erin, I thought. What confidential information had she given us? We couldn't come up with any answers.

I said, "How odd. For the record, Jill, Mara gave us more information than Erin did."

Darryl leaned toward Jill, pushing his elbows on the table. "That's right. There's the official story, and then there's the unofficial story. Let me tell you the unofficial one, which happens to be the truth and nothing but the truth."

He described the handling of this case from start to finish, telling her what we had seen, heard, and experienced. He told Jill everything, including Mara's lies, manipulations, and withholding of information, and how we had missed the hearing because Mara had informed us of the wrong location.

Jill wrote as Darryl talked, her forehead wrinkled the whole time. She said, "What happened is wrong. I'm definitely telling my supervisor about your concerns and complaints."

"The way this works," Jill went on to explain, laying down her pen, "is that after I tell my supervisor everything you've told me, she'll call you, probably for more information. Then she'll call Mara's supervisor."

She packed up her papers and folders and walked to the door. Turning back to us, she said, "It seems evident that Mara's shown bias in this case. That's not allowed. We'll work this out." She gave an encouraging smile and left.

We didn't hear back from Jill until several hours later. "Mrs. Clark? I spoke with my supervisor, Virginia Colbert, and got nowhere. I told her everything you told me. All she said to me in return is, 'I don't believe it. I know Mara Damian to be an upright person. She doesn't have a deceptive bone in her body.'"

I felt like I had just been slapped in the face and called a liar. My grip on the phone tightened. "Jill, does this mean that your supervisor isn't even going to entertain our concerns? Is she going to at least speak with us?"

"Nope."

"This makes absolutely no sense. Isn't our licensing agency supposed to be unbiased? Shouldn't everyone with concerns be heard? I mean, your supervisor doesn't know us, yet she's refusing to even consider speaking with us?"

"I know, Mrs. Clark. I hear ya. I did everything I could." Her sigh reverberated through the phone.

"Why are we the ones being demonized? We're trying to protect two innocent children, yet we're the ones pinned to the cross as the villains." I squeezed my eyes together in an effort to de-escalate the mounting anger.

"I don't know what to tell ya. I told my supervisor that you got a lot of your information from the former in-laws. She said you shouldn't have been talking with the former in-laws in the first place."

"Can someone please notify Mara of that rule?" I asked. "She's the one who gave us the phone number. I asked what the rules were for that, and she said she didn't care either way."

After my phone conversation with Jill, I found Darryl working in the office. I told him everything she had said to me.

Things didn't seem to be getting better. From all appearances, the caseworker, the guardian ad litem office, and our licensing agency were circumventing us and communicating behind our back. Allegations had been made about us that weren't true, and not one person had bothered to inform us of these accusations except our support specialist.

The next morning, bright and early, Darryl emailed Tonya McCallister at the guardian ad litem office. The tone of his email communicated a sense of urgency when he told her that we needed to meet. He didn't go into detail but simply let her know that, according to our support specialist, her office had made and filed allegations against us. He ended his email by stating that he didn't appreciate this unacceptable behavior.

A few hours later, Tonya responded to Darryl's request. They both agreed to a meeting in her office in two days.

With that out of the way, Darryl told me we needed to speak to Jill's supervisor and address her remarks.

I folded my arms in front of me while sitting at my desk in the office. "I think that at this point, it's not going to do the girls any good, just like Carla told us."

"Maybe. Maybe not," he said with a shrug of his shoulders. "I'm not giving up, and you shouldn't either. The truth—all of it—has to come out. One way is to tell as many people who will listen. The girls aren't gone yet. We still have a fighting chance."

I said, "Do whatever you want, but I don't think anyone cares either way."

"Well, if nothing else, we can clear our name."

Darryl then called our licensing agency and asked for Virginia Colbert. Within a few moments, she answered.

He introduced us, notifying Virginia that he had put her on speakerphone so that his wife could participate in this call. He laid the phone on the table between us and leaned forward to get closer to it.

"Ms. Colbert? May I ask why you weren't interested in speaking to us about our complaints?"

Virginia Colbert said, "Because I told Jill to speak to you about some of the allegations we had received about you. Honestly, I didn't think they were a big deal, like the one we got where you were too close to this case. I just thought that was understandable. I thought they could be settled once Jill addressed them with you."

Darryl leaned back in his chair with his body stiffened and his ankles crossed. "What about you tossing aside our complaints about the caseworker? It appeared that you weren't even interested in hearing what we had to say."

"Well, I know Mara Damian. I don't know if Jill told you, but I used to work with Mara and was once her supervisor."

Before Virginia had a chance to sing Mara's praises, Darryl leaned forward again and cut her off with more questions. "To start, did you know that she lied to us during our first phone call with her when she represented herself as the supervisor? Did you know she lied to us regarding the twelve-month judicial review hearing and the permanency review staffing meeting?" He went on with a few more examples of Mara's lies.

Virginia remained quiet. We took her silence as an invitation to continue.

Darryl did. For the next twenty minutes, he went through a slow, methodical process of laying out what had happened in the past twelve months. He also provided her with the sources of all of our information.

He said, "We have merely done what we were encouraged to do and documented everything. The end result is that we're knowledgeable foster parents. If all foster parents did everything they were not only encouraged to do but urged to do in order to get involved in their foster child's case, they would be just as informed."

Darryl told her the reason we had sent emails and explained that we were not trying to interfere with reunification. "We only tried to provide information on critical issues, especially when we saw all that had been withheld and the unresolved issues that could place the children at risk. Once we saw what Mara did in the permanency review staffing meeting, we couldn't remain silent."

Listening to him tell the story reignited my passion to right this wrong for the girls. I said, "Just for the record, Virginia, we are *so* beyond the issue of adoption. The only fight we're fighting is for those babies' safety and well-being. We'd rather the system give those children to a long-lost great-aunt in Milwaukee before giving them to the mother. I'm sure they'd be far safer."

Darryl gave me a slight nod, encouraging me to continue. "I believe Mara had so prejudiced those in the permanency review staffing meeting against us that they dismissed anything we mentioned as desperation. They most likely believed that if these issues existed and were as serious as we claimed, then the caseworker would've said something about them. The fact that she didn't even bring them up made it seem like we were just pulling at straws and making mountains out of molehills."

The stiffness in Darryl's body loosened, and he appeared energized. The revived fervor in his voice could have been mistaken as excitement. "It's important to keep in front of us the fact that this case is about much more than a desire to reunify a family, which in turn may save the state some money—in the short run. Rather, we should remain mindful of the fact that we're looking to protect the well-being of two very small and very dependent children. These aren't teenagers or even preteens who can, for the most part, care for themselves with less adult intervention. Instead, there's a small baby who's totally dependent on whoever's caring for her as well as her young sister."

Virginia asked many questions along the way, and we were quick with our answers. Darryl then told her that our input had been omitted in the judicial review report.

She said, "Hmm. I'm surprised because I'm the one who trained Mara to ask foster parents to write and submit their information in that section of the report."

With that, Virginia further confirmed our suspicions—Mara had intentionally excluded our information. We both just shook our heads.

Darryl then asked, "Virginia, knowing what you know now, if you were in that staffing meeting, what would you want to look at first before making a decision?"

Like Carla Mendes, Virginia didn't hesitate to respond, "The professional's report and recommendation."

She then expressed concern over the withheld information. Also like Carla, she thought that if all of this information had been presented, then the goal and recommendation for these girls could very well have been different.

Darryl nodded, his lips pursed.

Virginia said, "I'll admit that I also thought you were trying to interfere with the reunification process. But after hearing what you had to say, I now believe you're just trying to look after the best interests of these children. I'd be concerned about you if you hadn't been speaking up and making a lot of noise about this case."

We felt validated again by the time we finished speaking with Virginia. When people took time to listen to what actually happened with this case, their perspective always seemed to change.

Now, two people no longer thought of us as hysterical foster parents who were trying to sabotage reunification with a loving and nurturing mother.

But I didn't see how their changed mindsets would help save Graci-An and Molly.

The True Culprit

I had been dreading this meeting, not knowing what we would face.

All during the drive to the guardian ad litem office, I prayed. I didn't know what else to do at the time. The obstacles we had hit thus far made me realize that I could only trust in God.

Still, I was human. Knots in my stomach and an increasing heart rate seemed to dominate my physical body at that point in time.

On the one hand, I wished Darryl would just leave it alone because it seemed like we experienced extreme disappointment with everything we did in our pursuit of justice. On the other hand, his unceasing demand to reveal the truth prevented me from sitting idly by and feeling disheartened. It forced me to fight along with him.

I had been so caught up in my thoughts that I didn't realize we had reached our destination. Darryl and I stepped out of our car and onto the court parking lot where we were met with a blast of humidity like an angry army attacking us.

I shrugged it off. My attention had to stay focused on the upcoming meeting.

All the way through the parking lot, I continued to pray silently. We were about to butt heads with a powerful office, and I needed to have reassurance that God would be with us in the meeting.

I had already concluded that Celeste Poole would be there. After the trouble she seemed to be creating, I didn't get the warm fuzzies at the prospect of seeing her again.

Evidently, we had done something to make Celeste angry at us. I just didn't know what. If Erin had given us confidential information, which we would go to our graves denying, that shouldn't have been any reason to get mad at us. If we had gotten too close to the case, I couldn't see why that would make her angry either.

Maybe Celeste Poole was merely a complicated person. Regardless, I didn't have time to ponder what I perceived to be her emotional peculiarities. We needed to spend our time and energy on saving these little girls.

Entering the lobby of the building that housed the guardian ad litem office, we were greeted once again by a rush of cool air that felt like the arrival of allies coming to our rescue. I took in a deep breath, and I prayed more—for peace, for strength, for wisdom—as we continued to walk toward the security guard and gatekeeper.

As before, the security guard called up to the guardian's office. This time, a young woman came down to retrieve us.

Once we entered the reception area, she motioned with her arm toward the same chairs we had sat on before when we had met with Celeste Poole. That seemed like a lifetime ago.

About ten minutes later, a tall, slender, and attractive woman walked into the reception area, her quick, elongated strides gliding her to where we sat. She had pulled back her long blonde hair with a brown hair band that matched her well-tailored brown pantsuit.

Extending her right hand toward Darryl, she introduced herself as Tonya McCallister.

Darryl and I rose from our seats. Tonya turned toward me. Her shoulders were squared as she held out her right hand, her eyes staring directly into mine. I noticed that she had a firm handshake.

"Mr. and Mrs. Clark, thank you for coming. We're meeting in the small conference room. Please follow me." She motioned toward the same corridor that Celeste had once taken us down.

When we entered the conference room, we saw four other people sitting at the oval wooden table, waiting for us. We sat in the first two seats on the left. Tonya sat at the end of the conference table to our immediate right. She again thanked us for coming and introduced the other attendees.

Celeste Poole sat directly across from us. Nora Olsen, second in command, sat to Celeste's right. To our immediate left sat Frances Nelson, a staff guardian ad litem. To her left sat Leslie Frey, the guardian ad litem attorney assigned to the girls' case.

Tonya looked at Darryl. "Okay, let's get started. Mr. Clark, we need to know why you requested this meeting. How can we help you?"

Darryl brought up the topic of someone from the guardian ad litem office making complaints against us to our licensing agency.

He looked at Celeste, his eyes dark with anger. "I can only guess who made those allegations against us."

Celeste nodded, her face turning red. "Yes, I admit that was me. I didn't mean for them to be allegations. I only said something to them so they'd talk with you and explain protocol. I could see that your hearts would be broken when these girls were reunified with their mother."

Darryl's voice rose a few decibels. "Does that explain why you also sent them all of our emails? Not that we care, but it went overboard. What was the reason for that?"

She returned Darryl's stare. "Yes, I'll admit sending them could've been a little overboard, but I was trying to make a point with them. I was concerned about you because I could see you really love these girls."

Her eyes filled with tears and her voice cracked as she retold her story about losing her foster child several years ago. I thought she would break down and cry at any moment.

Regardless of how we might have construed her actions, mother to mother, I sympathized with her and forgave her. We still had Graci-An and Molly with us, and I couldn't yet imagine the pain associated with that kind of loss. I don't think anyone could unless they themselves had gone through such a horrific experience.

I looked across the table at Celeste, my own eyes filling with tears. "I believe you, Celeste, and I understand your intentions." Her eyes thanked me, mother to mother.

Darryl, on the other hand, exhibited a complete lack of sympathy and understanding. He stood with his chest out, glaring at Celeste. "Does that explain why you threatened to have the girls removed from us, on the basis of your *concern* that we had gotten too close?"

I've never seen him show that angry side except for when we were in the parking lot with Mara after the last hearing.

Tonya's shoulders jerked back, and she brought her eyebrows down. Celeste wore the same type of confused facial expression. I looked around the room. The other attendees looked just as puzzled.

Tonya shifted in her seat. Her voice matched the perplexity on her face. "We, the guardian ad litem office, cannot remove a child. We don't have that authority. The only one who has that authority is the caseworker or the court. That threat couldn't have come from this office. It must have come from the caseworker's office."

Darryl then confronted the allegations against Erin. "Our licensing agency told us that this accusation came from this office too."

Tonya and Celeste shook their heads, still with confusion written on their faces. In unison, they told us that those allegations also must have come from the caseworker because they didn't come from their office. They only received the allegations against Erin; they didn't make them.

There it was. Most of the charges seemed to have come from Mara. She had also been the one who threatened to remove the girls from us through our licensing agency. No wonder she left that crazy and deceptive voice mail, accusing us of refusing to return her supervisor's voice message regarding visitation.

My assumption had been correct. She had tried to set us up to make it look like we weren't complying and were trying to sabotage reunification. She would then have grounds to remove the girls.

I now saw that our complaint didn't lie with the guardian ad litem office but with Mara and the Community Children's Network. If Darryl hadn't insisted on dealing with the issues head-on, then we'd still be under the impression that the guardian's office had instigated this trouble.

After addressing our issues with the guardian ad litem office, Leslie Frey, the attorney, spoke. She had been silent until then. "You know, I wish all foster parents could be as dedicated and loving as you two are. If these children are reunified with their mother, I have many, many children who need to be adopted. I'd like to talk to you about them."

I thanked her for her compliment, but she didn't quite understand. If I lost Graci-An and Molly and the opportunity to make them permanent members of our family, they wouldn't be replaceable.

We didn't just want to adopt *any* child. These two girls had a huge piece of our heart, and we loved them dearly.

We couldn't pick up and move on simply by replacing them.

After the Case Plan Ends

Were they not going as well as hoped?

Carla had told us that she liked to give the unsupervised day visits two to three weeks to see how they worked out before moving to overnight visits. So far, the girls were in their sixth week of day visits with Gretchen. We hadn't heard about any plans for overnight stays.

Then we learned why they hadn't progressed to the next level. When Darryl brought the girls home from their last visit, Molly told him about things that were happening—things that showed Gretchen's life was pretty much a repeat of what it had been when the state first removed Graci-An from her.

I knew from talking with many, many people within the system that reunification couldn't even be *considered* unless these issues were resolved. Caseworkers emphatically stated that reunification under these circumstances was absolutely not allowed, pure and simple. When they heard that another caseworker was reunifying children with a parent who hadn't rectified these specific issues, they were appalled.

When Mara came for her next home visit a couple of weeks later, Darryl and I didn't hesitate to bring this to her attention. As we had predicted, she excused Gretchen's lack of progress by stating she was just getting back on her feet.

Darryl rolled his eyes and shook his head. "Mara, the time for her to get on her feet was during the twelve-month case plan, not after the case plan *expired*." (Yes, the case plan had expired after twelve months, despite how Dionne Kincaid had tried to extend it.)

I then shared with her the remarks and concerns that other caseworkers had expressed regarding the rules in this matter.

Mara's gaze dropped down to the table. "The mother's doing the best she can."

Darryl looked over at me before looking back at Mara. "Don't you see that Gretchen's currently repeating the same poor behaviors and actions she had before her children were removed? She's in the same situation that she was in when DCF first removed Graci-An. What about this makes it okay to put two defenseless little girls back in her care?"

Mara continued staring down at the table. "I think if a mother's trying, we need to give her a chance."

His chest heaved from another sigh of exasperation. "She had her chance for twelve whole months. Once the girls go back to her, what's the motivation?"

Mara didn't answer and changed the subject. She told us about an upcoming hearing in September for Gretchen. I assumed she had gotten a lot of flak for not notifying us about the last hearing.

Darryl declared that even if the girls were reunified with Gretchen at that time, he would still go.

The Unknown Had Taken Its Toll

We had a week to think about Mara's visit before Jill came to conduct her home visit.

She arrived a few minutes before her two o'clock appointment. Opening the door to let her in our home could be compared to opening a preheated oven. The late-July heat blasted through the doorway, trying its best to invade our air-conditioned home.

The dining room blinds remained closed in an effort to keep out the sun's penetrating rays. The room still had more than enough light spilling in from the kitchen window where the blinds were kept open. Their gaping vulnerability brought to mind our ongoing torment of not knowing from day to day what would happen to the girls ... and when.

Darryl gave Jill an update on the latest occurrences with the case and the reunification efforts. He sounded as if he were reciting a tragedy about some fictional person. But the tragedy belonged to Molly and Graci-An, both of whom were very real.

"I tell you what," she said, shaking her head, "I get more complaints from my foster parents about Mara and one other caseworker named Eunice than all of the other caseworkers combined. Yet upper management thinks they're wonderful, and Mara and Eunice think of themselves as wonderful. It's terrible. One of my parents told me that Mara Damien had better never set another foot in his house again."

We knew that as mad as Jill might get, she couldn't do anything. Her job as a support specialist didn't allow her to step outside of her limited scope of power and ability. Her title defined her job description: being a support system for us. She took on the role of being our cheerleader. But like cheerleaders at a football game, she couldn't carry the ball and run with it. She couldn't even touch the ball.

Still, we needed her shoulder to cry on. We had been going through the threat of having the girls removed ever since we heard the verdict for their lives. Jill couldn't do anything about that one either but listen.

Then another week passed, putting us at two months since the twelve-month judicial review hearing. No one had communicated to us regarding what to expect next. The lack of progression with the visits made us wonder if Gretchen couldn't prove herself capable of keeping the girls overnight.

We lived with the unknown. It was roughly comparable to having a terminal disease: once you've been given the diagnosis and prognosis, you can then start addressing the illness and making emotional and physical preparations.

But the precarious prognosis of these circumstances prevented us from preparing physically; we didn't know how much longer they would be with us. Our love for them stymied our efforts to prepare emotionally. Anyway, how does one prepare for something like this?

Both the intensity and duration of the mental anguish had proven to be unbearable. I became jumpy and unable to eat, my mind consumed with what-ifs and the pending possible loss. Darryl seemed to have his mind elsewhere as well. I suspected that I didn't have his full attention during the few times we spoke to each other.

I sent an email to Mara to get clarification on the status of the visitations. Since we were in the tenth week of day visits, I asked her how long we should expect them to last—or could they continue indefinitely?

I then asked Mara if she had an idea as to when we could expect the overnight visits to commence. They would affect our family, our schedules, and Molly's school, which was scheduled to start in a few weeks.

It came to the point that we needed to know either way. Otherwise, we would continue dangling in the air without any type of solidity beneath us.

Our hearts were breaking as we clutched tightly to that small thread of hope, praying for a miracle. Every day was precious, yet every day was agony, reminding us that what we now had might soon be gone.

The Plan for Reunification

"The professional has recommended overnight visits," wrote Mara in her response the next morning.

She continued with her email by compiling a schedule. The first visit would be from next Monday morning at nine thirty until Wednesday morning at nine thirty. The second one would be from Friday morning at nine thirty until Monday morning at nine thirty. Then on that following Friday morning at nine thirty, the girls would be placed in the parent's home for post-supervision.

Denial set in as my first reaction. Surely, she had written this email about some other children, not our Graci-An and Molly. It didn't make sense. Her plans didn't even follow the guidelines.

Mara was going straight from day visits to two "weekend" visits to reunification. Did the professional know that Mara had taken her overnight-visit recommendation and was abusing its intention? Mara didn't say anything about getting a recommendation for weekend visits or for complete reunification for that matter. Yet she planned both without conducting the required evaluation and again without any apparent recommendation but her own.

I showed the email to Darryl. He read it, and his jaw was clenched so tight that it would probably have taken a crowbar to pry it loose.

He said, "Do you mind moving from the computer and letting me sit here? I need to address this right now. I can't believe what she's trying to do."

I left the office to fold a load of laundry. When I returned, he had already written and sent the email to Mara.

I read it and saw that he had questioned this unexpected process: Shouldn't single overnight visits take place before three *successful* weekend visits? And shouldn't all of this take place before returning the girls to the parent? He expressed our confusion over not seeing a third weekend scheduled. He asked why there didn't seem to be a time set aside afterward to evaluate the success of these visits.

Mara responded, informing us that the third weekend visit would be the same as the placement date. Was that possible? Could she really do this?

The twelve-month judicial review report specified the word "successful" when referring to the three unsupervised weekend visits *prior to* reunification. How can something be determined "successful" without an evaluation?

Darryl sent an email back to Mara and copied Carla, reiterating in detail the reunification process Carla had told us. Mara's plans contradicted this. He again questioned Mara's decision to schedule the return of the girls full-time to the mother without first evaluating whether or not the three weekend visits went well.

He asked when this process had changed. Darryl asked Carla to reply as well.

About an hour later, Mara came back with her response. She told us that once the children were reunified and placed in the home, she and her agency would still be involved. Weekly visits would begin, and they would know what was going on during those visits.

She then told us that the schedule would allow us to have four days with the children for closure. She ended her email by telling us to address any further questions with her supervisor at her office.

Were we really supposed to have closure in four days? Was she an unfeeling robot who thought our relationship with the girls had been nothing but a short-lived day job in which we needed to tidy up loose ends?

We responded to her email. We said we wanted to meet with her and Carla Mendes, and we asked when we could do this. We needed clarification from Carla since what she had shared with us regarding the visitation and reunification process was different than what Mara was planning.

After my denial left, reality hit me like a ton of bricks. Once again, grief overwhelmed me. I cried until I couldn't cry anymore. We only had two more weeks with our girls.

Then they planned to take them away forever.

Breaking the News

The next morning, we picked up my three older sons from their summer visit with their father. The timing couldn't have been better after the news we'd received from Mara the previous day.

The boys were glad to see the girls but didn't seem surprised they were still with us. Now I had to tell them again that they would definitely leave our home in about two weeks. We decided to tell all four boys at the same time while the girls were visiting their mother.

After the boys settled in, I took advantage of having all four of them together in the same place. I walked into Devlin and Tristan's room to join them and sat on the edge of Tristan's bed.

Looking around at all of my sons, I patted the mattress. "Hey, come and sit next to me. I have something to talk with you about."

They stopped what they were doing and gathered around me with curious looks on their faces. I thought, *How do I do this? I'll have to just dive right in.*

I tried my best to sound as positive as possible, but inside, my heart was ripping apart. "Remember how we discussed the possibility that Graci-An and Molly may go back to their mother?"

I looked into their eyes one by one as they nodded their heads. Tristan smiled; Devlin's pulled his eyebrows together; Micah lifted his eyebrows, and Liam had a frown on his face.

"Well, they'll be leaving us in less than two weeks. The state decided it would be best if they went back to her." I almost made it through without showing any sadness, but my voice cracked with the last few words.

Their eyes were now large, looking at me in disbelief.

Devlin spoke first. "Uh-uh. Are you serious, Mom?"

Breaking the news to them had turned out to be tougher than I had imagined. I forced myself to smile when I looked at him. "Sweetheart, I wish I were joking."

Tristan's eyes stared without blinking. He lifted his chin in anger or defiance or both. "But that's not fair."

I wanted to tell him that fairness had nothing to do with the decision.

Devlin asked, "How can they do this? They're part of our family."

I said, "Well, I guess they feel that Graci-An and Molly need to go back to their other family."

Micah's lip trembled. "Why do you have to let them go? Why can't we just tell them no?"

If only it could be that simple, I thought.

"Baby, we don't have a choice. We just borrowed them for a short time. Our time is now up, so we have to give them back." I tried to smile again.

Micah's eyes had tears in them. "Will we ever see them again?"

"Let's pray that we do. Hey guys, we'll get through this. We'll be okay," I said, trying to encourage them. I felt hypocritical. Inside, I thought I'd never survive losing the girls.

Liam hadn't said anything. I asked, "Liam? You okay?"

He just nodded. His face held the same expression as when I first told them a few minutes ago, although his eyes appeared to be damper. I guess he had to process this news in his own way.

All the boys became quiet. After a few moments, I left them alone so that they could try to sort through their emotions. I hadn't made it two steps down the hallway when I heard crying.

The First Weekend Visit

The day for Graci-An and Molly to leave for their first unsupervised "weekend" visit had arrived.

As soon as Darryl left to drive them to Mara's agency, I already began to miss them. I couldn't stand the thought of not seeing them for forty-eight hours.

The whole time they were gone, I tried to stay distracted. Instead, I could think of little else except the girls and how they were doing.

The boys appeared different during their absence too. They didn't seem as energetic, almost like they were moping.

It was a long forty-eight hours.

And then finally ... Wednesday morning came. I couldn't wait for Darryl to pick up the girls and bring them home. I knew I'd jump out of my skin if I didn't see them again soon. I kept looking up at the red-and-white chef's clock above my kitchen sink, wondering at what stage in the process he was in retrieving them.

I scrubbed the pans in the sink, more as an effort to vent my nervous energy and keep my mind preoccupied. Then I heard the front door open and little feet scurry inside. I immediately stopped scouring the same pan for the sixth time and almost ran into the living room.

Molly entered first. She walked past me without acknowledging me.

Okay, I thought, *so far, not so good.*

Darryl carried in Graci-An. The smile that emerged on her face when she spotted me mirrored my feelings: total joy and complete relief.

I ran over to her. She held out her chubby arms. I grabbed her and held her close. She smelled like stale cigarette smoke, but I didn't care. I had her back in my arms.

By the afternoon, Molly had warmed up to us, although she wouldn't talk about the visit. It didn't matter. We were just glad she was here.

That night, we all sat around the table for dinner. Everything had gone back to normal.

I had my family back together again, if only for a short while.

An Overabundance of Power

Our time with the girls went fast.

Before I knew it, Darryl needed to take them back to the Community Children's Network for a second "weekend visit." We would retrieve them in seventy-two hours.

I had hoped this visit would be easier, but it was just the contrary. For many reasons, I found it much more difficult to let them go this time.

I prayed, "God, please keep them safe and bring them back to us."

I pulled out my journal to write. While I had it opened, I read through the previous pages. I was desperate to find something—anything—that could provide a smidgeon of logic about what was happening. I figured that if I could make some kind of sense out of this whole mess, then maybe I could find some acceptance and closure.

By the time I finished reading my year-plus worth of entries, I concluded that the dependency system had some people in it who were good, and some who were not so good.

I thought about how fear kept many foster parents from making complaints against caseworkers. Stories of foster children being removed from a home out of retaliation kept foster parents submissive. Undoubtedly, caseworkers had an overwhelming amount of influence over so many lives.

Even so, I realized that only a certain kind of person could fill that position. As a result, the system experienced constant caseworker turnover, causing a perpetual hunt to hire and train new ones. With such a low salary, those who took the job really loved children and wanted to make a difference or desperately needed a job or were young and fresh out of college or craved power.

As the years, not to mention the inherent dysfunctions of the system, wore on them, some of them became burned out. The responsibilities of the job became burdensome, resulting in sloppy work.

On average, a caseworker juggled around twenty to thirty-five cases at any given time. Such a large caseload demanded long hours.

Some caseworkers thrived in that environment, viewing the extra cases and extra hours as extra opportunities to flex their muscles. These were the ones who couldn't handle the power, so they allowed their professional immaturity, lack of integrity, or both to guide them in making decisions. This kind of caseworker was incapable of considering the true best interests of a child.

Supervisors like Carla Mendes managed several caseworkers, so their total caseloads could reach as many as 150 to 180 children. Carla had said that she didn't have a choice but to rely on the integrity and honesty of her employees regarding their cases. But if even one of her employees lacked these qualities, well, one could imagine the depth of destruction that could occur in the life of a child.

The caseworker had become all too familiar with this blind trust. The unscrupulous used it to their advantage to experience the ultimate power rush—when they witnessed important decision-makers sitting on the edges of their seats, hanging onto their every word and recommendation. They drank it all in as they sat upright on their perches, chest puffed out and feathers fluffed, and rendered their "omniscient" verdict derived from deceit and manipulation.

The attorneys for the state also fell prey to the integrity, or possible lack thereof, of the caseworker. They recited his or her inaccurate information in front of the judge, and no one was the wiser…no one but that caseworker.

The judge's time prevented him or her from investigating the merits of a case. If its file contained all of the documentation required, then the judge's job consisted of merely making a ruling based on information basically provided by the caseworker.

It wasn't hard to see that caseworkers were the crux of the system, but it was their overwhelming power that remained a best-kept secret. That is, until you became involved in this secret society

My fact-finding mission may have resulted in a greater understanding. As for logic, it simply didn't exist from my perspective.

Undoubtedly, the system malfunctioned at many levels, and our Graci-An and Molly were "positioned" to be its next victims.

Chapter Nine

The Shattering of Our World

It was seven o' clock Monday morning.

The birds' chirpings sounded like a musical alarm clock, their melodious rhapsody stirring me out of my dreams. My eyelids slowly opened, and then I remembered the girls were coming home this morning. Feeling immediately rejuvenated, I jumped out of bed and got dressed, smiling the whole time.

I could already smell the enticing aroma of an already-brewed pot of coffee, thanks to our coffeemaker's preset timer. My olfactory nerves followed the scented vapor stream to the kitchen.

The room was brightly lit by the sun's early morning beams cascading through its uncovered windows. After fixing my first cup of the caffeinated potion, I strolled to the sink to get a closer look outside. Our thermometer, hanging from under the roof's eave, displayed a strong seventy-five degrees. That would soon change, though, as the August heat forced that red fluid to make a rapid ascent.

Just past the thermometer was a squirrel that caught my attention. I watched as it grabbed some kind of treasure and scurried away. I was able to relate to its dashing escape. I wanted to grab my treasure—my family—and scurry away with them. I wanted to escape the train wreck that was "positioned" to happen.

Each time I contemplated Mara's insistence in returning the girls, my peace left. I wondered if Mara ever considered the pain she created with her lies.

Then the phone rang, startling me from my ruminations. I answered it before the ringing woke up Darryl and the children.

"Mrs. Clark? This is Carla Mendes. I'm sorry for calling so early, but I'm multitasking. This is the only time I could squeeze it in today. Is this time okay with you?"

"Sure. I was already up. I'll get Darryl."

I was sure she had become a bit annoyed with the emails and voice messages that Darryl had left her recently, but we didn't care. She hadn't responded to our request to meet with them. Darryl and I were fighting the clock because in four short days, the girls were scheduled to be reunified with Gretchen.

I walked into our bedroom and over to Darryl's side of the bed. Shaking his arm, I said, "Darryl, Carla's on the phone."

He jumped up like he'd just been bitten by a snake. Before he had a chance to run out of the room in his current disoriented state, I handed him the portable phone in our bedroom.

He smiled at me and took the phone. "Carla. Hi. I appreciate your calling us back. Time is of the essence, and we really need to talk."

"Is now okay? I've got a full schedule all day. In fact, I don't know when I'll be able to rise up and take a breath of air any day this week."

"Absolutely," Darryl answered. He sounded more jovial than I had anticipated, considering he had been in a deep sleep just moments ago.

"What's up?" Carla asked.

Darryl started to walk around the bedroom with the phone held against his ear. "I'm sure you know what's going on with the girls being reunified with their mother this Friday, right?"

"Yes, I'm aware of it."

"Do you believe that this is in the best interests of the girls? I mean, the guidelines given were *three successful* weekend visits. Mara's pushed up the date to return the girls to Gretchen before the time stipulated by the judicial review report. As soon as the professional gave the thumbs-up for unsupervised overnight visits, she jumped straight from day visits to weekend visits. She omitted the separate overnight visits that were part of the process and at the same time scheduled reunification placement. There's been no room for an evaluation to see if the visits were successful."

His eyes were focused on the floor in front of him as he paced. "Is Gretchen even prepared to take the girls? Has Mara prepared Gretchen for the return of the children? Gretchen may want to have them, but is she capable of taking care of them?

"No one has asked us to give instructions or share vital information that would make caring for the girls, especially the baby, much easier and less stressful for Gretchen and her boyfriend Bill. We're the ones who know more about the baby than anyone.

"Mara's attitude seems to be one of let's-just-get-this-done-and-as-quickly-as-possible. With the mother's history, it'd be vital that she doesn't get stressed."

Carla said, "Yeah, I do support Mara, but I have to admit that I've got some concerns about how quickly the reunification's being done. Unfortunately, that's the way it is with this system. It's been my experience that eighty percent of those children who are returned to their parents come back into the system. Those parents didn't get it the first time around."

Darryl stopped his pacing, looking like a deer caught in headlights. I returned Darryl's look of shock by rolling my eyes and shaking my head. Not much surprised me anymore, not even hearing how the girls would probably be thrown into that eighty-percent category.

He placed his phoneless hand on top of his head, his eyes wide with amazement. "So, you're saying that's it. There's nothing else we can do."

"I know this is hard for you," Carla said, "but it does look like at this point the girls are being reunified. It's not a perfect system, I know."

Darryl stopped as if his body had slammed into an invisible force shield. His desperation transformed into anger, and his voice shook with conviction. "Well, there's something we can do, Carla. I have no problem writing a letter to the judge and telling him all that's happened. I have no problem fighting this."

Carla remained calm. "Yes, Mr. Clark, you can do that. You can fight it, but you'd only be postponing the inevitable. It'll turn out the same anyway. By delaying the process for the girls, you'd simply be making it more difficult for them. Do you really want to do that, Mr. Clark?"

Darryl looked down. "No, of course not."

After our conversation with Carla, Darryl resumed his pacing, now with both hands on top of his head. "That's it. I've gotta do something to stop this from happening like this. It's obvious. Carla's not going to do a thing."

I hugged him. "Carla was manipulating us, but there's some truth to what she said. Nothing's going to change if we rely on those we've talked with so far." I shrugged. "They want this case over and done with."

I thought Darryl felt disappointed with Carla because he had regarded her as an ally. As for me, I had figured out a long time ago that no one in this system could be considered our friend and trusted.

We were probably considered troublemakers because we demanded accountability. We refused to put our tails between our legs and shuffle off with our heads bowed, saying, "Oh well, that's just the way it is. It's not a perfect system, I know."

The Last Four Days

I stood at the window, waiting.

I had been waiting for the last seventy-two hours, ever since they'd left for their last "weekend" visit with Gretchen.

I appreciated Darryl's willingness to take on the responsibility of driving the girls to and from the visits. I couldn't make myself do it.

Then I saw the car pull into the driveway. The rear door opened, and Molly jumped out and ran to our front door, giggling the whole way.

Darryl took Graci-An out of the car from the other side and carried her. She wrapped her arms around his neck and had a big smile on her face.

When Molly came through the door, she stopped as soon as she saw me. This time, she gave me a big hug as if she were glad to see me. She then ran over to the dog and gave him a big hug.

Graci-An came in next. Darryl put her down, and she toddled over to me on her chubby legs. She didn't have a doubt in her mind that I'd pick her up and hold her.

I didn't care that she smelled like stale cigarette smoke again. She was here with me, and nothing else mattered.

Oh yes, it was good to have them home.

We only had four more days with them, and I intended to take full advantage of every precious minute. From all appearances, we couldn't do anything more.

This Friday, our girls would be the next sacrificed children within this secret society known as the foster-care system.

The Last Night

Thursday night shoved its way into our existence.

I had never wanted to know what it would feel like to share the girls' last night in our home. But here we were. In just a few hours, they would be gone from our lives.

During Molly's bath time, I tried to explain to her again that she would be leaving the next day, and I might not see her again. I described what I thought she could expect.

"So tomorrow, you'll go to Gretchen's to live. First and foremost, always remember that I love you more than you'll ever know. This was not our choice. We didn't want you to leave. We love you so much, and we want you to stay. But it's not up to us. Other people say you need to go and live with your mommy."

"And then I come back here with you, right, Mom?" Molly looked at me with that big, beautiful smile.

"Is that what you want? To come back here and live with me?"

She nodded her head up and down emphatically. "I want to stay here with you and Daddy and go see Gretchen," she said, still wearing that big smile.

"Oh, baby, if only that could happen. I like it that way too. It seemed to have worked fine so far, you know, with you visiting Gretchen and then coming home to us. But other people don't see it the same way you and I do. They say you have to live with your mother now."

Molly's smile quickly transformed into a frown. "But I not want to live with Gretchen. I want to live here with you, Mom." Her smile returned as if what she wanted mattered.

"I know, baby girl. I love you, and you're going to have so much fun at your mommy's. I'll think of you all the time. Never forget that I love you. Nothing or nobody or even our being apart can ever change that."

Molly began splashing in the bathtub. She had already forgotten our conversation. The floating toy now had her undivided interest.

She was still young, so I didn't know if she would remember this conversation. I wasn't sure if she would remember us after many years.

My stomach did flip-flops when I thought about their leaving. I sat back on my heels and watched her play. I wondered what life would be for her as of tomorrow. Would she still be happy-go-lucky, playing in the bathtub? Or would that faceless enemy that had emerged after previous visits rear its ugly head?

The tears refused to be held back any longer. Fortunately, Molly was too busy playing with her toys to notice.

That night, I rocked Graci-An to sleep for the last time. I laid her in her bed and stroked her cheek. She looked so peaceful, her eyes closed, her body relaxed, her breathing even.

Would she be treated well at Gretchen's? I didn't feel in my gut she would be.

I sat and watched her for a long time as she slept. What would our life be without her? I couldn't imagine it because she seemed to have always been with us.

Denial set in again. I couldn't see past what I had already experienced. I couldn't visualize them not returning like they had for the past fifteen months. Self-preservation took over, preventing my mind from fully comprehending the truth—they wouldn't be coming back this time.

I believed that if I thought along those lines that night, I would literally die.

The Last Time

Lying in bed, I tried to pray, but my mind kept wandering. In a few hours, the girls would be gone.

I finally forced myself to get out of bed and stagger to the kitchen to make a cup of coffee, praying the whole time for strength and comfort, but mostly praying for a miracle. I needed some time alone before waking everyone.

I didn't see Darryl, so I assumed he was working in the office, probably something to do with business. Well, good for him that he was able to do something constructive to get his mind off of today's event.

I stood in the kitchen and stared out the window. I contemplated all of the good times we'd had with Graci-An and Molly. Graci-An had grown so big, and Molly had made so much progress.

My eyes welled up. I wondered if I would survive the morning. I wondered if I would survive at all.

I wrote a letter to Gretchen and told her some things about Molly and Graci-An that she needed to know. I wanted to ease the transition and process of her caring for the girls. I shared with her that taking care of her daughters had been an honor. Toward the end, I gave her our phone numbers should she have any questions or concerns and if she ever needed free babysitting for the girls.

I spent the rest of my time alone thinking, praying, and reading the Bible.

Finally, the time came to wake the girls. I planned to feed them a leisurely breakfast and then get them dressed for the last time.

"For the last time"—was that really true, or was I caught up in some kind of nightmare?

As usual, I had difficult waking Molly. I let her stir in bed while I pulled her favorite new outfit from her closet. When she managed to fully open her eyes, she'd find the black jumper and pink cotton blouse lying on her bed next to her and her brand-new black dress shoes on the floor at the foot of her bed. She was so proud of those shoes.

I then went to gather Graci-An's clothes. At fifteen months, she couldn't have cared less what she wore. Naked would have been just fine with her.

Gently, I nudged Graci-An. Her eyelashes fluttered before she opened her beautiful eyes. When she saw me, she gave me a big smile.

Before she had a chance to lift her arms to me, I reached down and picked her up out of her crib. I held her close as tears began to flow from my eyes unrestrained.

I carried Graci-An into the dining room and placed her in her high chair. I went into the kitchen to make her some cereal and fruit, taking advantage of the brief solitude to pull myself together.

By the time I came back out into the dining area, Molly was sitting at the table eating the breakfast I had prepared for her, still in her pajamas. I walked over to her and hugged her from behind. "Good morning, Molly."

After Graci-An finished breakfast, I picked her up and held her close. She had no idea that our time together was soon coming to an end.

With my mouth close to her ear, I said softly, "Oh, baby girl. Never, never forget how much we love you. You'll be leaving here soon, and I don't know if I'll ever see you again. You'll be in my prayers, and I pray that you'll return one day. I know that you don't have a clue about what I'm telling you now. Please don't forget me, and know that you'll always have a large piece of my heart wherever you may be. This is not my choice. I fought for you to stay, but there are people who are bigger that want to take you back to the mother who had you living in her tummy. I guess they just loaned you to me, but I never saw you that way. You were and are my daughter. I will always think of you as my daughter. For the short period of time you were with us, you were a blessing. It was a pleasure and a privilege to have you as a part of our family. And you will forever be a part of this family." I kissed her on the top of her head.

I carried her to the bedroom and dressed her. She looked absolutely adorable in her white dress, white bloomers, and white shoes. Molly got dressed, and she, too, looked beautiful.

My girls were leaving in just a few minutes. I stared at Molly and Graci-An, thinking that this was the last vision I wanted of them in my mind. I stared at them as though this would be the last time I would see them.

It was.

The Closing Door

I couldn't believe it; I would never hold my baby girl again, nor would I ever see Molly's beautiful smile.

I hugged Molly tight, reminding her that I loved her. She hugged me back and told me that she loved me and would see me later. She then ran out to the car. She was gone.

I picked up Graci-An and held her small body close to me, the last fifteen months flashing before my eyes: how tiny she had been when we brought her home from the hospital, her radiant smile, feeling her rub her face against my cheek, her trying to crawl, her laughter.

She smelled so good, so fresh. A bittersweet smile materialized on my face as I caressed her blond tufts. I wondered what she would look like when she finally got a full head of hair.

Holding her for the last time, I felt as if a cold knife were stabbing my body. Its sharp blade then ripped itself through major organs before stopping in my heart and holding its position without mercy.

The pain intensified when I thought about our future without her. I would never again hear that tiny voice say, "Mama" as her chubby legs waddled to me, arms outstretched, her body language making it obvious that she wanted me to pick her up.

I realized that never would I get to experience walking her to her first day of school. I'd never have the opportunity to talk to her about boys and dating. I'd never see Darryl walk her down the aisle on her wedding day. I'd never have that feeling of excitement as I rushed to the hospital to be with her while she gave birth to our grandchild. Never would I have the opportunity to be an overprotective mother, trying to keep her from the dangers of the world. No, I had failed at that all-important task.

My eyes overflowed with tears. I still couldn't believe this was happening.

Darryl gently tapped my shoulder. I jumped as if interrupted from a deep trance and forced myself to look at him. Although he tried to be strong, his cracking voice belied his calmness.

"Sherrie, you need to let her go and give her to me," he said softly. His hazel eyes blinked rapidly to stop the tears from pooling.

Shaking my head, I knew I couldn't do anything else. I gently and lovingly placed her in his arms. As he held her close, she looked even smaller against his broad chest. He turned to walk away with her for the last time.

The tears now poured from my eyes. The contented look upon her beautiful face will be forever etched upon my mind. She turned to look at me, her bright-blue eyes shining. She smiled at me as if saying, "See you soon, Mommy."

I stood in the dining room and watched as Darryl walked away with this little girl who had taken a huge part of my heart. Panic rose as the distance between us increased.

Feeling helpless, I cried uncontrollably. The soft closing of the door behind them was deafening, reminding me that I would never see my girls again.

My dreams died with the sound of that closing door. Over the last fifteen months, Graci-An had become my life, but she was now gone.

The mounting pain was more than I could endure. No one should ever have to experience this anguish. I couldn't control my emotions.

The boys had been standing nearby after they told the girls goodbye. Devlin and Tristan came over and wrapped their arms around me. They too were grieving, and we were doing our best to comfort each other. We were the bereaved consoling the bereaved.

After a few minutes, they pulled away. I told them I loved them and then rushed to my bedroom so that I could be alone. I didn't want to break down anymore in front of them.

Closing my door to ensure privacy, I fell to the floor in a heap, instinctively curling into a fetal position. The pain seemed to come from my very core. I cried for what seemed like hours, questioning God as to why he had allowed this to happen.

I was haunted by flashbacks of Graci-An looking at me, ever so trusting as Darryl carried her away for the last time. These images played over and over again in my mind like a scratched album skipping on a record player, repeating the same words and music. My final memory of her was tormented by her easy smile that told me there was no doubt in her mind she would be home in a little while to see me. She had no idea that she wouldn't see me ever again.

I had tried my best to prepare my sons, myself, and these innocent girls. I tried to explain to their young minds what was happening, but I knew they didn't understand. To them, life was good.

I also knew that soon, Molly and Graci-An would begin looking for Darryl and me to come and pick them up from what would now be their new home. Graci-An especially would become confused and hurt, wondering why we never came.

The senseless circumstances behind losing them made the loss that much harder to bear. We had tried to protect them from this moment ever happening, but we had confronted a much bigger force than ourselves. This force presented a danger within itself, not only to these girls but to thousands of other defenseless children as well. We fought hard, but we were unable to hold back the tidal wave of fate that came crashing down upon them.

At this time, the damage incurred was immeasurable, but it was just the beginning of the emotional toll that would be exacted upon us in both the short run and the long run. Everyone in our family would have to work through their own grief. Like a pebble tossed into a pool of water, there would be a ripple effect from this loss, and it would continue for many years to come.

We had raised Graci-An from birth. Darryl and I had walked the floor with her at night when she was sick. We received so much pleasure rocking her to sleep, listening to her breathing become deeper and deeper, and seeing a look of total peace upon her face as she gradually surrendered to sleep.

We went through the teething process along with her and were relieved when we saw a tooth finally peeking through angry gums. We experienced the same joy and pride she felt when she took her first steps. She might not have been blood of our blood, but she was without a doubt, life of our life.

Most of my pain came from knowing that she would suffer as a result of being separated from us. Images of her thinking we had abandoned her plagued me. She didn't understand DNA nor would she care if she had understood.

We were her family, and she loved us. We went to church together, ate out together, and participated in other family events together. She received an endless supply of love and nurturing. When she cried to signal a need, we were there to lovingly supply it. She called us "Mama" and "Dada."

A tight bond had formed between us as it would between any baby and any parent who was present and involved in her life. She and I were so connected that when she breathed in, I breathed out, and vice versa.

What we went through was comparable to experiencing the tragic deaths of our dearly loved children, but with a few differences. With a death, others come to mourn with the survivors. The survivors have the comfort of knowing their loved one is in heaven and in the care of the Father. There is a service, and there is closure.

We were not proffered these acts of solace after losing our loved ones. Very few mourned with us and came to comfort us. There were no flowers or sympathy cards. There wasn't a service to provide closure. People didn't seem to recognize these children as bona fide members of our family. Very few understood that just because I didn't give birth to them, they were no less our children.

The lack of acknowledgment from others intensified our grief. The pain couldn't have been more real or torturous than if our biological daughters had been killed by the hands of another.

Unlike the death of a loved one, we'll never have the opportunity to feel peace. We'll always be looking for them and keeping our door open just in case they come back to us.

Until then, we'll always wonder where they are. What are they doing? What do the girls look like? Are they being taken care of? Are Graci-An's cries being answered?

We won't ever know, and that in itself is a kind of perpetual hell that we'll always have to live with.

The Aftermath

The girls had been gone for less than two hours, but it felt like months. Every minute that ticked by seemed like a day.

Experiencing the loss of a child for the first time made me feel like I had been dropped into a dense and unfamiliar forest. I'd never been there before, and I felt utterly lost.

Dear God, I miss them already. Help me to survive the loss of my girls.

That first night after their departure, I lay in bed but didn't sleep. The next morning, I prayed to God about what had happened. I asked Him again the age-old question of *why*. I felt hurt and betrayed by the system and by my God.

Knowing that Graci-An would endure trauma disturbed me greatly. She'd be affected more than Molly, who had already lived with Gretchen in the past.

I cried as I again thought about the trust that had enveloped Graci-An's face the last time she saw me. I cried as I wondered what she'd think with each passing day when we didn't come to get her and bring her home.

I pushed myself to get out of bed. I needed a cup of coffee, so I lumbered down the hallway to the kitchen.

The dream I'd had several years ago of the two little girls I had found, one in the grocery store and the other on the side of the road, came to mind. It seemed that I now must relive that pain all over again. But losing Graci-An and Molly wasn't a dream from which I would awaken.

The similarities between that dream and reality couldn't be written off as coincidence. That dream could very well have told the future. I silently reminded God of his promise to bless me doubly.

As if on cue, Darryl came stumbling into the kitchen. His half-opened eyes found me leaning against the cabinet and sipping coffee from a large red mug.

He said, "I need to tell you about a dream I had last night."

Darryl never shared his dreams with me. I didn't even know he dreamed, so he definitely had my attention.

"In my dream," he began, "I was walking down the street, and a small compact car approached me very slowly. The driver was a guy who looked kinda like Jesse. In the backseat was a woman. She rolled down her window to hand something to me. It was a baby, but she looked much younger than Graci-An."

Did our subconscious minds create scenarios that reflected our desires—desires which were manifested in our dreams? Or did Darryl's dream serve as a confirmation of mine? They presented a small strand of hope, but I dared not place too much value on them. Our loss was too fresh.

For now, the girls were gone. Death had invaded our home and our hearts.

We needed to allow ourselves to grieve.

The Monster

Molly and Graci-An had been gone for two days.

I can only begin to describe the pain. I had experienced losses before in my life, but nothing, I mean *nothing* compared to this inexpressible torment. In between bouts of the most horrific grief came fits of anger. I liked to think of it as a righteous anger, and I preferred it over the grief. Being angry provided a lot less pain.

Still, grief inserted itself uninvited into my life and thoughts at every turn. When it did, I broke down. I missed them so much.

Nevertheless, I knew the power of anger. This God-given emotion could be used destructively or constructively. I chose the latter.

I wrote all of my feelings in my journal. Writing felt good, and I gladly surrendered to its therapeutic effects. The more I wrote, the more I remembered about the horror of what we had witnessed during our venture in the system. I wrote down my thoughts as fast as they came to me.

I felt anger toward everyone who had been involved in this case but had done nothing. I thought that if Gretchen had not waited nine months to do her case plan, it wouldn't have dragged out to this point in time. The bonding with the girls wouldn't have been as intense.

I blamed the biological mother for not getting off her duff sooner to do what it took to get her children back. I had never understood her lack of motivation. Then again, she might have known the system better than we did. Maybe she already knew she didn't have to do much work to get her children returned.

I blamed the state for enabling Gretchen by allowing her to procrastinate so long in starting her case plan. I blamed the state for coddling her and for not making her accountable.

The system bent over backward to protect the rights of those parents whose children were removed from them. What about the rights of the children to live in a safe and loving home?

I felt anger toward the system and its illogical push for reunification without first making sure the biological parents were truly prepared to accept responsibility for the child. Even if there were signs of *some* improvements in *some* situations, it didn't necessarily mean they had acquired the most basic of parenting skills.

I understood that most children who had lived with a parent possessed an intrinsic desire to be reunified with that parent. This was only natural.

But after nearly fifteen months of living with a foster family during a time frame that had begun days after birth, a baby undeniably and unavoidably formed a bond with her foster family. That, too, was only natural. To rip that baby out of that family's arms at this tender age was traumatic, even cruel. The system didn't "reunify" this baby with anyone or anything; it separated her from the only family attachment she knew.

The "reunifiers" looked good because they were able to show through their reports just how many parents they had "turned around," who were now on the parental road to glory. They returned the children to harmful situations for the sake of their numbers. They justified it by saying, "They're *working* their plan," referring to the biological parents.

These same parents were given a year to complete their case plan, but some didn't finish it by its expiration date. Yet the court deemed it okay to return innocent children to those parents who hadn't overcome the same issues that had caused their children to be removed from them in the first place.

I recalled Mara's let's-get-these-kids-back-as-soon-as-possible attitude, and Carla telling us that was the way it was with the system. Did the state not know or care that this type of mentality led to caseworkers looking the other way, excusing potentially dangerous behaviors on behalf of reunification? What about the federal Adoption and Safe Families Act of 1997 that stated, "The child's health and safety shall be the paramount concern"?

We had learned that the whole system—which included some judges, some within the guardian ad litem office, Mara Damian and her office, and many others—was apparently obsessed with reunification. Through it all, we had discovered that they had omitted or overlooked the most important factor, one that posed a simple question: What was in the best interest of the child?

Reunification itself wasn't the monster. In theory, reunification's a grand idea. Piecing a family back together must be extremely gratifying. The operative words here are "back together," referring to the idea that the parents once had their lives in order. But for some reason, something out of the ordinary had happened, and their lives began to go awry. During this period of time, having the children removed so that they could focus on recovering could be a huge help.

But what about children who were removed from parents whose circumstances had been the results of detrimental *life-long* behaviors or harmful compulsions? What if these parents continued to give in to these same old behaviors and impulses?

Placing children back in the homes of parents who had changed little, if any, merely perpetuated these parents' behaviors and compulsions. Admittedly, some needed to overcome tough issues. In the meantime, the state sent children back to a perilous life where they once again got caught in the midst of these problems. At best, these children were once again removed and sent back into the system for their own safety, and more "veteran parents" were added to the pile.

Sadly, the people in the system knew this when they made the decision to reunify. They held their breath and crossed their fingers. They hoped everything would magically work out for the sake of the parents and for the sake of the state, which spent money trying to straighten these parents out. Did they not understand that some parents were incapable of changing while others simply didn't want to change?

When the state held the parent's hand through the process and excused this person's lack of trying, it displayed nothing shy of codependent tendencies. It was in need of its own brand of rehabilitation. Moreover, the state wouldn't be there to indulge the parents and take responsibility for them after the case was closed.

The real culprit here was the system that allowed children to be reunified without the parents changing and being prepared. That was what qualified it as the monster. The monster was putting a small child back into that same culvert from which he or she was removed because the caseworker and agency were under pressure to "get these kids back as soon as possible." The system fought, and I mean it fought hard, to reunify a family.

In the beginning, the state took a child away from his or her biological parent for the sake of the child. In the end, the state returned the child to that same parent, but this time for the sake of attaining goals, reaching numbers, and maintaining a healthy bottom line.

The Quest

As the weeks went by, the pain refused to lessen. It became an alien resident that invaded my complete being.

I couldn't stop crying. Every day, I missed the two girls. Sometimes, something would remind me of them. Sometimes, nothing reminded me of them; I just thought of them.

The same questions haunted my mind, repeating over and over. Did Graci-An still look for me, waiting for me to pick her up and bring her back home? Did she wonder if I had abandoned her, thinking that she had caused me to reject her?

I had a hard time understanding this separation, and I was an adult. I could only imagine the confusion that went through the mind of that precious baby.

Thankfully, I had my sons. They kept me strong and grounded through it all. Still, I couldn't see any silver lining to encourage me in regard to Graci-An and Molly. The lack of hope fueled my anguish. I felt trapped in a holding pattern of grief.

As a result, my physical health suffered too. I experienced constant heartburn. You could literally hear my stomach churning. I began to buy over-the-counter heartburn medication in large quantities.

My chest hurt, and I honestly believed I could *physically* feel my heart breaking inside of it. This must be why it's called a broken heart.

I sometimes questioned whether I was having a heart attack. I didn't want to be like that one foster parent who'd had a stroke following the stress and grief she suffered when her seventeen-month-old foster baby, whom she'd had from birth, was removed.

I've always been the type of person who snaps back quickly when facing adversity. I couldn't do that this time. The injustice of this case prohibited closure. The irrationality of what had occurred and knowing what that baby must have gone through after she was ripped from our home prevented me from achieving any sense of peace.

I was angry at God. The cards appeared to have been stacked against Molly and Graci-An's case, but I had been confident that we had God on our side.

Since they were torn from us, I questioned God's part in this many times. I asked why he gave me these beautiful children. He knew we would bond with them, and they would bond with us, yet he allowed them to be taken away. I questioned why nothing appeared to be in their favor. I asked God why he didn't come to Molly's and Graci-An's defense.

God was all we had, but where was he? He knew I had depended on him totally to protect these little ones. Had I not prayed hard enough or long enough? Did I not pray the right prayer? Was it totally my fault because I didn't do something I should have done?

Instead of running away from God, I had an almost compulsive need to chase after him. I wrapped my arms around his ankles and refused to let go until he told me why he had allowed all of this to happen.

I wanted to know if we needed to hang on to their return or if we were never to see them again. Should I move forward in life with hope or introduce closure so that I could begin the healing process? Regardless of my incessant quest, I didn't get any answers but was left to drown in the grief that I kept hidden from everyone except my God.

Jeremiah 29:11 came to mind, reminding me that God knows the thoughts and plans he has for me. These plans are not to harm me, but to help me prosper and to give me hope in my final outcome.

Each time I had read that scripture in the past, I zeroed in on the prosperous part. Who didn't want to focus on those words of encouragement? But now, the part that said "and not to harm you" lit up in my mind like a flashing neon sign. Had God removed the girls from us because he foresaw harm? Was their removal for our protection?

I acquiesced to the knowledge that God had me where he wanted me. I had no other choice but to continue to rely on him.

During the last few months with the girls, I assumed that God had sent this or that person across our path to change things for Graci-An and Molly. In a way, they had changed things, but perhaps the changes were supposed to take place inside of us in order to increase our reliance on him. Perhaps these people were brought into our lives to show me that it was only him and through him that changes could be made and miracles could happen.

God knew the standing of our hearts and how we had turned everything over to him. I believed that he allowed me to feel his heart and his disgust as he looked down upon the dependency system and what was happening to his kids. These were the very orphans spoken of in James 1:27.

I sensed that what had been taking place in the foster-care system sickened God. I sensed that he had been saying to me, "These are *my* kids, and what are you going to do about it?"

Perhaps God did need a willing vessel. Biblical history was full of stories of God using common people because they were willing with open hearts.

But they all had a price to pay, and ours had been heavy.

Eyes Wide Open

Some people reading this may think, "Shame on you. You knew she was a foster child. You took her based on the possibility she'd be returned to her parents. She should be returned to the woman who gave birth to her. You went into this with your eyes wide open. Now you're boo-hooing because you lost her."

Part of this line of thinking is absolutely correct—with regard to the beginning of the process. We did take Graci-An into our home with our eyes wide open, knowing that we might have her only temporarily. We knew we might only have her in our lives for three hours, three days, or three weeks.

Having her removed from us after days or weeks would have been much easier. Even losing her after three months would have been far less painful than losing her after almost fifteen months.

All along the way, until the tenth month, those within the system who were close to this case gave us tidbits and sometimes large morsels of hope that she'd be ours forever. We heard little talk of Graci-An and later Molly being returned to their mother.

The more we were made to believe that the chances were good we'd be able to adopt them, the more emotionally and psychologically bonded we became.

As a result, we had held on to the very end.

Chapter Ten

Coming Out of the Pit

The leaves were turning colors, and the nights were turning cooler.

Fall festivals were popping up in many of the churches. Scarecrows, multicolored corncobs, and pumpkins decorated homes and businesses alike.

The agony of losing Graci-An and Molly continued with a cruel intensity beyond description. I loved Molly with all my heart, but I shared a special bond with Graci-An that I shared with no other. She was my first daughter.

I still cried at the mention of their names. At other times when I thought about them, I'd have to leave the room to go somewhere in private so that I could cry.

Every shower included my own waterworks where unbridled tears flowed freely down my face. There, I cried out to God, begging him to bring them back to us.

The boys appeared to have moved on with life, but once in a while, one of them mentioned the girls. One day, Micah asked me why I never cried for Graci-An.

I sat him down and explained that I couldn't stop crying since she'd been gone. I still cried over her. I had to make myself stop crying around him because I didn't want him to see me sad all the time.

I didn't know I'd been pulling it all together so well, if only on the outside.

He Speaks

The calendar page flipped from October to November.

Thanksgiving decorations came out of attics and closets. Fortunately, the weather corroborated the start of the holiday season by providing lower temperatures.

I was in my office and had just finished talking on the phone with my mother-in-law about the Thanksgiving Day menu. Our conversation prompted me to search for a recipe I had saved on my computer.

While scanning the file names, an old journal of mine caught my eye. Seeing the date, I realized I hadn't visited or written in it for over three years. For some reason, I decided to open it.

I scanned through the many years of thoughts, events, and dreams I had once entered into this diary of sorts. One particular entry seemed to jump off the screen.

Almost four years earlier, I'd had a dream where God reminded me that he had blessed me with four sons. He told me that he was now going to bless me with a daughter to teach in his ways and prepare for the Kingdom of God.

I sat there in awe, my mouth open, tingles going up my spine and down my arms. I realized that God *had* heard my many cries. He now answered them. I took this as a sign to not give up and to hold onto hope.

I felt that he had guided me to my journal. It was as if he had said, "My child, let me remind you of my promise."

The timing of reading that one entry couldn't have been better. I had come across it during a time when I was begging him for either hope or closure. It wouldn't have had the same effect if I had read it a year earlier or six months later.

Did this mean Graci-An and Molly would be coming back to us?

I knew this wasn't a coincidence. He had spoken to me that day! His word says in Psalm 91 that if we call out to him, he will answer us.

I had tested him on his word, and he had come through.

Reopening the Closed Door

It's human to sometimes forget promises, especially when we don't see them fulfilled immediately.

This mindset applied to me too.

Time went on. The world continued to spin, dragging us along with it. Before we knew it, we found ourselves smack-dab in the middle of the Christmas season.

It didn't feel like Christmas, though. The weather warmed back up, too much so, considering we'd already entered December. Floridians were running around in shorts and T-shirts.

Every time I saw families with little girls participating in Christmas activities, I'd be reminded of Molly and Graci-An. My heart broke all over again. I wanted to crawl under a rock for the duration of the holidays, but I had the rest of my family to think about.

I spent as much time as possible with my sons. We didn't talk about the girls much anymore. When the subject came up, they changed the topic within moments. I figured either they had processed it in their own way, or they would come to us when they wanted to talk.

I understood. Everyone processed grief differently. For my part, I kept a vigil near our phone, expecting a call to tell us that Graci-An and Molly were back in the system and to ask if we would mind taking them again. I couldn't give up.

Still, I couldn't deny the expanding void in my heart either. I knew God had a daughter for us because I experienced too many incidents that confirmed it. A desire to adopt a child had begun growing inside me years earlier, and it had taken root. I couldn't ignore the possibility that God might have someone else for us. The more I contemplated this idea, the more it bore witness with my spirit.

I needed to talk to my husband about this turn of events. While we were working in the office a couple of days later, I walked over to him and squeezed the top of his shoulders.

"Darryl, I know you're going to find this hard to believe, but I've been feeling that there may be someone else who God wants to put in our lives. I feel that we shouldn't close the door to that option."

There. I finally said it.

Darryl's hands froze on the keyboard. His eyes didn't leave the screen. "Okay. Are you sure?" He turned to look at me. "What if we get attached to another child, and then she's taken away? I don't think any of us can go through that again."

"Darryl, I don't know if we'll ever see Graci-An and Molly again. What if, just *what if* God has someone who *he* wants us to have?"

His body relaxed, and he looked at me. "You're right."

He'd also been going through his own grief. I don't think he could comfort me the way he used to before they left. I think doing so just caused him more pain.

He had met with people he believed could make a difference in the foster-care system, and I tagged along. He recognized the possibility that our girls might be gone, but he wanted to prevent other children from going through what they did.

The head of the lead foster-care agency, Family & Children Connections, personally asked me to come up with a proposal for change. I did. In fact, I came up with two ideas, both of which he loved and wanted to implement.

First, I suggested a Foster-Care Specialized Investigative Team. Its members would consist of individuals independent of the foster-care system, and they would ensure that case integrity would not be compromised.

Secondly, I suggested resurrecting the Florida Citizen Review Panels (F.S. 39.702) in the dependency system. The panel would objectively review and monitor foster-care cases.

Our mission took our minds off the girls temporarily. In addition, I couldn't let go of this new sense of urgency growing inside of me. We had decided to jump back on this path, and I didn't have any idea where it would take us.

I got the impression that I shouldn't sit by and wait for Placement to call and ask us to take in another foster child. I chose to be proactive and took matters into my own hands. I went to my bedroom and dialed the number to Placement. Someone named Holly answered my call.

Introducing myself, I asked Holly if she could put us on the list for foster families wanting to adopt.

She said, "I can do that, but we first place adoptions with families who'd be able to adequately take care of a baby or young child."

I took offense to what she said. "Excuse me? We took excellent care of both Graci-An and Molly when they were with us."

Holly said, "That's not what I mean. I'm sure you did. What I'm saying is that you've got four other children, right?"

Now I was offended *and* confused. "Yes, and what does that have to do with it?"

"Well, we prefer to give adoptions to those who don't have as many children. Also, there have been families waiting a long time to adopt. They get first priority."

Now I was offended, confused, and hurt. "Then why should anyone with children get involved in the system if that's the prerequisite? If those with children are at the bottom of the list, then they'll stay at the bottom. You're always going to get childless couples or families with one or two children who want to adopt coming through your door. We'll never surface to the top."

I forced myself to take a deep breath before continuing. "Holly, we've also been waiting a long time to adopt, for almost two years. That's why we became foster parents. Our file should show our status as 'foster-to-adopt.' Have those on your list been waiting longer than us?"

"Well, not necessarily."

I began to shake, afraid that we'd never be offered an adoptable child. Silently I prayed, *God, I don't understand this. I truly believed this was you wanting me to do this. I guess I missed it because it appears our adopting a child will be a miracle.*

I then spoke again. "Why didn't anyone tell us that our being able to adopt was less likely because we already had children? That's just not fair, nor is it right. We wanted to adopt the last little girls we had, but they went back to their mother when they shouldn't have." I told her about our losing Graci-An and Molly and how it had broken my heart.

"Holly, we can't go through the pain of bonding with another child, only to lose her again."

Her voice and demeanor softened. She began to open up to me about her loss of a foster child and how it had broken her heart. Somehow, we ended up forming a kind of camaraderie. She and I had finally made a connection, mom to mom.

By the time Holly and I ended our call, my spirit was lifted a little. But my heart still held the sharp arrow of disappointment.

Clarification

The name "Janna" kept coming to mind.

I personally didn't know a Janna, although I gave this name to one of my secondary characters in a novel I was writing. Still, it didn't explain why this name kept pushing itself into my thoughts.

Out of curiosity, I conducted some research and discovered that "Janna" meant "the Lord is gracious" in Hebrew, and it meant a blessing and a gift from God.

What gift?

According to Holly, our chances of adopting a child were slim to none. We didn't even have a foster child in our home.

That didn't keep support specialist Jill Moseley away. She still needed to come to our home every month to make sure we remained in compliance with our foster-care license.

When she stepped inside, I noted that she was wearing a cute pair of cotton Capri pants and a sleeveless top, unusual for mid-December … unless you live in Florida. Her summer attire clashed with our Christmas decorations.

Jill, Darryl, and I sat down at our dining room table and made small talk. We didn't have much to say.

She asked if Placement had called us to take in a child since her last visit. We assured her that they hadn't, but we believed we might finally be ready to take one into our home.

This topic reminded me of something that had been nagging at me since I had made that phone call to Placement a week earlier. I brought it up to Jill simply out of curiosity and for clarification.

"By the way, Jill, why don't they tell those families who want to adopt that their chances aren't that good if they already have children?"

Her eyes opened wide. "What are you talking about?"

I told her about my conversation with Holly and how they shouldn't withhold this bit of information from families wanting to adopt.

She shook her head. "No, that's not right. A family with four kids has just as much right and priority to adopt a foster child as a couple with no kids.

"Mrs. Clark, what she told you is not how it's done here."

From the Mouths of Babes

This Christmas season … well, it was a tough one.

I found it so tough that I tweaked my prayers. I still prayed for the girls' safety and for their return. But now I also prayed, *God, if your will is for us to have another child, please bring her to us by Christmas.*

In the meantime, I tried to focus extra hard on making this time of year festive and creating memories with my family. The boys' excitement, of course, made this venture more enjoyable. They were counting down the days until they could open up the growing pile of presents under the tree.

Before we knew it, they had counted down to seven—seven more days until Christmas Day. Thankfully, the temperature started taking a slight dip, bringing us back to a more Christmassy feel. According to the weatherman's extended forecast, the colder temperatures planned to hang around for a while. That was good. We preferred wearing sweaters instead of shorts when opening Christmas gifts.

That evening while I prepared dinner, Micah and Tristan were talking to me about one of their video games. Then out of the blue, Micah made a statement that had nothing to do with our conversation.

"Mommy, I miss Graci-An."

Tristan chimed in. "Yeah, I miss her too."

That same old pain started throbbing in my chest. Finally, though, they had brought her up. I had prepared myself for this happening, but the conversation swerved down a completely unexpected road.

Tristan said, "I want a baby sister, and I want her by Christmas."

Micah then said, "Me too. I want her by Christmas."

Whew. Instead of a heavy conversation, they wanted to talk about something optimistic, and something I'd been feeling as well. I couldn't help but laugh, both out of relief and at how wonderfully their young minds worked.

"Wouldn't that be great? I tell you what: Why don't you both pray to God for that to happen?" I suggested.

Yeah, it would be nice, but my logical, adult mind wasn't convinced it could happen.

They had no idea I'd already been praying for a child by Christmas. But I didn't know if God had been listening to me.

My sons possessed the faith of children. In their minds, they wanted a baby sister this week and didn't see why it couldn't happen.

When my friend Faith Mead called that evening, I told her about my conversation with Tristan and Micah. We both laughed.

She said, "Well, you'd better get yourself busy if you're going to make that happen in a week."

I put it out of my mind and wrote it off as one of those cherished memories of our-children-can-say-the-darndest-things incidents.

However, we should never discount the prayers of children.

An Unexpected Call

It needed to be fixed, not unlike my heart.

Whoever came up with the adage "Time heals all wounds" had never experienced a tremendous loss.

Otherwise, its author would have said, "Time does *not* heal all wounds; it just allows you to cover up your pain better."

I knew this all too well. Although it had been awhile since Graci-An and Molly had left our home for the last time, I still missed them as much as I did yesterday, as much as I did last month, and as much as I did the day they were removed from our home.

It was only by the grace of God that I didn't spiral down into the pit of depression. Many days, I felt myself teetering on the edge of that dark hole, fighting the urge to fall in.

This day was one of those days. Christmas was just around the corner, and the memories of this special family time with the girls flooded my mind. I again forced myself to think of other things, which was easier said than done.

I reapplied my smile that Friday morning and went grocery shopping for Christmas dinner. Being productive raised my mood considerably.

Around four thirty that afternoon, while I was talking to a friend on the phone, a beep came through on the line, notifying me that someone else was calling. I almost ignored it since I was involved in an intense conversation.

Then I remembered I had left a message for Darryl. Maybe he was returning my call.

I brought the phone away from my ear to look at the caller ID on its handset. The small screen read "Family & Children Connections."

I made the decision to let the call go into voice mail since I really wanted to continue my phone conversation with my friend. At the last moment, however, I found myself telling her to hold on and clicking over.

"Mrs. Clark? This is Holly from Placement. DCF just called because they have a newborn baby girl who's still in the hospital. She's about to be discharged and needs to be placed in a home."

Oh, my. This sounded so familiar. My heart raced. Did I dare hope?

Holly continued. "It looks like she could go to adoption, but I can't promise. You know this system. Unfortunately, you can't count on anything with it."

I froze, afraid that any movement would keep me from hearing her exact words.

"So… the reason for my call is to see if you'd be interested in taking her."

A Special Gift for Christmas

Did she just say *adoption*?

The kitchen began to spin, and my body went numb. I stared at the colorful assorted fruit on the tan wallpaper in front of me. It reminded me of how I had stared at the mounted swordfish at the restaurant when I first got the call to take Graci-An.

The strong smell from the cooking cabbage probably worked much like smelling salts, keeping me from collapsing.

Were we to get back on this same train, the same one we had climbed aboard another lifetime ago … the one that crashed, making us and two little girls casualties of its bloody wreckage?

Then it dawned on me: this was what I'd been praying for … a child for Christmas.

"Wow, Holly. I'm excited. If it were up to me, I'd take her right now. But I've gotta call my husband and ask him first." I remembered my friend was still holding on the other line.

"No problem. I understand. I tell you what. I won't call DCF until I hear back from you."

Inside, I breathed a sigh of relief. "Great. I'll call you within five minutes."

I clicked back over to my friend and apologized for keeping her hanging for so long. After promising to call her back later, I dialed

Darryl on his cell phone. My hand trembled the whole time. When he answered, I repeated everything Holly had told me.

"Is this what you want to do?" he asked.

Is this what I want to do? I halfway expected to implode from the excitement. "Yes, especially if we can adopt her. I promised the boys that I wouldn't bring another child into our home unless we could adopt her. But I do realize this may be a gamble."

"I know. Then you do whatever you want."

After getting Darryl's blessing and agreement, I dialed Holly. She answered on the second ring.

"Holly? This is Sherrie Clark. I just spoke with my husband. He said yes, and so do I. So yes, yes, yes!" Oh *yes*. I was ecstatic.

Holly laughed before saying, "Okay, I'll call the CPI. The baby can be released from the hospital tonight or anytime this weekend, really. They said they'll keep her until Monday if they need to. When do you want to pick her up?"

I thought for a few moments, allowing the logical side of my brain to take over, if only for long enough to answer this question.

First, Darryl would have to get the crib out of storage and put it back up. The crib linens needed to be washed so that they could be nice and fresh for when she came home. Then we needed to find her car seat and clean it.

It was getting late in the day. I didn't think bringing her home tonight would be possible, not that I didn't want her right then.

"Holly, we probably need to do some things first to prepare. Everything's been packed away from when our last baby left. Tomorrow would be better for us."

"I agree," she said. "I think it would be better all the way around. I'll let the CPI know that tomorrow afternoon, you guys can take the baby."

"Thank you, Holly, for understanding. I am so happy!" I pinched myself. *Oww!* Okay, I was fully awake.

"Me too," she said. "This was so weird. We were all about to leave for the long Christmas weekend when this call came in from DCF. Anyway, when this baby came across my desk, I went through a list in my mind of whom to call. For some reason, I thought about you."

I smiled at the confirmation her words just provided. "You know, Holly, my calling you a couple of weeks ago could've been just one step in God's ultimate plan. Thank you so much."

"Yep, you never know how God's going to work. I won't be back in until Wednesday, so I'll call you then to see how it's going. In the meantime, I'll call the CPI and give her your information so that she can call you. Oh, Merry Christmas!"

Oh yes, Holly was absolutely correct. It would truly be a merry Christmas!

A Divinely Guided Path

The kitchen clock crept to the 4:57 position.

What if Holly couldn't get a hold of the CPI before leaving work?

I couldn't wait any longer, so I called her, and to my surprise, she answered her phone. Under my breath, I thanked Jesus.

I forced myself to speak with something that I hoped resembled composure. "Holly, it's just about five when most people start their weekend. No one's called me. I wasn't sure if this was normal or if maybe I missed the call. I just wanted to check before everyone locked up and left."

Her upbeat voice calmed me. "I left a message on the CPI's phone. She's probably in the hospital and had to turn off her cell phone. By the way, the CPI's name is Callie Ricker."

Well, at least we had her name. "Holly, I know you want to get home for the holiday weekend. What if she returns your call, but you've already left?"

I realized I might be pushing the envelope, but I couldn't keep silent anymore. I could no longer accept whatever they told me without asking questions to get all of the details. I'd become quite a bit wiser since first getting involved in this unique world of foster care.

"No, I'll be here until I hear back from her."

I thanked her, feeling much better.

When Darryl came home, we sat the boys down to tell them the news.

I couldn't keep from grinning. "Tristan and Micah, do you remember how you told me on Monday that you wanted a baby sister by Christmas?"

They both looked down and nodded with smiles on their faces.

"Well, the Lord must have heard your prayers. We're getting you a baby sister for Christmas!"

They jerked their heads up and looked at me to see if I was serious. Then all four boys cheered and started talking to each other, shouting questions: "When?" "How old is she?" "What does she look like?" "How big is she?" They went on and on.

That night, the atmosphere in our home lightened up significantly as we all looked forward to getting what we now considered our family's Christmas gift.

But by seven o'clock, I still hadn't heard anything from the CPI. I called Holly again. I got her voice mail and left a message, giving my cell phone number as an alternate number.

The unknown made me very anxious. Why hadn't I heard from anyone? Maybe the CPI had gone to a Christmas party and planned to call me tomorrow. By the time I went to bed, I still hadn't heard from Holly or the CPI.

Frankly, Holly calling us in the first place to take this baby had surprised me because of our last conversation. According to her, we didn't qualify for a pre-adoptive child since we had four other children.

But I truly believe that without that first conversation, Holly wouldn't have chosen us for this baby. We would've continued to be just another name on a list.

I thanked God for prompting me to take the initiative and call her. Evidently, she and I had needed to talk.

Otherwise, Holly wouldn't have had the opportunity to hear our story … and listen to my heart.

Holes in the Hearts

I woke up early thinking about the baby.

What did she look like? Would we be able to keep her? That last question dampened my excitement a bit. I didn't like the prospect of going through another fifteen months of a case plan, becoming attached and bonded, and then having her removed from us.

I looked over and saw that the clock on the nightstand read 7:02 a.m. I still hadn't heard back from Holly or from the CPI.

My mind played the what-if game: What if Holly didn't talk to the CPI last night, and Callie Ricker didn't know about us? What if Callie had to call the weekend Placement, and they put this baby with another family? What if, what if, what if ... the questions kept coming.

At the moment, I couldn't do anything about it but pray. I've been told that if God has something for you, then nothing can keep it from you.

With that piece of encouragement, I got out of bed to make my way to the kitchen for my first cup of coffee. The sound of the whipping wind slapping the drizzly rain against the windows made me want to crawl back in bed for a few more minutes.

I fought the temptation, knowing I needed to prepare for the arrival of a baby. Supposedly, we'd be bringing her home this afternoon, and I didn't have any supplies for a newborn. But what if we didn't get her after all? My distrust of the system began to overpower my excitement.

I decided to only buy the basics. If we didn't get her, then I'd return everything. I'd rather be prepared with some unneeded merchandise than pick up a newborn baby without any of the necessities. I made a list, got dressed, and left for my shopping spree.

With Christmas three days away, stores opened exceptionally early, allowing me to get an early start. I just wanted to buy my items and get back home, away from the sky's dreariness.

The abnormally heavy traffic for this time of morning slowed me down. Furthermore, I was forced to contend with the rain's inability to make up its mind as to whether it wanted to come down in sheets or merely be an annoyance by placing mist after mist on the windshield.

My shopping expedition did nothing to elevate my mood either. Meandering through crowds of last-minute Christmas shoppers exhausted me physically and mentally. Evidently, the possibility that we might not get this baby had affected me more than I wanted to admit.

I needed some good news. After buying everything on my list, I called Darryl on my cell phone. He reported that there still hadn't been any word. I made a mental note to call Placement once I got home.

I pulled into our driveway at 9:57. Walking toward my house, I heard the phone ring. I ran to the front door, opened it, and rushed inside. It stopped ringing just as I reached it.

The name on the caller ID read "Callie Ricker." I thought, *Oh no*.

Disappointment flooded my entire being from head to toe. I picked up the phone to call her back and was relieved to hear Darryl's voice on the other phone.

My heart started racing again. "I'm here, Darryl."

"Oh, great," he said. "Callie, my wife's here now."

Callie talked to us some about the baby, reiterating what Holly had said. "I don't know where this case is going, but probably to adoption and quickly. I went to the shelter hearing this morning, and the parents left. I don't think I'll see them again."

Wow! Callie shocked me with what she said. We had fought so hard and for so long for Graci-An and Molly, yet it seemed this one was being handed to us on a silver platter.

"The baby's name is Mary Webster. Right now, she's in the Neonatal Intensive Care Unit. She does appear to have a hole in her heart and something like a floppy airway. The hospital assured me that she didn't need a medical home, though."

We then made arrangements with Callie to meet at the hospital at two o'clock to pick up the baby. Now that we had finally talked to the CPI, I could hardly contain myself.

About an hour later, Callie called us back. "Mr. and Mrs. Clark? I talked with the hospital social worker. The baby won't be discharged until after the doctor comes in on Monday. Anyway, the hospital staff wants to work with you over the weekend regarding how to take care of the baby."

A little disappointment seeped in, but at least we were talking to the CPI about definitely taking this baby. "We can work with that, Ms. Ricker. Of course, we're eager to bring her home, but we can wait an additional two days."

"Okay. Good. Can you still meet me this afternoon? I can do the paperwork while you're getting acquainted with the baby."

"Yes, ma'am," I said. "We'll meet you at the same two o'clock time."

For the next couple of hours, we stayed busy. We had cleaned all of Graci-An's baby things the previous night, so we only needed to set everything up. Darryl put the crib together. I put clean sheets on it and organized the items I'd bought earlier. Darryl secured the car seat in the van right before we left for the hospital. We wanted to be prepared either way.

By then, the weather had done a complete turnaround. The sun came out of hiding, and the day turned out to be beautiful.

Darryl and I arrived a little early. We met Callie in front of the hospital pharmacy. We rode together on the elevator to the second floor and walked into the Neonatal Intensive Care Unit (NICU), scrubbed in, and then Darryl and I followed behind her.

I had never been in a NICU. This one had its walls and carpeted floor covered with earth tones, creating a warm atmosphere that was matched by its temperature. We walked by several units with metal tracks on the ceiling to pull curtains for privacy. Each section was exposed in its entirety, though, including the clear bassinets holding tiny babies.

Each "room" had a set of upper and lower supply cabinets built onto the wall and a spacious countertop that would be envied by most kitchens. Multiple tubes and wires from the various machines reached into the bassinets, attaching themselves to these tiny beings.

Finally, Callie's steps ended. From where I stood, I saw the top of a tiny head covered with dark-brown hair, lying in a bassinet. Callie made herself at home in the cabinet area, putting her files on top of the counter.

I walked around to the side of the bassinet, holding Darryl's hand. I gasped when I saw her. She took my breath away. She looked so much different from Graci-An. Not only did she have dark hair, but she had darker skin, more of a tan color.

She seemed so tiny and defenseless, but what struck me the most was how alone she looked. Could she, at her young age, sense that her parents had left her?

The nurse asked us if we had ever held a newborn baby. Darryl and I just smiled and told her yes. She then put Mary in my arms. Oh my, she felt so light. The nurse then handed me a bottle to feed her. I sat down in the rocking chair next to the bassinet and placed the bottle's nipple in her small mouth.

Callie looked up from her paperwork and watched us with Mary. "This baby must have some kind of guardian angel. Her being born prematurely was actually the best thing that could've happened to her.

Because she needed to stay in the hospital, we had an opportunity to thoroughly investigate the situation."

She went back to work on the numerous forms. She spoke to us without taking her eyes off the papers in front of her. "Since you're taking her straight home from the hospital, she won't need a seventy-two-hour medical visit. She's gotten such excellent care here that it won't be necessary. Just make sure they give you her medical records when you leave."

Darryl stood next to me and gazed at Mary with a tender smile. When he spoke, his voice was almost a whisper. "Can I hold her now?"

I reluctantly handed her over to him.

I asked Callie why Mary had been removed from her parents. She told me that the reasons were confidential but that the hospital doesn't call DCF for nothing.

I don't know why she wouldn't tell us, but I didn't argue. I now knew that we would soon find out why.

Darryl and I stayed with the baby for almost two hours. The nurse asked if I would come back the next day so that she could go through the checklist and see if I knew how to bathe her, feed her, change her, take her temperature, etc. At this point, I didn't even raise an eyebrow. She could've asked me to come tomorrow to see if I knew how to breathe, and I would've done it. I planned to come back anyway and would be there every day until we could bring Mary home. Whatever this nurse had on her checklist was fine with me.

When we got home that afternoon, all of the boys met us at the front door, repeating their same questions. Of course, they knew we should be able to answer them now since we had seen the baby.

My friend Faith Mead called me not long afterward. She too asked all kinds of questions about the baby. I answered each one with a smile on my face. I knew that I already loved Mary.

Faith said, "Sherrie, she came to you with a hole in her heart. And she came to you with a hole in your heart.

"Together, you can help each other mend and heal."

Divine Purposes

As it turned out, Mary wouldn't be discharged from the hospital on Monday either.

I visited her every day for the next several days, twice a day, holding her, rocking her, feeding her, and changing her. Sometimes, if I was good, the nurse let me give her a bath.

On Christmas morning after we unwrapped presents, Darryl went to the hospital to stay with Mary while I cooked Christmas dinner. I then visited her that evening.

The inconvenience of traveling to and from the hospital was a small price to pay for the uninterrupted time I had with Mary alone, enabling us to bond. Mostly, I didn't want her to be by herself in the hospital, even though the nurses gave love to all of the babies. I wanted her to have a special someone who loved only her.

During one of Mary's feedings, I gazed into her eyes. I saw something very special about her, but I couldn't put my finger on it.

When I came home that evening, I told Darryl, "She has a sweet spirit. God has his hand upon that baby, and she's got a calling on her life. I don't yet know what it is, but it's there."

Darryl just smiled.

Before I knew it, I spoke again. "Her name is to be Janna, for the Lord is indeed gracious."

The Homecoming

The boys were so eager for us to bring Janna home.

We weren't allowed to take them to the NICU because of their age. They had to get to know her through our reports.

When we walked through our front door with Janna two nights after Christmas, they converged on us like bees on honey.

They marveled at how tiny and beautiful she was. Devlin remarked on how much different she looked from Graci-An. This time, I didn't cry when I heard her name.

I let them spend some time with Janna. Even though they should be getting ready for bed, I cut them some slack because they had waited all week to see her. They too called her Janna.

That first night, I didn't get much sleep. I guess Janna and I were getting used to each other. She woke up twice, but she was still very young.

I couldn't help but think of Graci-An. I reflected on how she woke up three or four times a night up until the time she left.

Janna, though, began sleeping through the night within a couple of weeks after we brought her home from the hospital.

It appeared that we had been blessed with a baby who was perfect in each and every way.

The Silver Platter

Janna had been living in our home for almost two weeks when Christy Middleton from The Children's Village called. She introduced herself as Mary's caseworker and sounded quite stern.

She asked, "Is the baby in daycare?"

"No, ma'am, she's still quite young."

"Then are you home with her all day?"

When I told her yes, she said she needed to come by our home before Friday to see her. "I have to go to court Wednesday morning for a TPR advisory hearing on the case."

I couldn't believe my ears. In two days, there was a hearing to discuss terminating parental rights?

I wanted to remain calm, cool, and collected, but my shocked tone betrayed my best efforts. "A TPR advisory hearing?"

She ignored my question. "Says here you may be interested in adopting her."

"Yes, ma'am, we are." This time, I managed to keep my tone flat and not come across as too eager. I had learned my lesson with Graci-An.

"Well, we'll have to talk about that when I come to your home."

We set an appointment for Wednesday at two o'clock after the hearing. I asked her if I could attend the hearing, and she said that I didn't need to go to this one. I sensed that was her way of telling me no.

Come Wednesday, Christy ended up calling at a nine fifteen that morning, wanting to know if she could come to our home at ten o'clock instead. Thank God, Darryl was home with me. We both dashed around the house to straighten up.

At ten minutes before ten, Christy knocked on our door. I forced myself to be composed when I opened it. On our porch stood a woman of average height and average weight with short black hair, big brown eyes, and a frown on her face.

I thought, *Oh no, here we go again. Another Mara. We can't lose Janna. We just can't.*

I smiled, hoping she couldn't see my insecurities. I invited her inside and asked her to have a seat at our dining room table.

She obliged. She then started rummaging through her black leather attaché case and pulled out some papers.

Darryl came in the room to join us and smiled as he walked to where she sat. He extended his hand to her. "It's nice to meet you, Ms. Middleton."

She looked up from her papers and shook his hand with a slight smile. Then she went back to writing on the forms in front of her.

I asked her how the hearing went. Without looking up from her papers, she said, "Fine."

When I asked if the parents were there, she did look up. Her eyebrows pulled together in the middle, and she said, "No."

Christy then held up a manila envelope with a deadpan expression on her face. "I brought an adoption packet if you're interested."

If we were interested? I almost jumped across the table and grabbed it from her. Instead, I just looked at it, not knowing if she was merely showing it to us or actually giving it to us.

"I take it you've never done this before," she said, still holding on to that much-coveted packet.

"No, ma'am, not this," I answered. My eyes must have been as big as doughnuts.

She gave another slight smile and laid the adoption packet in front of her on the table. "Okay, I'm gonna write everything you need to do on the front of this envelope."

I liked that. It reminded me of checklists, and I do very well with them.

She emphasized the necessity of getting the packet and checklist done—and getting them done now. "The sooner you get this in to me, the better. Otherwise, there are a lot of people who'd like to adopt a baby."

Talk about giving me a swift kick to the rear end. I nodded in an effort to convey that I completely understood. "I'll start working on it as soon as you leave."

She began writing on the envelope. "The baby has to be in your home for ninety days before the adoption can be finalized. When was she placed with you?" She looked at me. Christy might have sounded brusque, but I saw that her eyes held kindness.

"December twenty-first, but she was in the hospital until the twenty-seventh."

"I'll have to use the twenty-seventh as the placement date. Or they may use the date of the TPR, which was today," she stated with about as much enthusiasm as one would use to explain the law of gravity.

TPR? Today? Darryl and I exchanged a look of surprise, but I think we succeeded at keeping our excitement under control. We had no idea that it moved that fast.

Christy continued speaking, but she almost sounded as if she were thinking out loud. "Of course, since this is an expedited TPR, they may waive the ninety-day requirement and do it sooner."

She pulled out her planner and made appointments for more home visits, one for February and one for March. "The adoption should be finalized by then," she said.

Christy flipped through more pages in her planner. "I shouldn't need to come in April, but I'll schedule an appointment anyway, just in case."

Then she asked to see where the baby slept. We took her into our bedroom and showed her the beautiful crib decorated with animals. She seemed satisfied.

We returned to the dining room table, and she gave me the green home-visit form. Before signing, I read through her remarks. It said the parents had surrendered their parental rights at the shelter hearing. Callie Ricker had only told us they left the hearing. I didn't know they had signed off on their rights and given them up.

After Christy left, Darryl and I looked at each other and grinned. He came over and hugged me. "It looks like we're adopting Janna." His words sounded more contrived than convincing.

I understood. We'd been here before, and it had almost destroyed me. Mara had never given us an adoption packet, though.

I went through its contents and realized it wasn't as bad as I imagined. I then took the checklist that Christy had written on the envelope's front and broke it down further.

I got on the phone and made doctor appointments for our physical exams and called the vet to notify them that I'd be by to pick up our pets' shot records. I sent out reference letters to three people after calling them, and I scheduled a day to get fingerprinted. The last detail on Christy's list involved completing the application. I needed to figure out a time to sit down with Darryl for about an hour so that we could go through it together.

Janna had been asleep in her car carrier. I looked at her face and the peacefulness of her expression. I loved her. The thought of making her an official member of our family filled my heart with joy and excitement. At the risk of sounding like an ingrate, I still missed the girls and wanted them back too. I wanted them all.

Although Janna's adoption provided a lot more promise, we knew we needed to tread cautiously. We couldn't afford another heartbreak.

Then I remembered the dream Darryl had the night after Graci-An and Molly left us. He said that the woman in the car passed a baby to him through the car window. That baby appeared to be much younger than Graci-An, yet Graci-An was only fifteen months old when we last saw her. So, the baby must have been an infant.

Perhaps Darryl did have a prophetic dream, one that the Lord used to give us hope at a time when we had needed it so much.

Chapter Eleven

Through a Tiny Baby Girl

"**G**irl, you'd better not tell anyone that baby's available for adoption."

I was shocked at my friend Rose O'Neil's emphatic warning. She had been a foster parent for many years, so she knew more than most.

I shifted the phone to my other ear while placing Janna on my shoulder to burp her. "Why? I mean, she's in our home, and we're considered to be the pre-adoptive placement by the court."

"I know, but I've seen some vicious people who'll do anything to get a baby."

My concern started rising, although her words didn't make sense. "Why? If someone told me they were about to adopt a baby, I'd say, 'Congratulations.' I wouldn't do anything. I wouldn't think I could do anything. I wouldn't want to do anything. That seems sacred."

"I know, but you'd be surprised."

I still couldn't understand how other foster parents could take Janna away from us now. Regardless, I planned to heed Rose's words of wisdom.

Her warning did bother me. When our support specialist, Jill Moseley, came about a week later, I wanted to see what she had to say about it.

Even though Jill might not have any influence in the court system, I'd learned that her position enabled her to keep her ear to the ground. She heard just about everything that went on system-wide.

But first, I wanted to share the good news with her. She of all people had a right to hear it because she had been there as a shoulder to cry on when we lost the girls.

When she knocked on our door to conduct her home visit, I opened it with a big smile. She walked inside and looked at Janna in my arms. "My, oh, my, she sure is a cute one."

I closed the door behind her before joining her at the table. "Yep, she's already trying to hold up her head, and she just turned a month old. Oh, Jill, she's perfect. She has such a curious and loving disposition. I have so much fun shopping for her, I think because she appears to be so appreciative of everything I buy for her."

My grin grew bigger. "And guess what? We may be able to adopt her. Her caseworker was here last week and gave us an adoption packet. They've already TPR'd her."

Jill just smiled. "After our last visit, I was upset at what you told me. You know, how Placement told you that those without children were considered first when it came to adopting a child. I told my supervisor, who told her supervisor, and it all went uphill. They were very upset about that too. They emailed Holly's supervisor, correcting her and telling her to let their employee know she was wrong and she better quit telling foster parents that stuff.

"The next thing I know, Holly emails me, telling me that you had taken what she said the wrong way. Yet she wrote things in her email that she said she told you. What she wrote confirmed what you told me.

"So, you were right. I don't even know why she sent me that email. It didn't do her any good. But evidently, someone had a talk with her because she called you about this baby."

Jill, our cheerleader, not only could touch the ball, but she could run with it and score a touchdown. It turned out that Jill was quite capable of doing more than being a shoulder to cry on.

I gave her a big hug. "Thank you, Jill." Even as I said them, I knew those words would forever be inadequate.

I thanked God that I had asked Jill my by-the-way question that day concerning Holly's supposed Placement policy. I thanked God as I began to see the steps taken behind the scenes that led us to Janna without our knowing they were being taken.

I shared with Jill what I had been told about babies who had been TPR'd. "Do you think my friend was overexaggerating or being paranoid?"

Jill's eyebrows went up. "It can and has happened. A lot of foster parents don't come to the association meetings because they have to take their foster children. They're afraid to bring them because of the other foster parents who may try to take them away."

"Wow! That's really cold and cutthroat. It reminds me of vultures circling until the prey dies or sharks circling the weak for the kill."

Jill nodded. "One foster parent took her foster child to one of those adoption seminars, and someone there saw the child and ended up adopting him."

"This is deplorable. To think that you have to hide a foster child for fear that he or she will be stolen from you."

She pressed her lips together. "What could hurt you, though, is if they find out how you went all the way up the ladder to make complaints regarding the two little girls you had."

The mere idea of what she had said infuriated me. "Seriously, Jill? You mean to tell me that stepping up to the plate with legitimate complaints about a caseworker's ruthlessness and indiscretions would cause us to be blackballed? Are you kidding? No wonder we have such a system of secrecy and dysfunction."

Fear rose within me and almost turned to panic. "If that happens, then I'll go to Judge Rothman. I heard how he had announced in court that if he ever heard of a foster parent being blackballed because of complaints against workers in the dependency system, then he'd personally place sanctions against that agency and the employee who did the blackballing. He encouraged any foster parent who had a problem with agencies and their employees to come to him."

I hugged Janna tighter. "I'm tired of being jerked around by this system, Jill. We love this baby, and this is not a game. Not to us! I'm not threatening. This is critical. If it comes down to it, I *will* take the judge up on his offer."

Cinderella's Slipper

The following week, I called Christy Middleton, Janna's caseworker. I needed to know whether the state required physical exams on the children for the adoption packet. She told me yes.

"By the way, Mrs. Clark, I was planning to call you. I wanted to let you know that your foster baby has a great-aunt in New Jersey who wants her. We'll have to investigate the aunt, and that'll take about a month. Then the adoption specialist will do a home study to determine the best fit for the baby."

I began to get sick from the rapid churning in my stomach. What did she mean by the "best fit"?

What was Janna, the proverbial glass slipper that had been left behind? Was the system playing the role of the prince? Were the prospective parents playing the role of the fair maidens, hoping and praying that their foot would easily glide into the glass slipper so that they could be deemed "the best fit"?

I couldn't believe this. My head spun as anxiety tried to consume my body. I felt like we were reliving the case with Graci-An and Molly. The wind got knocked right out of me.

Using every bit of strength I could muster, I pushed aside the negative thoughts.

I had to remind myself that at least with Janna's case, we were contenders.

The Answer

She had something wrong with her eyes.

A hazy film covered them. Janna wouldn't respond to my smiles, and when one of the boys put his hand near her face, she wouldn't so much as blink.

Was she blind?

When she had her follow-up appointment with one of her specialists, I decided to ask him about my concern. He brought it up before I had the chance.

While examining her, he frowned. "What's wrong with her eyes?"

He called the nurse over to get her opinion. She agreed that Janna's eyes looked odd.

He then referred Janna to an ophthalmologist. I knew the process of getting a referral approved took time, but I felt a sense of urgency. Something within told me that she needed to be examined by an eye doctor now.

I prayed, *God, she's in your hands*.

During dinner that evening, I told the boys about Janna's doctor visit. "So, he referred Janna to an eye doctor. Let's hope everything turns out fine."

Devlin said, "Mom, we don't care. We love her anyway."

His words and support meant the world to me. I've heard that sometimes when a child gets diagnosed with a disability or impairment, those who had once considered adopting him or her no longer felt they could… or wanted to.

But even with Janna being such a blessing to our family, I still questioned God every day as to why he had allowed the girls to be taken. It was only when we found ourselves facing medical problems with Janna that I felt he answered my unceasing question.

I had come across a pink toy bunny that belonged to Graci-An and washed it before passing it onto Janna. When I took it out of the dryer, memories inundated my mind. I could still see her dragging it around by the ear and hugging it and poking at its glued-on plastic eyes. I brought it to my nose and smelled its clean scent.

"Why, God?"

What came to my spirit—immediately—was, "Janna needed you more, and you needed her more. Graci-An is fine. Don't you trust me to take care of her?"

"Lord, I don't know if this is you or not. If it is, please give me confirmation."

God didn't wait long to provide it.

The very next day, I went to lunch with Rhonda, a close friend of mine.

"How are you doing these days, now that you have that little one?" she asked from across the wooden restaurant table.

I shared with her my joy of having Janna and some of her more notable exploits. I found myself always smiling when I thought about her. "She has the biggest eyes, and she is so loving. She's very sensitive to touch. When I massage her tiny back, her little body relaxes, and she rolls her eyes back."

Rhonda's smile left her face, and her eyes centered on my own. "How are you doing regarding the girls?" She knew their loss had devastated me.

I squirmed in my seat and looked away. "That's a whole different conversation. I still feel a deep pain over losing them. I miss them so much, especially Graci-An." I looked back at my friend. "Don't get me wrong. I have no doubt that God gave us Janna, and I love her so much, much more than I thought I could ever love again. But I can't get over Graci-An. I just can't, no matter how hard I try. I keep thinking about how she's possibly being treated."

Rhonda's smile returned, and her eyes held compassion as she touched my forearm. Leaning toward me, she asked, "Don't you trust that God is taking care of Graci-An for you?"

I had chills. The hair rose on my arms; tears filled my eyes. I told her about my conversation with God. She, of course, didn't know that had occurred. She didn't know what he had told me or that I had asked him to confirm his words. Her question gave me all the affirmation I needed.

I then made the conscious decision to let the girls go, and in particular, Graci-An. Doing so would be a process. I couldn't help them anymore, but God could.

Although I didn't know if I would ever see Graci-An and Molly again, I knew one vital fact: Janna's arrival had saved my life.

At the same time, Janna needed us.

We didn't know if she had a serious medical problem, and if so, whether or not she would suffer from it permanently. We did know that we loved her for *who* she was, not for *what* she was.

She got stronger each day and responded to the sounds of our voices. Her smiles became more frequent.

Already, she possessed a wonderful, fun-loving disposition. I sang silly songs to her, and we danced together, me holding her in my arms while I moved to the music.

I was rocking her one night when she was about two and a half months old. She laid her head on my chest, and I kissed the top of it. She pulled her head back and looked up at me with the sweetest smile I think I've ever seen. I kissed her again, and she repeated her actions.

Janna had become so precious to me. I loved her with all my heart; for that, I was certain.

The Unofficial Diagnosis

While we waited to see the eye doctor, the pediatrician wanted to see Janna.

He examined her eyes and gave me the unofficial diagnosis.

Turning to me, his eyes on mine, he said, "Janna may have cataracts, or she may even have glaucoma."

I closed my eyes for a moment. "But isn't glaucoma for the elderly? I've never heard of a baby with it."

He leaned his head sideways and studied my face. "Unfortunately, babies can be born with it. Try to get her in to see the ophthalmologist as soon as possible."

By the time I got home, Janna was sleeping in her car carrier. I went online and researched both cataracts and glaucoma in infants. The three symptoms of glaucoma were extremely large eyes, eyes that tear frequently, and a cloudy covering over the eyes. Janna had all three.

I continued reading and learned that this disease had no cure and must be monitored for life. Surgery could only stop the vision loss from progressing, but any vision loss prior to surgery couldn't be recaptured.

My heart broke as I thought about what Janna had gone through in her very short life. Her parents had left her. Whereas most babies were enjoying the newness of this world and everything their eyes could capture, Janna's world was limited to what she heard and felt.

The question now lurked as to how much vision loss she had experienced. This baby needed help, and she needed help now.

Waiting on the insurance company to approve her appointment with an eye doctor was stripping her of precious time.

A Sense of Urgency

The great-aunt refused to give up her pursuit of adopting Janna.

Knowing that the foster-care system's wheels still churned with plans to determine the "best fit" sickened me. I couldn't help but think that if Janna's biological parents had given up their parental rights, didn't that automatically terminate the rights of the other members of Janna's biological family? I felt as if my wounds that had been healing since Janna's arrival were slowly being reopened.

I couldn't think about that now. I needed to focus my energy on Janna's eyes.

I called the ophthalmologist. The nurse reported that Janna's referral had been approved, that she was in their system, and that we could go ahead and set up an appointment. She told me the doctor had an opening in six weeks.

That seemed so far away. This sense of urgency wouldn't leave.

I asked, "Do you have anything sooner?"

"Are you thinking that she can't wait that long?" She sounded like she genuinely wanted to help.

"Oh yes, ma'am, I truly don't believe she can. There's something wrong with her eyes, and I feel that every day counts for stopping any vision loss that may be happening. Her pediatrician thinks she may have glaucoma or cataracts."

"Okay, then. Hmm. Let me see. I can work her in this Thursday morning at nine thirty."

"Perfect!"

Matters of the Heart

Christy seemed warmer toward us during her next home visit, a vast contrast from the first one. Her face and body looked relaxed.

I didn't know what had changed. Maybe the interactions she had with all kinds of people in her job made her skeptical of everyone. Maybe she had needed to wait to see if she could like and trust us.

Whatever her reasons, I was thankful that we were on the right footing.

Christy asked me about Janna's health. I went through the various issues she faced.

She took notes as I explained each one. She said she'd do some research on them. "I'll need all her medical reports. I also need to make sure the great-aunt knows about these potential health problems."

Darryl stretched his neck toward Christy, his eyes peeking over and down at what she was writing. "Speaking of, what's going on with the investigation of the great-aunt and her home study?"

Christy stopped writing and looked at Darryl. "I don't know where that stands right now. I'll try to track it down. I can tell you that I've talked with the aunt. I mentioned to her that she could visit with the baby if her foster family adopted her. She told me that she wasn't interested in just visiting the baby. She said, 'Why should I do that when I can have her?' By law, you know that the state is required to consider relatives first."

My heart sank before beating hard and fast. My mouth became dry.

Christy glanced over at me and made warm eye contact. Her voice softened. "I want to thank you for all the work you're doing and the doctors' appointments. Most foster parents wouldn't go to this extent."

She even referred to Janna as "your child" and then smiled. "I do feel that you have a good chance of adopting her, but be prepared for the what-ifs. This may take some time. Family & Children Connections denied the expedited investigation since this is an adoption home study. I guess they want it to be thorough."

What about in the meantime? An indisputable fact existed: the longer we had Janna with us while they tried to determine the "best fit," the more bonded she became to us.

Christy leaned toward us, her eyes going back and forth between Darryl and me. As if she had read my mind, she said, "Bonding is an important issue in determining where the child should go and who should adopt her." She pressed her lips together as she closed her book. "Anyway, the great-aunt hasn't called me to get your phone number to check on the baby. I'm making notes of all this in my report."

This caseworker demonstrated a completely different outlook regarding Janna than what we had experienced with Mara regarding Graci-An. Unlike her predecessor, Christy strongly considered how quickly a baby could bond with a family. She realized the importance of that bonding *to that child.*

She was fighting to work with us, not against us.

It was as if Christy had introduced a whole new concept into the foster-care system—thinking of the child for once.

A Different Kind of Monster

My muscles stiffened like a shield of armor, protecting my body from the assault attempted by February's cold and bitter airstrikes.

Thankfully, Darryl had already started the van so it could be warm by the time Janna and I got in it.

We arrived early at the ophthalmologist's office. After a lengthy wait in the reception area, a nurse finally called Janna's name.

We followed her down a short hallway and into a long and sterile-looking room. The back of it contained the patient's chair and the kind of eye examination equipment seen in a typical ophthalmologist's office.

To one side of the exam area, a computer sat on a desk with upper and lower cabinets. A variety of supplies stood neatly arranged on the counter next to the computer.

A few minutes later, the doctor came into the room. A tall, thin man, he had kind eyes and a gentle and compassionate manner. He looked at Janna the whole time he asked me questions.

He then performed several tests on her eyes. I didn't know what any of them meant.

When he finished, he studied me a moment before giving her diagnosis. "Her eye pressure is extremely high. She has congenital glaucoma."

He sat down in front of the computer to type his notes. He then stood and turned to face me. "I want to operate on her eyes as soon as possible to stop any further vision loss. My next surgery date is this Tuesday. I think we should try to do it then."

I had difficulty fully grasping what he had just said.

The doctor called one of his nurses in the room and introduced her as Sue. "She schedules the surgeries."

When Sue found out that Janna was a foster child, she told us that they would need an affidavit from the state giving them permission to perform surgery.

Her eyes matched her warm smile. "Can you give me the caseworker's name and telephone number?" She had her pen poised at the top of her clipboard, ready to write. "I'll go back to my desk and call her to let her know what we need. I'm afraid that she needs to get a judge to sign the affidavit."

I must have had a panicky look on my face. "What if she can't get this done in time?"

She leaned toward me and touched my arm. I looked into her face to see an encouraging smile. "Don't worry. I've done this before. They're pretty good at working with us, especially if the situation is dire and an emergency. I need to go and get started working on this."

When she left, the doctor said, "It's good that you came in when you did because glaucoma can be a progressive disease. I've gotta be honest. Surgery may or may not correct it."

"What's ahead for her? What can she expect?" Concern had evolved into overwhelming worry.

"It's hard to treat children who are born with it. Janna will have to go through a series of surgeries. I'll perform surgery on her right eye first because it's the worse. The next one will be in a couple of weeks. I only like to do one eye at a time.

"If I can drain the fluid and pressure from her eyes during surgery, she may very well have pretty good vision. I hope that's what happens. At her age, I just can't offer any prognosis because it's hard to tell how this will end up. Yes, she can still go blind anyway."

He paused a moment, probably so that I could process this information. He said, "I'd like to get a genetics consult, possibly while she's in the hospital, to see what the underlying causes of all of her physical problems are, like the hole in the heart, the floppy airway, and the congenital glaucoma."

I said, "The pediatrician's office already did a referral for her to see a geneticist. I've called them, and now I'm waiting to hear back so that I can schedule an appointment."

"Oh, good. Let me know when you talk with them, please," he requested. "In the meantime, you'll need to schedule a pre-op appointment with us for Monday. Also, she'll have to have a cardiology consult before Tuesday. Because of her heart condition, he'll have to say she's okay to go under anesthesia before we can do the surgery. I know this is a lot to get done in such a short period of time." He gave me an understanding smile.

While we waited for Sue to return, I called the pediatric cardiologist. Thankfully, the pediatrician had already submitted a referral for Janna to see him too. I explained the situation to the nurse and asked if the appointment could be scheduled within the next day or two. She said they could work her in at eight o'clock Monday morning.

Sue came back to the room. "Okay, I spoke with the caseworker, Ms. Middleton. She said that she has to go to court this afternoon. If you can bring her the medical affidavit as soon as you leave here, she can hopefully see the attorney then and give it to him to draw up. He can then get the judge to sign it. She thought that it could be signed by the end of tomorrow."

The doctor said, "Here, take it and go. You can come by here after you see the cardiologist on Monday so that we can do the pre-op. Just call before you come."

By the time I left their office, I was emotionally worn down. Still, I needed to rush to get to the other side of town to hand deliver the documents to Christy.

I had to do my best to make it there before she left.

Striking Back at the Monster

Everything, miraculously, went off without a hitch.

Christy got the signed affidavit from the judge. Janna's cardiology examination showed her heart to be fine—built differently—but nonetheless fine. The pre-op appointment with the ophthalmologist went without incident.

The next day, we needed to arrive at the hospital exceptionally early.

Janna came through the surgery like a real trouper. A nurse came out to the waiting area to tell me Janna's room number. "You can go ahead and go on up there. They should be bringing her at any moment."

I had just walked into her hospital room when another nurse wheeled in her crib. She looked so tiny in it. Seeing the wires attached to her and the metal patch taped over her right eye broke my heart.

I spent the night with Janna and refused to leave her side. I couldn't imagine how frightening this experience might be for a young infant. She wasn't even three months old.

Darryl came to see us at every opportunity. I was amazed at how much he had fallen in love with Janna. He looked at her with such adoration in his eyes and with such awe. His feelings seemed different toward her than Graci-An. Perhaps he felt comfortable letting loose with his emotions and not holding back.

He gave me reports from the home front. The boys asked about Janna and begged to come to the hospital so that they could see her. On the last day of her hospital stay, he decided to give in to their pleas.

I could feel—and hear—their exuberant energy from all the way down the hall. They spilled into Janna's room, each trying to be the first one in. Janna was sleeping, but that didn't deter them from surrounding her crib.

I think that like Darryl and me, they felt differently toward Janna than they had toward Graci-An. All of us seemed to have a special kind of bonding with her.

As I watched her sleeping with four smiling boys surrounding the big hospital crib that held her diminutive frame, I had an epiphany.

My family was complete, even if the girls never returned.

Letting Go

Janna recuperated wonderfully after her first surgery.

We had been home for a couple of days when Jill, our support specialist, came for her next home visit.

I said, "We haven't been told that we'd be able to adopt her for sure. With this great-aunt wanting her, you'd think we'd be more cynical after what we went through. But I feel like she belongs to us."

Jill smiled. "You know I can't tell you what's going to happen, but don't you remember I told you that God had a special child for you? I told you. I don't think anyone would do a better job with her than you. It's like she was made for you."

After she left, Darryl and I began talking about our future plans with the foster-care system. Our license would be expiring soon. Judging from the way things were going, it didn't look like the adoption would be finalized by the time it lapsed. We needed to go through the renewal process again.

"We can't take the chance, Darryl," I said. "We would never forgive ourselves if they took Janna from us because our license expired."

Darryl nodded and then sighed. "But once we adopt her, let's not take any more children."

I grabbed his hand and smiled as I searched his face. "I totally get where you're coming from. Why don't we do this? We've gotta get our license renewed; it'll be good for another year. We won't take anymore new foster children, but let's keep our home open, just in case Graci-An and Molly get put back into the system."

Darryl tilted his head to the side, the outer edges of his mouth turned down. "Okay. We'll keep our doors open for them only."

"Thank you, honey. You know, I've often thought about how we almost quit the foster-care system after losing the girls. What if we had let our pain and anger get the best of us, and we turned in our license then?"

Chills went down my spine as I contemplated how much more we would have lost from such an emotional decision. "Do you realize that we never would have gotten the blessing of having Janna in our lives? Looking back, I can see how God maneuvered everything. This was his plan. *She's* his plan. I'm so thankful to him."

I realized that I had finally let go of Graci-An; it had been a difficult process. She would always have a place in my heart, but holding onto her like I had been doing wasn't healthy for anyone. She had become a ghost who haunted my dreams and my waking hours. I recognized that Janna needed my time and attention more than my tormenting memories did.

For what seemed like too long, I had cried out to God, begging and pleading for him to remove that agony.

Finally, and in his own time, he mercifully gave me the one thing that would transform my pain from an excruciating grief to pure and unconditional love and joy.

Pray for Peace

Janna made it through the second surgery just fine.

The doctor admitted her to the hospital for observation. Darryl brought the boys to see her the next day. They were just as excited to see her as they had been after the first operation.

Post-op turned out to be a full-time and complicated job. The instructions required that different drops be administered at different times to different eyes. I found that I needed to construct a chart to keep from getting confused. None of this included the three to four appointments with various medical specialists every week.

About ten days after her second surgery, her ophthalmologist called around five o'clock in the evening. He said that the eye pressure hadn't really decreased any. He foresaw having to perform two more surgeries at the very least and maybe as many as four more.

"I'm afraid that she's lost more vision than I had hoped," he said.

To us, Janna was perfect whether she could see with twenty-twenty vision, could partially see, or was totally blind. Her big, beautiful eyes did not define her.

He continued. "I've already scheduled her for another surgery next week."

I quickly did the math in my head. That would make it only eight days since her last surgery.

Then I got a call from Christy, her caseworker, the next day. She informed me that they had been working hard on this case and that the great-aunt still wanted the baby.

"It might be good if the aunt could call you," she said.

I didn't particularly like the idea, but I would do anything to help. "Sure, Christy, you have my permission to give the great-aunt our phone number. Let her know she's welcome to call us anytime."

I then told Christy about the medical challenges Janna faced. If the great-aunt truly wanted her, she needed to fully understand everything involved in raising this baby.

Almost overnight, Janna had become a special-needs child and would be for life. The aunt needed to know that caring for this baby would require total commitment as greater demands would be placed upon her. It meant more appointments with more specialists, surgeries, medication, special equipment, time off from work, etc., etc., etc.

When we hung up with each other, I prayed, *Lord, I thank you for our blessing in Janna. I believe that you gave her to us. But God, could you work on the heart of this great-aunt? Please give her peace that Janna should stay with us.*

I didn't pray his will be done because I believed from the depths of my soul that his will was for Janna to be with us.

All I could do at that point was to put her in God's hands and leave her there.

The Wheels of Justice Turn

There I was again, walking through the doors of the Cypress Boulevard courthouse for another judicial review hearing.

This time, I didn't have any apprehension.

I met my attorney, Brook Kingston, in front of the same courtroom where a travesty had once occurred. I stood in the same place where I had confronted Mara about giving us the wrong location for another hearing. That all seemed so long ago.

Court was not in session, so Brook went into the courtroom and retrieved the judicial review report. She brought it back out to the waiting room where we both read it together. I noted that several times throughout, it stated how the baby was very bonded to us.

Christy needed to attend another hearing on the other side of the building, but she thought she'd be finished in time to make it to this one. When the court officer called the case of Mary Webster (a.k.a. Janna), I looked around one last time for Christy before walking into the courtroom with Brook. The hearing would have to proceed without her.

Brook told the court that the foster mother/pre-adoptive parent was very eager to get this over with. She mentioned the baby's medical problems.

Brook then said the caseworker had sent her an email less than a week ago. The great-aunt's investigation and home study had been completed, and she was waiting for the results.

Good, I thought. *This process is moving forward.*

Brook reported that the caseworker had informed her of her recommendation for the child to stay put. The attorney for the state requested the court assign a guardian ad litem in case it came down to the Manifest Best Interests of the Child; the guardian could then provide information from both sides.

Afterward, Brook shared with me that the hearing went fine.

I appreciated Brook's encouragement, but I believed Janna's fate belonged to a higher court.

The Nine-Month Plan

Christy called and asked me to fax over the contents of Janna's red folder.

While doing so, I reread some of its documents and Janna's medical records of her premature birth. Out of curiosity, I took her birth date, the number of weeks and days she was born early, and determined her actual due date. The day's number sounded familiar.

I counted backward from her due date to see when she probably had been conceived. By the time I got to nine months, I came to a marvelous realization. Exactly nine months before her due date—to the day—the state conducted the girls' permanency review staffing meeting. In other words, on the same day when the state made the recommendation for Graci-An and Molly's reunification with Gretchen, Janna was conceived. I couldn't dismiss this as a coincidence.

I marveled at God's goodness and his perfect timing. He saw ahead and knew I'd be losing a baby I adored. He then allowed the conception of the baby he had specifically chosen for us.

While we went through the anguish of that meeting, I had no idea that several months down the road, we'd get a call for the perfect blessing. I didn't know an event that almost destroyed me would be the forerunner to something that would repair my shattered heart.

Looking back to that permanency review staffing meeting, I could almost hear God saying, "My child, you're about to go through a journey of tremendous heartbreak and pain. But fear not, and do not be anxious, for I am now creating a very special blessing, one that I have customized especially for you."

An Answered Prayer

Exhaustion overcame me.

The unusual heat from the mid-afternoon April sun didn't help my energy level. It depleted what little get-up-and-go I had.

Janna had just undergone her third eye surgery. For the past two nights, I had stayed with her in the hospital and tried to sleep on a pullout chair.

Turning into our driveway and seeing Darryl waiting for us sure did feel good. He got Janna from the backseat and carried her inside while I gathered our belongings.

I took my time going inside. After having confined myself to a hospital, I enjoyed the treasures the outdoors offered, almost as if it were saying to me, "Welcome back." I took in a deep breath of fresh air and allowed myself to appreciate the aroma of spring flowers and fresh grass.

Unfortunately, indulging my senses did nothing to stimulate me out of sleep deprivation. I forced myself to go inside and begin to tackle the pile of work waiting for me.

I grabbed a bottle of soda for the caffeine effect before heading into our home office. While I sorted through the last three days of mail, the phone rang. Darryl was also working in the office and answered it.

He said, "Phyllis Hinds? May I ask who you're with? Oh, you're Mary's great-aunt." He looked at me, eyebrows raised.

I cringed. I wasn't ready to talk with her, not with the clutter of cobwebs in my brain.

Darryl put his hand over the receiver and whispered, "She wants to know how the surgery went."

I pressed my lips together, gave a short nod, and held my hand out to him.

He removed his hand from over the receiver and put the phone back to the side of his face. "Ms. Hinds? Here she is."

I took a deep breath before taking the phone from him.

"Mrs. Clark? I'm Mary's great-aunt, and I wanted to know how the baby's doing."

I told her, "Fine," and left my answer vague.

We talked for a couple of minutes, and then boom, she came out and asked, "So what are your intentions with Mary? Do you want to adopt her?"

Was this a trick question? Time was speeding but standing still at the same time. "Yes," I said, wondering if she could hear my heart pounding. "Yes, we do. We love your great-niece very, very much."

"Well, I really wanted her, but I've been praying and praying over it and crying over it and wrestling with it and decided that she'd be better with you." I could hear her voice crack over the phone. "I have peace with that decision."

I couldn't speak. I tried to repeat her words in my mind, making sure I hadn't missed something or hadn't heard her incorrectly. The tears poured from my eyes as it dawned on me what had just happened. God had answered my prayer, and her words repeated my request to God almost verbatim.

When Darryl saw my tears, his eyes widened, and his mouth opened. He looked scared. I smiled and winked slightly.

I gave Phyllis a simple response, knowing that whatever I said would never be able to effectively convey my deep appreciation. "Thank you. Thank you so much."

Now I was fully awake. A weight had just been lifted. I felt so, so light, lighter than I had felt in a long time.

Phyllis and I talked. I learned about Mary's biological family and that Phyllis was a strong Christian. She and I hit it off.

She told me she wanted to have communication with Mary and develop a relationship with her.

I assured her that my husband and I would be fine with that. God was in this, and if he wanted Janna's great-aunt in her life, then so be it.

Afterward, I couldn't stop thinking about how God had answered my prayers to soften the heart of this great-aunt.

If there were any doubts as to whether God had given Janna to us permanently, they all dissipated with that phone call.

Redemption

Nothing could have knocked me off my cloud of elation.

Christy and I talked the next day. We discussed the great-aunt's decision and the next steps toward adoption.

I then called Brook, my attorney, to give her the good news. Someone had gotten to her first because she answered with "Congratulations." I could hear her smiling through the phone.

I asked, "Who told you?"

"Actually, I knew a day or two earlier that the aunt had come to that decision. I wanted to call you so badly but decided to wait and see."

I understood Brook's reluctance in calling. She didn't want to get our hopes up and then have them dashed by the possibility that the great-aunt would change her mind.

I called my friend Faith Mead to share the good news.

"I am so happy for you," she said. She listened to me gush with excitement.

After monopolizing the conversation for several minutes, I asked her how she was doing.

She said, "Well, your call actually came at a good time, made me feel a little better about renewing our foster-care license. I just finished my licensing paperwork, and I was sick when I signed the agreement that stated, 'Being a foster parent is not a right. It's a privilege.' How dare they say this is a privilege?" I could hear the indignation in her voice.

I could appreciate her annoyance. "I agree," I said. "It's not a right. I get that. But a privilege? Taking in a child with behavior issues, taking her to the doctor probably more than our own child because she may need extra services, counseling once a week, visitation that could be a fifty-five-mile round trip once a week or twice a month, people coming into your home all the time to inspect you and the child and your home, etc., etc., at fifteen dollars a day is *not* a privilege. It's not even a job."

Faith said, "Being a foster parent's a sacrifice. It's a worthy calling, just like being called to work in a third-world country as a missionary. Both are huge lifestyle changes and definitely have their rewards. The word 'privilege' bothers me because it's the definition that gives them the right to treat foster parents like cheap labor with no respect but with all of the liability."

I shared with Faith our decision to not take in any more foster children and only leave our home open for Graci-An and Molly's return. Otherwise, Janna would be our last foster child.

Our time as foster parents had basically come to an end. Through our journey in the foster-care system, we learned a lot of lessons, maybe too many in such a short period of time, relatively speaking.

The dependency system is not an all's-well-that-ends-well system. We were blessed with our final ending, but that's not always the situation. We had Janna put in our lives permanently, but we also saw and experienced the ugly and unforgettable corrupt side. We witnessed the sacrifice of too many children.

It's a crapshoot when you get a foster child. It could have a good ending or a bad ending. We experienced both. You don't know which it will be when you take a child. A lot of what happens depends upon the caseworker. We learned this fact firsthand.

Thank God for Christy Middleton because it was through her and only through her that the system redeemed itself.

The Call

Never again would that dark cloud loom overhead and follow us everywhere, even into our sleep.

Just a little while longer, and we would never again have that fear of our foster child being taken away from us.

The fact that we were in spring was appropriate since that's the season that denotes new life. Mother's Day brought a new specialness, knowing that although we hadn't officially adopted Janna, she was a part of this family, forever and always.

Over the next several weeks, all of the required documents for the adoption were pulled together. Of course, several glitches cropped up along the way. Of course, we wanted it done yesterday.

Janna belonged to us, and we belonged to her. She had all of me, completely and fully, without any trepidation.

I never got tired of watching her. Clearly, she loved to smile and laugh. When she started laughing, I laughed, which made her laugh harder, which made me laugh harder, and on and on. She would also cry for me.

The Lord was right. Janna needed me, but God knew I needed her more.

Then we got THE phone call telling us that the adoption hearing had been scheduled. It was funny how this whole adventure had started with an oh-so-important phone call.

Now, that part of our life would end with an even more important phone call.

The Reality of a Dream

At last, we adopted Janna.

It happened so fast. We had prepared for years for this day, yet the event lasted about four minutes.

The hearing started off with Darryl and me being sworn under oath. Brook, our attorney, asked us several questions. We weren't given a heads-up about what questions would be asked. We didn't even know we would have to answer any questions for that matter. We didn't know what to expect. We didn't care.

During the inquiry, Brook told us to think about our answers before giving them. I don't know why. They were all fairly simple.

She came to the last question. "Why do you want to adopt this child and make her part of your family?"

I didn't have to think about or debate that one either. I looked down at Janna, so peaceful, sleeping in my arms. In a knee-jerk reaction, I blurted out my answer. "Because we love her."

After that, we were swept up from our chairs. Our children were told to come over and stand with the adults. The judge stood behind us. Cameras were pointed at us, flashes went off, and voila, it was done.

Despite the fact that this hearing took less than five minutes, it forever changed the lives of at least seven people. It didn't involve any drama; it didn't have any fanfare. It was just a short-but-sweet hearing unlike any I had ever sat through.

Feeling surreal, I turned around to the judge and asked, "So that's it? She's ours forever?"

He laughed. "Yes, ma'am, that's it. She's yours."

Like Christmas morning, after much anticipation, our time before the judge, our time of officially making Janna our daughter, all came and went within what seemed like moments. Our lives had been transformed in so many ways. And … we had our daughter!

We celebrated by going out to dinner at the same restaurant where I had taken Devlin for his birthday almost two years. That seemed like a lifetime ago.

This was the first time we had gone back to that restaurant since that fateful day. I sat there, looking around at my growing family, and something came to mind.

I looked at my oldest son and said, "Devlin, two years ago, almost to the day, you and I came here to celebrate your birthday. While here, I received our first phone call from Placement asking us to take Graci-An. It was here that we began our life as a foster family.

"And it's here that Janna begins her life as an official member of our family."

A Conclusion

The Beauty from My Ashes

So much had happened during our short tenure in the foster-care system.

Halfway through our journey, I thought I'd literally die. At times, I felt as if I came close.

I'll never be the same person who made that first phone call to gather information on how to adopt a child. I was now a veteran, and I had the war scars to prove it ... scars which were no longer wounds ... scars that can't be seen.

Our God is faithful and good. With our daughter, I was pulled ever so slowly out of the heap of ashes into which we had been dumped headfirst. For out of our ashes, he gave us beauty in the form of a tiny baby girl whom he named Janna.

> *To appoint unto them that mourn in Zion, to give unto them beauty for ashes, the oil of joy for mourning, the garment of praise for the spirit of heaviness; that they might be called trees of righteousness, the planting of the LORD, that he might be glorified. And they shall build the old wastes, they shall raise up the former desolations* (Isaiah 61:3–4).

Afterword

Janna's Impact on the World

With a personality larger than life, Janna is growing up and is a happy, well-adapted girl. (We can no longer call her "little girl" because she keeps insisting that she has passed that era.) To say that she is the perfect daughter would be an understatement.

For sure, Janna was indeed God's choice for our family. I still think of Graci-An and Molly, wondering what they're doing and how they're being treated.

By now, I can agree with the adage "Time heals all wounds." I've come to realize that it does take time to process a great loss. After all, it took seventeen months before I allowed myself to be wholly healed, completely getting over my anger toward God for losing the girls.

What I learned was that His grace is sufficient. It took even longer before I could replace all of my pain and anger with understanding, acceptance, and a special gratitude to the Father for going to such measures to bless us with the honor of raising his little princess.

As for the foster-care system, well, Darryl and I have never regretted our decision to let our foster-care license lapse and close our doors. Leaving our roles as foster parents didn't mean we were quitting the foster children but rather solidifying our commitment to our own five children, one of whom used to be a foster child. Quality took priority over quantity.

A little after Janna turned one, I was driving her to a doctor's appointment. Third Day's song "Show Me Your Glory" played on the radio. As I listened to the words, I said silently, *Lord, please show me your glory.*

A soft voice answered. "You have seen My glory, and she's sleeping in that infant car carrier in the backseat."

Her life has been atypical, however. For the first eighteen months, she was under the care of nine specialists, and over the years, hospitals, clinics, and specialists were the rule, not the exception for Janna. She has undergone surgery after surgery and EUA's (exams under anesthesia) so many times that I've lost count. For each one, she has come out a real trouper.

One time, I told her, "Janna, you are so brave. I could never do what you've done."

I'll never forget the look she gave me, one of such shock. She responded, "What? Would you have freaked out?"

The truth is, yes. She has no idea the example of courage she has set before me. It's a very high bar and one that I doubt I'll ever be able to reach.

Beyond the valor she has exhibited time and time again, Janna is a typical girly-girl. She loves to wear pretty clothes and to be sprayed with "smell pretties," a name she uses in place of perfume. She plays dress-up with my clothes and my shoes, combs my hair, and she has helped me in the past pick out what to wear for meetings and conferences, taking delight in the process and my attending these events.

She rides a bike (with a little guidance), plays with dolls (with absolutely no guidance), and has a BFF (best friend forever) who is also visually impaired. Those two have been inseparable since Janna was three years old. They play dolls and talk about Jesus and love to go to church.

They don't even think about defining themselves by their impairment. They insist on becoming independent, grooming and dressing themselves and doing chores. They understand their limits, but the world is their oyster. They have dreams just like any child. Whereas the BFF wants to be a teacher, Janna wants to be a writer, editor, illustrator, and publisher. Both girls plan to use their braille abilities for books so that the blind and visually impaired will be able to read more of them.

Another one of their dreams is to be able to see, yet they never complain that they don't have vision like other children. On the contrary, they get excited at a classmate for just being able to see light. They are probably the most positive kids I've ever known, choosing to look at everything optimistically and with the glass-half-full perspective. I tell them that many children who can see could learn a lot about life from them.

Janna is the social butterfly of the family, of her school, and well, everywhere she goes. I've always said that she has her shoes parked by the front door as she waits for the first party or social invitation to come her way.

For sure, she makes a mark wherever she goes. She is herself. Because of her visual impairment, she doesn't see social cues, so being the free spirit she is, she feels free to be Janna. She enthusiastically enters a room or building, greeting everyone with genuine excitement, making each feel like the most important person in the world, regardless of age, size, or appearance. She has always had this gift of making everyone feel special.

People respond to her nonjudgmental attitude toward them and sense her love for them, but they just can't put their fingers on it.

Instead, the common responses have been "There is something about that girl I love."

One day while in a grocery store, she struck up a conversation with one of the managers. He had lost his teenage daughter in a tragic vehicle accident a couple of months earlier. While Darryl and Janna stood in the checkout line, he tapped Darryl on the shoulder, handed him his cell phone, and asked him to read a text. He then waved his hand in Janna's direction and said, "Because she moved me."

Darryl complied and read an older text from around the time he had lost his daughter. Darryl was stunned to learn that this man had donated his daughter's eyes so that someone out there could now see…all because of Janna!

Other times, strangers have given her money because they saw something different in her and were drawn by it. It had nothing to do with her blindness but everything to do with that anointing the Lord told me about when she was a newborn. It's still just as strong today, if not stronger, than it was back then.

Unfortunately, though, the glaucoma has been vicious throughout the years, although Janna has fought back hard. She has recently been diagnosed as permanently blind in her left eye, and she has very, very little vision—if any—in her right eye. She accepts her condition a whole lot better than me.

All through the years, people have told us how blessed she is to have us. Maybe so, but we don't and never have looked at it that way. In our minds, we're the ones who are and have been blessed. For if not for Janna, we would have been deprived of experiencing life through her eyes, the eyes of an almost-blind child who sees the world a lot clearer than us.

About the Author

Sherrie Clark

SHERRIE CLARK is the author of the best-selling books ***Behind Her Miami Badge***, ***Behind Her Special Agent Badge***, and ***Behind Her Criminal Investigator's Badge***. Through her unique creative writing style, she brings reality to stories by putting readers in the shoes of the characters so that they can experience what the characters see, hear, and feel.

With many books she writes and edits, she draws from her past experiences as a NYPD police officer and Licensed Clinical Christian Counselor through NCCA. ***Small Voices Silenced***, a bestseller on Amazon, came from her personal journey through the foster-care system. She studied the activities and laws of the foster-care system in depth and supplemented her knowledge by talking with other foster parents. Her position on the area's foster/adoptive parent association board of directors allowed her to acquire a more extensive education in the foster-care system's enormity and power. She enjoys speaking on this topic as well as law enforcement and issues concerning communications.

She's a best-selling and award-winning author, ghostwriter, editor, author coach and consultant, and book publisher. Sherrie's mission is to continue to raise up best-selling and award-winning authors. As the CEO of Storehouse Media Group and creator of Book Concept 2 Best Seller and the 8-Hour Author Program, she works with busy and aspiring authors to pull out stories and messages and craft them in a way that gives her clients credibility and value.

She loves to share her expertise and knowledge, so she educates authors through conferences and online classes on how to write their books in a simple step-by-step, tried and proven formula and then how to develop them to page turners.

Before tackling books, Sherrie started sharpening her professional writing skills in 2004 by writing copy for marketers, businesses, non-profit organizations, and authors. She's a proud member of the Professional Writers' Alliance.

As a visionary, she knew in late 2012 that podcasts were the wave of the future. Armed with her experience of working with victims and her Masters of Arts in Clinical Christian Counseling, she created, produced, and hosted the live weekly podcast *God, Where Were You When?* that became part of Lester Sumrall's LeSEA Broadcasting Network.

Although she has enjoyed each role and phase of her life, she feels each one has contributed to where she's at now, living her dream, doing what she's most passionate about, and fulfilling the adage, "Do what you love to do, and you'll never work a day in your life."

When not writing and working with other authors, Sherrie enjoys spending time with her family.

You can reach Sherrie for speaking events at www.sherrieclark.com and for help in writing your page-turner book at www.StorehouseMediaGroup.com.

www.ingramcontent.com/pod-product-compliance
Lightning Source LLC
Chambersburg PA
CBHW030050100526
44591CB00008B/83